The Record Shelf
Guide to the Classical Repertoire

How to Order:

Quantity discounts are available from Prima Publishing & Communications, Post Office Box 1260REC, Rocklin, CA 95677; telephone (916) 624-5718. On your letterhead include information concerning the intended use of the books and the number of books you wish to purchase.

U.S. Bookstores and Libraries: Please submit all orders to St. Martin's Press, 175 Fifth Avenue, New York, NY 10010; telephone (212) 674-5151.

The Record Shelf Guide to the Classical Repertoire

Jim Svejda

Prima Publishing & Communications
P.O. Box 1260REC
Rocklin, CA 95677
(916) 624-5718

Typography by Coghill Book Typesetting Company
Editing by David Manley
Production by Bookman Productions
Cover design by The Dunlavey Studio

The radio version of "The Record Shelf" is produced by Public Radio Station KUSC, Los Angeles, a broadcast service of the University of Southern California and is distributed nationally via AMERICAN PUBLIC RADIO.

Prima Publishing & Communications
Rocklin, CA

Library of Congress Cataloging-in-Publication Data

Svejda, Jim
   The record shelf : guide to the classical repertoire / Jim Svejda.
     p.   cm.
   Includes index.
   ISBN 0-914629-47-6
   1. Music—Discography.   I. Title.
ML156.2.S95   1988
016.7899'12—dc19   88-15204
                                                     CIP
                                                     MN

89 90 91 RRD 10 9 8 7 6 5 4 3
Printed in the United States of America

For Louise, who did everything but write it.

Foreword

I admit that I am not impartial when it comes to Jim Svejda. Long before I met him, I was an ardent fan of his radio program, *The Record Shelf*. His musical taste, his sardonic wit, his urbanity, and his unique connection with his listeners I find unequaled. And I am not alone. I have since learned— not from him—that of some three thousand letters received each month by KUSC, fifteen hundred are for Jim.

Four years ago, after conducting the Minnesota Orchestra, I had made dinner reservations with some musician friends. I couldn't budge them. They refused to go until they finished listening to that week's *Record Shelf*. To my surprise and ensuing delight, Jim began the program with a lusty Teutonic male choir, developed a comparison with my Sing A Longs, and concluded by featuring my oboe and English horn recordings from 1947 to 1951. Over the air, Jim anointed me his favorite oboe-English horn player of all time. The compliment was better than dessert.

When we finally did meet, my impressions were more than confirmed and we became instant friends. He truly loves music, being a former oboe player himself. The breadth of his knowledge is extraordinary. He thoroughly understands every kind of music, every conductor, composition, and nuance of performance, from early jazz through the entire classical repertoire. His taste is consummate; his integrity, unswayed by today's musical hype.

Sure, I am prejudiced, but so will you be after referring to this book for your recording needs. You may not always agree, but believe me, you'll *never be wrong* listening to Jim Svejda and *The Record Shelf Guide to the Classical Repertoire*.

MITCH MILLER

Acknowledgments

This book grew out of the comparative survey programs that are a regular feature of my weekly radio program, *The Record Shelf*. A production of KUSC, the radio station of the University of Southern California, *The Record Shelf* is distributed nationally by American Public Radio. For their invaluable help and support, I would like to thank my friends John Curry of the University of Southern California and William Kappelman, Acting General Manager of KUSC. To my closest musical friends, Kevin Mostyn, Robert Goldfarb, and Henry Fogel, no amount of thanks can adequately repay what I owe them. I am also deeply indebted to my friends and colleagues of the KUSC Programming Department, especially Gail Eichenthal, David Letterman, Dennis Bade, and Arthur Cooke for allowing me to shamelessly pick their brains over the years. I also owe a special debt of gratitude to Dr. Christian Rutland, without whose encouragement this book might never have been begun, and to Dr. Karl-Heinrich Vogelbach, without whose timely intervention it might never have been completed. Finally, for her expert and creative editing, unfailingly sound advice, marathon bouts of proofreading, and superhuman patience, I can't thank Louise Fasana enough.

Introduction

When I first began collecting records several centuries ago, record collecting was a trivially easy hobby. I had what at the time seemed an infallible system: I bought records entirely on the basis of their covers. I would search, innocently mind you, through the bins of the Roxy Music Shop in La Porte, Indiana, after my weekly oboe lesson, and spend my hard earned allowance on the most lurid, suggestive record jackets I could find. This was long before an adolescent could muster the courage to buy one of Mr. Hefner's forbidden magazines. Thus I had to content myself with the odd edition of National Geographic and what must have been, at the time, the most complete collection of *Scheherazade* and *Belshazzar's Feast* recordings possessed by any thirteen year old in the world.

Eventually, after I passed out of my early "Record Collecting as an Excuse for Smuggling Home Soft-Core Pornography" phase, my requirements for records slowly began to change. I gradually became able to make distinctions between recordings I liked and recordings I didn't like, and thus was well on my way to becoming the opinionated, elitist snob I am today. (Actually, all the arrogance is merely a pose, as is the elitism, and I can prove it. The *one* thing which a lifelong Detroit Lions football fan cannot be, by definition, is an elitist or snobbish *anything*.)

Now, as then, performances that offer nothing but all the notes neatly in place are crashing bores. Worse than bores, they are a disservice to the composer, the listener, and the very spirit which animates music itself: the desire for the human spirit to express its highest aspirations through that five century tradition of serious music, which may well be Western man's unique and most enduring contribution to the civilization of this planet. All of which is a rather grandiose way of saying that whatever else they may be, none of the recordings recommended in this book are boring.

Unlike other recording guides, this one does not pretend to be all-encompassing or objective. Following the pattern of the comparative survey programs that turn up regularly on my weekly radio program, *The Record Shelf*, I have tried to include something pointed, interesting, amusing, or enlightening about each work, and then suggest which of the many available recordings you should buy.

Although my enthusiasms will become obvious very quickly, it might be prudent and more fair to spell them out, just in case you happen to be one of those strange people who actually reads Introductions, and on that basis actually decides whether or not to buy the book. (I in fact went to college with such a person, who I believe is now living off the hospitality of the state of Michigan for ax-murdering some relative, or local politician. I've forgotten the details.)

In essence, this is clearly a book written by someone who was born fifty years too late. In general, I find that while the level of music making today has reached a phenomenal state of technical perfection—made all the more so by the magic of editable recording tape—from an emotional point of view, recordings have had increasingly less and less to say.

My great musical heros, from Wilhelm Furtwängler to throwbacks like Leonard Bernstein, all have one thing in common. Unfortunately, *that* commodity—an instantly recognizable musical personality—is becoming increasingly rare. This book is an attempt to separate the personal, the interesting, even the quirky and outrageous, from the dull, the routine, and the merely professional. It also attempts to do what probably can't be done: select the *one* recording of a given work that is the most exciting, probing, and unique on the market today.

With the enthusiasms, even the casual reader will quickly discover a number of apparent prejudices that crop up throughout. As a matter of fact, I have no musical "prejudices" whatsoever. The contempt that incompetent bozos like Nikolaus Harnoncourt have elicited, or even the hatred that beasts like Herbert von Karajan have evoked, has been earned honestly and over a period of many years. I even remain a great admirer of Karajan's early recordings, in spite of the numberless, musical atrocities he has perpetrated in the last twenty years and his activities during the Second World War. (Rumors have persisted through the years that he once conducted in an S.S. uniform.) In short, I find him despicable on both human and musical grounds.

As a consumer's guide to classical recordings, the prospective buyer of this or any of the recommended recordings, should be aware of a few important facts of life. First and foremost among these is the melancholy fact that the long-playing record—like the 78 before it—is, if not a dead, then at very least a dying issue. The compact disc is now so obviously the wave of the future that many recording companies, with their typical "buyer-be-damned" approach to business, have ceased releasing LPs entirely. One can hardly blame them, of course, for wanting to make a buck. But to leave those of us who still *like* long playing records high and dry is more than a little disconcerting. To add insult to injury, they are charging even more exorbitant prices for compact discs, in spite of the fact that they are *cheaper* to produce than LPs. The moral of the story is, that while I have tried to recommend LP, compact disc, and cassette tape versions of all the works that are herein considered, in many cases it was simply impossible to do so.

On a few rare occasions, I have given two possible choices for a work, or have recommended other worthy contenders within the discussion of the piece. This is not because I have any trouble making up my mind, but because there are often several astonishing, though utterly different interpretations, and each, in my opinion, belongs in every recording library. In addition, given the sad state of affairs for LP lovers, many selections may simply be hard to find or already have slipped out of print.

Given the limitations of space, time, and my own endurance, the selection of works covered in this book is, of necessity, limited. Even so, the book is nearly twice as long as originally intended. Nevertheless, many items I would have liked to discuss have gone undiscussed, and much music that doesn't really interest me failed to make the final cut. For instance, with the exception of Bach and Handel, very little baroque music is included, and even less of the music of our time. I frankly admit that I don't understand very much modern music, although it's safe to say that 99 percent of it is either ephemera or trash. (This should not be read as an attack on modern music, since, as everyone knows, 99 percent of all the music produced during *any* given historical period was trash.)

I hope you will find what follows more useful in putting your recording library together, or in enhancing your existing one, than buying merely on the basis of lurid record jackets, familiar, much touted artists and labels, or spurious record store sales. Aside from this, and earning a *lot* of money for the author, this book was written with no other purpose in mind.

Bach, Johann Sebastian (1685–1750)

Ask a thousand serious music lovers to name the greatest composer in history, and all but one or two of them will mention Johann Sebastian Bach with Pavlovian immediacy. (The only other possible candidates, Mozart and Beethoven, will be mentioned nearly as often.) Unfortunately, I am one of those rare musical perverts who is simply unable to love Bach with the same heated passion that the rest of the world manages to generate. Knowing his music as intimately as I do, I realize he is unquestionably one of the greatest composers who has ever lived, yet his music has never interested me very much. For instance, with a handful of exceptions, the Cantatas and Passions seem to me among the most leaden and stultifying works ever written. My general lack of enthusiasm in recommending recordings of his music is—again with a handful of exceptions—all too genuine. Therefore, the following opinions are offered with abject apologies to Bach lovers everywhere.

Brandenburg Concertos (6), S. 1046/51

Academy of St. Martin-in-the-Fields, Marriner. Philips
412105-1 [LP], *400076-2* [CD], *400077-2* [CD],
412105 [T].

English Concert, Pinnock. Deutsche Grammophon
423317-1 [LP] or *ARC-410500/1* [CD];
ARC-410501/1 [CD], 423317-4 [T].

Just as Johann Sebastian Bach is the final summation of all that the baroque era gave to music, the *Brandenburg Concertos* are the apotheosis of the Concerto Grosso, that most diverse and important of all baroque instrumental forms.

For years the standard recordings of the *Brandenburg Concertos* were those wonderfully musical performances from the 1930s by the Adolf Busch Chamber Orchestra, an interpretation that can still be found on several European import labels. While not for baroque purists (the *continuo* is realized on a piano by a very young Rudolf Serkin), the playing is marvelously virile and delightfully old-fashioned: a memorable souvenir of the days when Bach was generally considered a stylistic contemporary of Robert Schumann.

Another persuasively romantic interpretation—my favorite modern recording of the *Brandenburgs*—is the lush and stylish account turned in by the English Chamber Orchestra conducted by Benjamin Britten, a classic recording that London Records has inexplicably withdrawn from its catalogue. Eternal optimist that I'm *not*, I still hope to see it reissued eventually on a London compact disc.

If baroque "authenticity" is an absolute necessity, the best choice is the English Concert and Trevor Pinnock on Deutsche Grammophon. Although this recording has drawn extravagant praise from both the English and the American press, I find much of it rather prissy and effete. Nevertheless, the English Concert version is an enterprise that deserves to be taken seriously, unlike the inept and embarrassing scandal perpetrated by Nikolaus Harnoncourt and his abysmal Concentus Musicus of Vienna.

Until Britten's recording returns to the catalogue, the strongest available alternative is Sir Neville Marriner's engaging Philips recording. Using modern instruments, judicious tempos, and a group of soloists who play with individuality and feeling, Marriner—like Britten before him—has no theoretical or stylistic axes to grind and simply allows these great works to speak eloquently for themselves.

Violin Concerto in A minor, S. 1041; Violin Concerto in E Major, S. 1042; Concerto in D minor for 2 violins, S. 1043

Mutter, Accardo, English Chamber Orchestra, Accardo. Angel DS-37989 [LP] or *CDC 47005* [CD].

It's hardly surprising that of all Bach's innumerable instrumental concertos, these three works for the violin should remain among his most popular works in the form. Lyrical, dramatic, and overflowing with rich and memorable melody, these concertos were often taken up as vehicles by Fritz Kreisler, Eugene Ysaye, and other important turn-of-the-century violinists whose performances of any baroque music tended to be as scarce as hockey players' teeth. Another sure sign of the enduring popular appeal of the violin concertos is the recent enlistment of one for a key dramatic role in the hit film, *Children of a Lesser God*.

For years the most completely satisfying recording of three concertos was the unabashedly Romantic account by David and Igor Oistrakh that is still available on Deutsche Grammophon. Those achingly beautiful performances would have remained my first choice in a very crowded field had it not been for the release last year of an even more lush and lovely interpretation by the young German violinist, Anne-Sophie Mutter.

When Mutter first arrived on the scene a few years ago, I admit I took little notice. I assumed that, as the latest in a long line of Herbert von Karajan proteges, she would inevitably develop along the same cold, impersonal lines. Fortunately— if this marvelous Angel recording is any indication—she has shed all vestiges of Karajan's reptilian influence to become a most magnetic young musician.

Stylistically, Mutter's performances of the Bach concertos are throwbacks. Cast on a large scale and full of late-Romantic gestures (has anyone since Kreisler made the slow movement of the E Major concerto sound as languorously sexy as this?) the interpretations are a perfect complement to her immense tone and seamless technique. As conductor and second violinist in the Double Concerto, Salvatore Accardo brings his usual wealth of warmth and experience to what I suspect may become *the* indispensable Bach concerto recording of the 1980s.

For collectors of LPs and tapes, Itzhak Perlman's ripe and dashing performances with Daniel Barenboim and the English Chamber Orchestra (AM-34726, 4AM-34726 [T]) are the most enjoyable after Mutter's.

*G*oldberg *Variations*, S. 988

Gould, piano. CBS M3X-38610 [LP], MX3T-38610 [T]. (1955 mono version; 1981 Digital Stereo version; 1982 interview.) CBS IM-37779 [LP], *MK-37779* [CD], IMT-37779 [T]. (1981 version)

Pinnock, harpsichord. Deutsche Grammophon ARC-2533425 [LP], *415130-2* [CD], 415130-4 [T].

The most cogent thing ever said about that mystery wrapped in an enigma, Glenn Gould, was an offhand wisecrack dropped by the conductor George Szell shortly after he had performed with the late Canadian pianist for the first time. "That nut is a genius," Szell was heard to mumble, and history should probably let it go at that. Willful, unpredictable, eccentric, reclusive, and maddeningly brilliant, Glenn Gould is easily the most provocative pianist of his generation and one of the great musical originals of modern times.

The 1955 recording of the *Goldberg Variations* introduced Glenn Gould to an unsuspecting world and opened an entirely new chapter in the history of Bach interpretation. Legend has it that the *Goldberg Variations* were originally written as a soporific for a music-loving nobleman who was a chronic insomniac. In most recordings of the work, which as a rule are rather stultifying, the legend can certainly be believed. Gould changed all that with driving tempos, a bracing rhythmic vitality, and an ability to clarify and untangle Bach's dense contrapuntal lines; Gould's feast was, and remains, amazing.

After twenty-five years of further study, Gould rerecorded the work in 1981, and the result is every bit as controversial as his original recording. While sacrificing none of the razor-sharp clarity of the earlier performance, the interpretation becomes more profound and reflective. Tempos not only are dramatically slower, but also are chosen—according to the pianist—to help each of the variations fit into a more homogeneous, integrated whole.

For a half dozen years, I've been trying to choose between the youthful brashness of the original or the mature, studied brashness of the Revised Standard Version without much success. Although only the 1981 recording is available on a compact disc, CBS has conveniently packaged both performances, together with a typically zany and illuminating interview with the pianist, in a handsome boxed three-record set.

For those who insist on a harpsichord (though *I* am forced to agree with Sir Thomas Beecham, who said its sound reminded him of "a pair of skeletons copulating on a corrugated tin roof") I suggest the alert, intelligent performance by Trevor Pinnock.

Mass in B minor, S. 232

> Monteverdi Choir, English Baroque Soloists, Gardiner.
> Deutsche Grammophon Archiv ARC-415514-1
> [LP], 415514-2 [CD], 415514-4 [T].

> Nelson, Baird, Dooley, Hoffmeister, Opalach, Schultze,
> Bach Ensemble, Rifkin. Nonesuch 79036/4D [LP],
> *79036-2* [CD], 79036-4 [T].

The baroque revival of the 1960s was a very shrewd marketing ploy of the recording industry. Compared to operas or Mahler symphonies, baroque music is far easier and, more important from *their* point of view, far *cheaper* to record. Torrents of music by composers who for centuries had been little more than names in a book, along with well-intentioned but generally lamentable recordings by organizations like the Telemann Society and stellar European ensembles like the Pforzheim Chamber Orchestra of Heilbron, inundated us.

The Baroque Boom was further complicated by the emergence of the Baroque Authenticity Movement, whose exponents argued—at times persuasively—that for baroque music to make the points the composer intended, it had to be presented on instruments of the period. Like all such upheavals, the period instrument revolution spawned its fair share of frauds and fanatics: untalented, uninspired charlatans who forgot that making music *does not* consist entirely of making physically repellant noises and arcane musicological points.

In the work of three English musicians, Christopher Hogwood, Trevor Pinnock, and preeminently, John Elliot Gardiner, we finally have convincing evidence that the Authenticity Period Instrument Movement has at last grown up: for each of the three finest antiquarians before the public today is a musician first, a musicologist second. Gardiner's recording of the Bach *Mass in B minor* is as stirring and compassionate as his exhilarating recordings of the Handel Oratorios. He mixes grace, finesse, and dramatic grandeur into an immensely satisfying amalgam, while managing to coax more physical beauty from those old instruments than has any other conductor.

For an interesting companion piece to Gardiner, try Joshua Rifkin—a versatile and vastly gifted musician who helped persuade the musical establishment to take Scott Joplin's music seriously—and his controversial Nonesuch recording with the Bach Ensemble. Rifkin's recording of the *Mass in B minor* is a radical experiment that audaciously assigns only a single voice to each of the choral parts. From a musician of lesser stature, the project might have easily degenerated into yet another Baroque Authenticity gimmick. But Rifkin, in a brilliantly argued essay and an even more convincingly argued performance, proves that "authenticity" has far less to do with editions and instrumentation than with the authentic gifts of the performers.

Suites (6) for Solo Cello, S. 1007/12

Tortelier, cello. Angel *CDC 47090/3* [CD].

Ma, cello. CBS I3M-37867 [LP], *M2K-37867* [CD], IMT-37867 [T].

In the right hands, Bach's six Suites for Solo Cello can be an ennobling, thoroughly rewarding experience; in the wrong hands, they can be a crashing, unmitigated bore. There is certainly nothing boring about Pablo Casals' legendary recordings from the 1930s, which are still available as an Angel three-record Angel set. While professional musicians tend to admire them without reservation (Mitch Miller once told me that he developed his wonderful singing style on the oboe by trying to emulate the long lines that the cellist achieved on those famous old discs), my reaction to Casals' playing has always been similar to Igor Stravinsky's reaction: "Of course, he is a very great man. He is in favor of Peace, against General Franco, and plays Bach in the manner of Brahms."

My own introduction to the Solo Cello Suites was that superb, now deleted Mercury recording by Janos Starker. His more recent interpretation for the tiny Sefel label, while as polished and controlled as the older recording, lacks much of its fire and daring.

The eagerly anticipated account by Yo-Yo Ma, the most accomplished cellist of his generation, is a considerable disappointment. While the playing itself is thrillingly beautiful, a certain sameness in the performances leaves one flat, as though one had overheard a youthful run-through of what undoubtedly will be a great interpretation a few years down the road. Nevertheless, Ma's version is still to be preferred in both the LP and tape formats.

The magnificent 1983 recording, reissued on compact disc, made by the late French cellist, Paul Tortelier, is a robust, impassioned interpretation in the Casals tradition. His performances also manage to communicate a hefty dose of Gallic urbanity and wit. Tortelier's rich, red-blooded playing probably will not appeal to the baroque purists—which is probably why I have always loved it so.

Orchestral Suites (4), S. 1066/69

**English Baroque Soloists, Gardiner. Erato 75076 [LP],
    88048/49 [CD], T-75076 [T].**

**Academy of St. Martin-in-the-Fields, Marriner.
    London 414 505-1 [LP], *414 505-2* [CD].**

Nikolaus Harnoncourt's pioneering period instrument recording in the late 1960s established his reputation as an interpreter of Bach's music. I remember buying it and being moderately enthusiastic at the time. Listening to it again, after nearly two decades, I realize what a woefully uncritical listener I was twenty years ago. It still seems the best of Harnoncourt's recordings, but that's a bit like determining which root-canal procedure bothered one the least. You should not waste your money buying this recording, but the next time you hear it on the radio, notice how crude and lifeless the playing is. In fact, in his driven, humorless approach to everything, Harnoncourt suggests nothing more than a kind of technically inept Toscanini of the baroque.

Among the many fine versions of the Suites currently available, the admirable recordings by John Elliot Gardiner and Sir Neville Marriner stand out from all the rest.

The first of Marriner's three separate recordings to date, the London version, is a reissue of that dazzling Argo edition prepared with the help of the late English musicologist, Thurston Dart. As in Marriner's interpretation of the *Brandenburg Concertos*, the playing is brisk and ingratiating with memorable contributions by every solo voice.

A choice between Marriner and the equally gripping period instrument version by Gardiner and his English Baroque Soloists is an extremely difficult one. Like Marriner, Gardiner makes the music bubble over with an irresistible enthusiasm and freshness; his trumpets and timpani have a wonderfully obstreperous cutting edge, while the baroque violins sound uncommonly smooth and warm. If the Gardiner recording has an advantage over the Marriner, it is its slightly superior recorded sound.

The Well-Tempered Clavier, S. 846/93

Gould, piano. CBS D3S-733 [LP]; D3M-31525 [LP], *M4-42042* [CD], M4T-42042.

Gilbert, harpsichord. Deutsche Grammophon Archiv ARC-413439-1 [LP], *ARC-413439-2* [CD].

In a charming one-page essay called "Masters of Tone," the great American newspaperman, iconoclast, and linguistics scholar, H. L. Mencken, summed up the music of Johann

Sebastian Bach as "Genesis I:1." Nowhere is Bach's seminal importance to the development of Western Music more obvious than in that most significant of all baroque keyboard collections, *The Well-Tempered Clavier*. Beginning with a disarmingly simple C Major prelude that makes Beethoven's *Für Elise* seem like the Third Rachmaninoff Concerto, *The Well-Tempered Clavier* moves triumphantly through all the major and minor keys with forty-eight masterworks encapsulating the entire scope of baroque contrapuntal thinking and epitomizing the essential greatness of Bach's mature keyboard style.

Like *The Art of Fugue*, *The Well-Tempered Clavier* was probably never intended for public performance and is, in fact, dedicated to the "musical youth, desirous of learning." Despite this intention, major keyboard artists of the Twentieth Century, beginning with Wanda Landowska and Edwin Fischer, have left immensely personal visions of this towering monument, which continues to exert an irresistible fascination for performers today.

As a performance, the most staggering modern interpretation could be heard on a Melodiya/Angel recording, now long out of print, by Sviatoslav Richter. Like Serge Koussevitzky's rendition of Beethoven, Richter's conception of *The Well-Tempered Clavier* may have very little to do with the music of Bach; as a lesson in the art of piano playing given by the most fabulously complete pianist of the last forty years, it has never been approached.

As in his recording of the *Goldberg Variations*, Glenn Gould's performance remains a model of imaginative musical brinkmanship. In spite of all the eccentricities—which include some of the fastest and slowest performances the individual preludes have ever received—the playing is a triumph of Gouldian textural clarity and pizzazz. The way he manages to make the most complicated fugues sound so trivially easy will leave the jaws of the ten-fingered dragging on the floor.

For a less personal, though by no means anonymous, vision supplied by one of today's preeminent harpsichordists, the Deutsche Grammophon recording by Kenneth Gilbert offers many quiet and unexpected revelations. With playing alternately relaxed and pointed, Gilbert—without ever letting us forget that we are in the presence of a major artist—allows us to focus our entire attention where it properly belongs: on the music itself.

Barber, Samuel (1910–1981)

Adagio for Strings (from String Quartet, Op. 11)

**Los Angeles Philharmonic, Bernstein. Deutsche
Grammophon 423169-1 [LP], *413324-2* [CD],
413324-4 [T].**

Even before achieving its current celebrity as "The Love
Theme from *Platoon*," Barber's moltenly beautiful *Adagio for
Strings* had acquired many powerful non-musical associa-
tions. In fact, the case can be made that its moving use during
Franklin Delano Roosevelt's funeral established Samuel Bar-
ber's popular reputation.

Of the many recordings of the *Adagio*, none comes
within hailing distance of the live performance, preserved
superbly by Deutsche Grammophon, that Leonard Bernstein
gave a few years ago with the Los Angeles Philharmonic.
Bernstein adopts a tempo so measured that the music is
almost guaranteed to fall apart. With vast dignity and deliberation he wrenches the last ounce of pain and pathos from the
Adagio, while building to one of the most devastating climaxes any piece has received in recent memory. The Barber is
clearly the principal selling point, but Bernstein's equally
thrilling interpretations of his own *Candide Overture*,
William Schuman's *American Festival Overture*, and Aaron

Copland's *Appalachian Spring* make one of the most exciting recordings of American music released in a decade.

For those interested in the ravishing String Quartet from which the *Adagio* was taken, a searing performance by the Concord String Quartet is available on Nonesuch 78019.

*A*dagio for Strings; Essay No. 2 for Orchestra; Overture to "The School for Scandal"; *Medea's Meditation and Dance of Vengeance.*

New York Philharmonic, Schippers. CBS Odyssey Y-33230 [LP], YT-33230 [T].

Except for the powerful and powerfully original Symphony No. 1 (which has never had a completely satisfying recording since Bruno Walter—of all people!—left his blazing account during the 78 era), this treasurable Odyssey release contains most of the works upon which Barber's reputation as a composer of orchestral music will probably rest.

The late Thomas Schippers' credentials as a Barber conductor were, to say the very least, impressive. An intimate friend of the composer, Schippers was responsible for perhaps the finest of all Barber recordings: an ineffably tender account of the composer's masterpiece, *Knoxville: Summer of 1915.* (Shamefully, RCA Victor has allowed that luminescent recording, with soprano Leontyne Price, to slip out of print.)

In this recording, the New York Philharmonic is on its best behavior, and Thomas Schippers is at the very top of his form. This *Adagio* is the only one that bears favorable comparison to Bernstein's version, the Overture crackles with gaiety and wit, and *Medea's Meditation and Dance of Vengeance* is unleashed with such horrifying intensity that it makes listeners think Mother's Day should be canceled. The gem of the collection, however, is the reading of the Second Essay for Orchestra, in which lyricism, passion, and architectural integrity are kept in nearly perfect equilibrium by one of the most strangely underrated conductors of his era.

Bartók, Béla (1881–1945)

Concerto for Orchestra

**Chicago Symphony, Reiner. RCA AGL-1 2909 [LP],
5604 [CD].**

**New York Philharmonic, Boulez. CBS MYT-37259
[T].**

Like his near contemporary George Szell, Fritz Reiner
was one of the consummate orchestral technicians of the
twentieth century. There was little that his minuscule, but
infinitely varied beat could not express, and even less that
escaped his hooded, hawk-like eye. He was also a humorless
despot who terrorized orchestras for more than fifty years.
Once, at a Reiner rehearsal, a jovial bass player whipped out a
huge brass telescope and shouted "I'm looking for the beat."
The man was fired on the spot.

Like Szell—of whom one hears the same nonsense—
Reiner was frequently accused of being rather chilly and aloof
in his performances: a kind of radioactive ice cube who sacri-
ficed depth and emotion in favor of brilliantly polished surface
details. Dozens of Reiner recordings ably refute such a preposterous contention, but none more convincingly than his
stupendous version of Bartók's *Concerto for Orchestra*.

Reiner's association with the *Concerto* in fact began
before the piece was written. Without Bartók's consent or
knowledge, Reiner and his friend, Hungarian violinist Joseph

Szigeti, persuaded Serge Koussevitzky to commission the work from the destitute, dying composer in 1942. Reiner made the first commercial recording of the *Concerto* with the Pittsburgh Symphony, and the very first stereo recording with the Chicago Symphony in 1955.

In its new compact disc format, this ageless performance sounds as though it might have been recorded a few years ago, instead of at the very dawn of the stereo era. Reiner's characteristic combination of complete flexibility and cast-iron control can be heard in every bar of the interpretation, from the dark melancholy of the opening movement to the giddy reaffirmation of life in the *Finale*.

If Sir Georg Solti's more recent Chicago Symphony performance on a London compact disc offers clearer sound and slightly better orchestral execution, the brusque and intermittently vulgar reading is no match for Reiner's. In fact, Reiner's only serious competition comes from Pierre Boulez. In one of his finest New York Philharmonic recordings, Boulez offers a brilliantly analytical yet glowing performance, marred only by the occasionally slipshod playing of the Philharmonic brass. The Boulez recording is, by a comfortable margin, the first choice among all available cassette tapes. Still, Boulez (to say nothing of every conductor who has recorded the piece) is up against a force of nature in this music. And since the Reiner compact disc offers as a bonus the most hair-raising of all recordings of the *Music for Strings, Percussion and Celesta*, it constitutes—at something over 65 minutes—one of the few authentic bargains on the market today.

String Quartets (6)

Juilliard Quartet. CBS 31196/8 [LP].

Takács Quartet. Hungaroton *HDC-12502/04* [CD].

Excepting the quartets of Dmitri Shostakovich, Arnold Schoenberg, and Leos Janácek, Béla Bartók's are the most significant contribution by a twentieth century composer to the form. Each of these adventurous masterworks is an important signpost in the evolution of Bartók's stylistic development: from the folklike elements which pervade the early works, to the astringent flirtation with atonality in the middle two, to a more direct and simple mode of communication in the last two works of the series.

For more than three decades, the cycle has very nearly been the private property of the Juilliard String Quartet. They were the first ensemble to record the quartets in the 1950s and have subsequently recorded them twice. It is their second version that captures more of the color, ferocious intensity, and subtle poetry of these works than any other recording. Listen, for instance, to the Juilliard's diabolical playing in the second movement of the Second Quartet, a performance of such frightening precision and wild, gypsylike abandon that you will want to close all the windows and lock all the doors.

This irreplaceable recording should be a prime candidate for a compact disc, but until it appears in that format, the Hungaroton recording by the brilliant Takács Quartet will fill the gap quite nicely. While no match for the Juilliard's whizbang virtuosity and interpretive savvy, the four young Hungarians play with poise, individuality, and a refreshingly youthful impetuosity and ardor.

Sadly, no tape version of this pivotal cycle of twentieth century chamber works is currently available.

Beethoven, Ludwig van
(1770–1826)

Concertos (5) for Piano and Orchestra

Fleisher, Cleveland Orchestra, Szell. CBS M4X-30052
[LP], *M3K-42445* [CD].

Schnabel, London Symphony, Sargent. Arabesque
Z-6550 [CD], 9103-4 [T].

Since the extravagantly gifted William Kapell died in a
plane crash near San Francisco in 1953, the careers of America's finest pianists have been the cause of great sadness,
consternation, and alarm. The mercurial, highly strung Byron
Janis began canceling appearances on such a regular basis
that his brief but brilliant career was over almost before it
began; similarly, the unjustly maligned Van Cliburn, after
years of abuse from the critics, lapsed into a stony silence
from which he has yet to emerge. Gary Graffman has been
plagued in the last decade by a crippling neurological disorder, as has the most accomplished American pianist since
William Kapell, Leon Fleisher.

The recent CBS compact disc reissue of Fleisher's classic
account of the Beethoven Concertos with George Szell and the
Cleveland Orchestra is a major cause for rejoicing. Rarely, if
ever, have a pianist and conductor shown more unanimity of
purpose and execution in this music. The rhythms are consistently crisp and vibrant, the phrasing is meticulous almost to a

fault, and the hair-trigger reflexes of the Cleveland Orchestra are a perfect complement to Fleisher's once fabulous technique. Although some listeners might find the approach uncomfortably patrician, Fleisher and Szell manage to scrape off so many layers of accumulated interpretive treacle that we are able, in effect, to hear these familiar and frequently hackneyed works as if for the very first time.

If state-of-the-art recorded sound and mechanical perfection are not absolute necessities, the recordings made in the 1930s by Fleisher's great teacher, Arthur Schnabel, are still the standard by which all other recordings must be judged. Never a pianist's pianist, Schnabel's technical imperfections were the butt of countless jokes among his colleagues. When told that Schnabel had been exempted from military service for physical reasons during the First World War, that mordant turn-of-the-century virtuoso Moritz Rosenthal quipped, "Naturally, the man has no fingers." Nevertheless, the force of Schnabel's personality virtually rediscovered Beethoven's piano music in the 1920s and 1930s, and in Arabesque's immaculate transfers these impetuous, headstrong, and always deeply personal interpretations emerge as touchstones of twentieth century keyboard art.

Concerto for Violin and Orchestra in D Major, Op. 61

Menuhin, Philharmonia Orchestra, Furtwängler.
Angel CDC-47119 [LP], *47119-2* [CD].

Perlman, Philharmonia Orchestra, Giulini. Angel
DS-37471 [LP], *CDC-47002* [CD], 4XS-37471 [T].

It has been argued persuasively that Yehudi Menuhin has yet to make a finer recording than his 1932 version of the Elgar Violin Concerto, made when that extraordinary child prodigy was only sixteen years old. And in the last couple of decades, Menuhin's olympian technique has eroded alarmingly. Although his warmth and musicianship are still there in ample supply, his digital dexterity is now a mere shadow of its former self.

This famous recording of the Beethoven Concerto ranks with the Elgar as the violinist's greatest achievement. In it, this unique musician's high-minded nobility and melting tenderness are conspicuously on display. Add to that the surging yet impeccably disciplined accompaniment provided by Wilhelm Furtwängler in one of his final commercial recordings, and we are left with something very close to a Beethoven Violin Concerto for the ages.

For those who require more up-to-date sound—although in Angel's compact disc transfer the 1954 acoustics are remarkably detailed and warm—the best modern version comes from Itzhak Perlman and Carlo Maria Giulini. The violinist offers his usual blend of exuberance and arching lyricism, while the conductor's elegant yet probing support confirms his reputation as one of the great modern accompanists.

Fidelio, Op. 72

Ludwig, Vickers, Frick, Berry, Philharmonia Orchestra and Chorus, Klemperer. Angel AV-34003 [LP].

None of Beethoven's works would ever cost him as much time, pain, and backbreaking labor, but more than 180 years after *Fidelio*'s first successful production, the composer's one and only opera still provokes heated debates. Is the rickety rescue melodrama worthy of the magnificent music that fleshes it out? Is *Fidelio* a successful *opera* at all, or simply a breathtaking collection of musical essays in the composer's mature middle-period style?

No one ever made a stronger case for *Fidelio* both as music and as musical theatre than Otto Klemperer, whose legendary recording from the early 1960s features some of the noblest conducting ever captured on records. With a monumentality and scope that truly dwarfs the competition, the Klemperer *Fidelio* is also a gripping dramatic experience. Leonore's *Abscheulicher!*, Florestan's second act aria, the Dungeon Scene, and the exultant *Finale* all crackle and pop with an immediate and vivid realism, beside which all other recorded performances seem flaccid and pale.

Obviously, Klemperer was aided and abetted by an exemplary cast of singers: the ink-black Pizarro of Gottlob Frick, the intensely moving and musical Leonore of Christa Ludwig, and the incomparable Florestan of Jon Vickers, who clearly is the greatest dramatic tenor since the end of the Second World War.

There is no acceptable compact disc alternative to this astonishing achievement, but given Angel's past enlightened policy of reissuing Klemperer recordings, we can no doubt expect a compact disc version soon.

Missa Solemnis in D, Op. 123

> Moser, Schwarz, Kollo, Moll, Hilversum Radio Choir, Concertgebouw Orchestra of Amsterdam, Bernstein. Deutsche Grammophon *413780-2* [CD].

> Popp, Minton, Walker, Howell, Chicago Symphony Chorus and Orchestra, Solti. London 411842-1 [LP], 411842-4 [T].

During his tenure with the New York Philharmonic, Leonard Bernstein made a splendidly dramatic recording of this greatest of Beethoven's choral works, a performance which is now superseded—as is every other recording in the catalogue—by this sublime interpretation pieced together from two live performances given in Holland a few years ago.

Bernstein's name still conjures up images of glitz and glitter for some people. For three decades his public persona has certainly not encouraged many to take him seriously, and a recent shallow and vulgar biography hasn't helped matters. Yet beneath it all, Bernstein has always been a profoundly serious musician, and this recording only confirms what I have suspected for many years: Leonard Bernstein is the most consistently interesting and, in all probability, the greatest conductor the world has seen since Wilhelm Furtwängler.

Like Furtwängler, Bernstein frequently turns the act of music-making into a deeply spiritual, often mystical experience: an experience we feel from first note to last in this transcendent *Missa Solemnis*. The performance itself is by no means perfect: the soprano soloist is barely adequate in her brutally demanding part, and even the normally flawless Concertgebouw Orchestra has the occasional, if barely noticeable, slip. Of course, such minor quibbles hardly matter. It's extremely unlikely that any recorded version of the work will ever come close to this one's depth and ethereal beauty.

For record and tape collectors, Sir Georg Solti's vivid and dramatic London recording is the best alternative to the otherworldliness of Bernstein's phenomenal achievement.

Overtures

Philharmonia Orchestra, Klemperer. Angel *CDC-47190* [CD], 4AE-34441 [T].

Cleveland Orchestra, Szell. CBS MP-38758 [LP], MT-38758 [T].

These are two invaluable collections of Beethoven's most popular overtures. The Klemperer performances are characterized by an all-encompassing grasp of the musical architecture and imposing strength of character; the Szell performances, by an appealing nervous energy tempered by the conductor's storied technical control. Both recordings offer all three of the *Leonore* Overtures and the *King Stephen*.

Klemperer provides an epic account of the *Prometheus*, and Szell's performance of the *Egmont* is arguably the most exciting ever made.

Quartets (16)

**Alban Berg Quartet. Angel *CDC-47126* (Op. 18) [CD];
CDC-47130 (Op. 59, 74, 95) [CD]; DC-3973 [LP]
or *CDC-47134* (Op. 127, 130, 131, 132, 135,
Grosse Fugue) [CD].**
Talich Quartet. Calliope 1631/40, 4631/40 [T].

If in his nine Symphonies Beethoven became the composer who had the most seismic impact on the development of nineteenth century music, then in his astonishing series of sixteen string quartets we are introduced, more revealingly than anywhere else, to the man inside the public figure. Beethoven reserved the most personal and intimate of his musical thoughts for his chamber music, and in his chamber works the most restlessly original composer in the history of music became his most consistently adventurous.

Since the days of those pioneering, magically effective 78 recordings by the Lener Quartet, virtually every important ensemble has come to terms with the cycle, and none more successfully in recent years than Vienna's Alban Berg Quartet. Named after the great Viennese composer, the Alban Berg Quartet is probably without equal in the world today. They play with a finesse and finish that only the Guarneri Quartet, at the height of its fame, could begin to match. The Berg Quartet's technical prowess is reminiscent of the young Juilliard, and the engaging warmth and mellowness of its physical sound has not been heard since the disbandment of the great—and greatly lamented—Quartetto Italiano.

For the audiophile or the novice listener, the Berg Quartet's recording of the complete Beethoven quartets is a nearly perfect introduction to the cycle, and even the most jaded collector will find much here that seems startlingly fresh, original, and new. The Opus 18 collection sparkles with a suitably Haydnesque wit and charm; the middle-period quartets are appropriately tempestuous and heroic. If in those final mysterious masterworks the Quartet is unable to probe quite as deeply as the Busch Quartet did a half century ago, its performance still leaves most of the current competition far behind.

For the LP or tape collector, the performances by the brilliant Talich Quartet, while not quite as polished as the Berg Quartet's, are full of character, bite, and youthful enthusiasm. Their recording also has the distinction of being one of the few which is not solely available on compact discs.

*P*iano Sonata No. 8 in C minor, Op. 13 "Pathetique"; Sonata No. 14 in C-sharp minor, Op. 27 No. 2 "Moonlight"; Sonata No. 23 in F minor, Op. 57 "Appassionata."

Rudolf Serkin, piano. CBS MY-37219 [LP], *MYK-37219* [CD], MYT-37219 [T].

Rudolf Serkin has often told an amusing story about his Berlin debut in the 1920s, when he performed Bach's Fifth Brandenburg Concerto with the man who would eventually become his father-in-law, Adolf Busch. Following the audience's warm reception, Busch invited the young pianist to favor them with an encore. Serkin responded with the whole of Bach's *Goldberg Variations*. As Serkin later recalled the scene, "At the end of the evening there were only four people left in the hall: Adolf Busch, Arthur Schnabel, (the musicologist) Alfred Einstein, and me." Throughout his career, there has been an endearing, almost boyish earnestness in Serkin's playing, and to the music of Beethoven, Mozart, Schubert, and Brahms he has always brought a special authority and integrity that no living pianist can match.

In this attractive collection of three of the most popular Beethoven piano sonatas, Serkin's lofty, thoroughly committed approach serves this familiar music extremely well. The performances are vastly intelligent without ever becoming pedantic, selfless though never self-effacing, impassioned yet never overblown. Until some recording company is canny enough to reissue Ivan Moravec's impossibly beautiful Connoisseur Society recording of the "Moonlight" Sonata, Serkin's will remain the standard performances of all three.

Sonata No. 9 in A Major for Violin and Piano, Op. 47 "Kreutzer."

Huberman, violin; Friedman, piano. Danacord
141/146 [LP].

Perlman, violin; Ashkenazy, piano. London *410554-2*
[CD].

I have had countless heated arguments with violinist friends over the years whenever I made so bold to suggest that Jascha Heifetz was not, as far as I was concerned, the great violinist of the twentieth century. Granted, his was probably the most phenomenal technique since Paganini's, but with a handful of recorded exceptions—the Second Prokofiev Concerto and the D Major Concerto of Erich Wolfgang Korngold—I have always found his playing heartless, distant, and cold. When challenged to name a finer violinist, I typically supply a list of at least a half dozen possibilities. The list invariably begins with Bronislaw Huberman.

Like Fritz Kreisler, Jacques Thibaud, Joseph Szigeti, and other giants of the era, Huberman was never a note-perfect player, nor was he a paragon of consistency. More often than not, his performances were flawed by the most elementary kind of mistakes, even though his technical finish could be nearly as impressive as Heifetz' whenever the occasion arose. For Huberman's generation of violinists, technique was never an end in itself: always a great musician who only *happened* to play the violin, he was far more deeply concerned with what lay between and beneath the notes.

Compare this justly celebrated 1930 recording of the "Kreutzer" Sonata with any of the several versions that Heifetz left, and you'll begin to understand the difference between flesh-and-blood music making and mere superhuman facility. In spite of some minor slips and the errant sour note, Huberman invests every bar of the piece with passion, profundity, and an instantly recognizable musical personality. It is an interpretation riddled with rubato, *portamenti*, and other Romantic liberties, yet a performance of such conviction that everything sounds utterly natural, inevitable, and right. The playing of pianist Ignaz Friedman more than lives up to its almost mythic proportions. In addition, this priceless six-record collection preserves virtually all the commercial recordings ever made by the legendary Polish pianist.

The most completely satisfying modern version of the "Kreutzer" is the London compact disc by Itzhak Perlman and Vladimir Ashkenazy, who also turn in a delectably verdant account of the composer's "Spring" Sonata.

Symphony No. 1 in C Major, Op. 21

English Chamber Orchestra, Thomas. CBS IM-39707 [LP], IMT-39707 [T].

Philharmonia Orchestra, Klemperer. Angel *CDC-47184* [CD], 4AE-34423 [T].

Here is a pair of superlative recordings which will help to demolish the preconceptions that many listeners have about the two conductors involved: the adroit but essentially lightweight Michael Tilson Thomas, and the stodgy, ponderous Otto Klemperer, who toward the end of his life made recordings as weighty as Easter Island monoliths.

Using an ensemble whose reduced forces are those of the standard Mozart orchestra, Thomas turns in a beautifully proportioned, refreshingly vigorous interpretation of the work, and Klemperer, who most assuredly *never* was lethargic, responds with the same light and delicate touch that characterized his admirable Haydn recordings. Until Philips sees fit to reissue that spontaneous wonder Sir Neville Marriner and the Academy of St. Martin-in-the-Fields, unleashed a decade and a half ago, these are the recordings that will probably dominate the catalogues for years.

*S*ymphony No. 2 in D Major, Op. 36; Symphony No. 8 in F Major, Op. 93

London Classical Players, Norrington. Angel DS-47698 [LP], *CDC-47698* [CD], 4DS-47698 [T].

The thought of a group of musicians actually going out of their way to wrestle with those treacherous and invariably vile-sounding antiques has always reminded me of my quasi-Hippie, back-to-the-basics friends of the 1960s, who took such inexplicable pride in outdoor plumbing, home-ground grain, and miserably inefficient—to say nothing of vastly malodorous—wood-burning stoves. Thank goodness times have changed. It's now possible to dismiss such nonsense without people suspecting you of having been a secret supporter of the Vietnam War.

Imagine, then, my dumfounded amazement at being so thoroughly swept away by this electrifying period-instrument recording, further heartening proof that the Authenticity Movement has finally moved out of the finger-painting stage. The London Classical Players are obviously cracker-jack musicians one and all, as opposed to the hacks and second-raters that the phrase "period instrument" always seemed to imply. They play with genuine polish and fire and, urged on by Roger Norrington, deliver two of the most ferociously exciting

Beethoven Symphony recordings released in years. Had such recordings been available when the period instrument revival began, I might have given up eating Wonder bread years ago.

Symphony No. 3 in F-flat Major, Op. 55 "Eroica"

Vienna Philharmonic, Furtwängler. Angel *CDC-47410* [CD].

Cleveland Orchestra, Szell. CBS MY-37222 [LP], *MYK-37222* [CD], MYT-37222 [T].

From 1922, the year he succeeded Arthur Nikisch as music director of both the Berlin Philharmonic and Leipzig Gewandhaus Orchestra, to his death in 1954, Wilhelm Furtwängler was the most potent and eloquent spokesman for a style of interpretation that could trace its roots to Richard Wagner, the major conducting force of nineteenth century music. In Furtwängler, Wagner's radical theories about phrasing, tempo modification, and the idealized image of the interpreter as an artist on equal footing with the composer were given—depending on one's point of view—their final grotesque or glorious expression.

For those who grew up under the spell of Arturo Toscanini's new Objectivism, Furtwängler was an anachronism: an unpleasant reminder of a time when Romantic excesses practically made a composer's intentions unintelligible. For those who were unpersuaded by the Italian conductor's manic though essentially simpleminded approach, Furtwängler was one of the last heroically subjective individualists: a man whose mystic, almost messianic faith in his own ideas transfigured all he touched with the sheer force of his personality alone.

If any other recording of Beethoven's "Eroica" does more to justify the Symphony's subtitle, I have yet to hear it. Only Otto Klemperer found a comparable grandeur in this music; however, along with the titanic *scale* of Furtwängler's performance comes a dramatic power and animal magnetism that remains unique. No one has ever transformed the funeral march into the stuff of such inconsolable tragedy, nor has any conductor found such individuality in each of the final movement's variations or galvanized that movement into such a unified, indissoluble whole. In short, this is one of the great recordings of the century.

For a more brilliant modern version of this popular work, George Szell's recording with the Cleveland Orchestra—like all the performances from his memorable Beethoven cycle—has stood the test of time magnificently. The sound in all three formats, especially the compact disc, simply refuses to show its age.

Symphony No. 4 in B-flat Major, Op. 60

Bavarian State Orchestra, Carlos Kleiber. Orfeo
S-100841 [LP], *C100841A* [CD].

Columbia Symphony, Walter. MY-37773 [LP],
MK-42011 [CD], MYT-37773 [T].

Robert Schumann inadvertently invited posterity to think of the Fourth as something of a weak sister among the Beethoven symphonies when, in one of his poetic moments, he described it as a Greek maiden standing between two Norse gods. If so, this volcanic souvenir of a live Munich performance suggests the maiden is one hell of an interesting girl.

With his customary flair, Carlos Kleiber virtually rethinks this essentially light and graceful symphony. The outer movements, especially the finale, rush by at a breakneck clip, while the slow movement and *scherzo* are invested with an uncommon significance and weight. Given the extraordinary demands he makes upon them, the courageous Bavarian Radio Symphony's playing is exemplary. Listen especially to the principal clarinet and bassoon who, in their cruelly difficult Finale solos, sound like men born with the snakes' tongues.

For cost-conscious collectors who can't quite bring themselves to spend hard-earned money on any recording, however spectacular, which offers barely a half hour of music, the best alternative is Bruno Walter's gentle yet potent interpretation with the Columbia Symphony. In the LP format, the filler is an equally affecting version of the Eighth Symphony; the compact disc edition comes with a slightly less successful, but still utterly enjoyable run-through of the Fifth.

Symphony No. 5 in C minor, Op. 67

Vienna Philharmonic, Carlos Kleiber. Deutsche Grammophon 2530516 [LP] or *415861-2* [CD], 415861-4 [T].

Dozens of recorded versions of this popular symphony have come and gone since the mid-1970s, when this withering recording introduced a most electric musical personality. For more than fifteen years, only one other version—that majestic and tremendously adult interpretation by Carlo Maria Giulini and the Los Angeles Philharmonic, also on Deutsche Grammophon—has seriously challenged what may be the single most exciting Beethoven recording of the stereo era.

The first movement is a triumph of cataclysmic energy and hushed mystery, while the ensuing *Andante con moto* has never seemed more poetic and refined. Yet it is in the Symphony's final movements that Kleiber leaves the competition panting in the dust: The *scherzo* is transformed into a diabolically grotesque witch's sabbath, and the *Finale*, with the incomparable Vienna Philharmonic in full cry, sweeps all before it in a flood of C Major sunshine.

As in his recording of the Fourth Symphony, Kleiber's Fifth offers fewer than thirty-four minutes of actual playing time. Still, considering the quality of this historic issue, either the LP or the compact disc—to coin a cliché—would be a bargain at twice the price.

Symphony No. 6 in F Major, Op. 68 "Pastorale"

Columbia Symphony, Walter. CBS MY-36720 [LP], *MYK-36720* [CD], MYT-36710 [T].

Symphony No. 7 in A Major, Op. 92

Columbia Symphony, Walter. CBS *MK-42013* [CD].

Like dogcatchers, truant officers, old-time sideshow geeks, and syndicate hit men, recording company executives have always had a rather unsavory reputation: cost conscious bureaucrats whose meager artistic standards have always taken a distant back seat to the pursuit of the almighty bottom line. In fact, with a slight change of gender, their behavior has reminded many musicians and music lovers of Dr. Samuel Johnson's pronouncement on Lady Diana Beauclerk: "The woman's a whore, and there's an end on't."

And yet the recording executive at Columbia Records (now CBS) who in the late 1950s turned the eighty-year-old Bruno Walter loose on the heart of his repertoire, deserves a medal or at least our undying gratitude and admiration. For like the homeric series of recordings that Otto Klemperer made in London during the final years of his career, Walter's protracted recording swan song is an enduring monument to one of the greatest twentieth century conductors.

For more than six decades—and Walter had been conducting professionally for three years *before* the death of Johannes Brahms—the "Pastorale" Symphony was one of his most famous house specialties, and the freshness, wide-eyed innocence, and vivid nature painting of this beautiful recording has never been approached.

Similarly, a finer recording of the A Major Symphony does not exist. If the tempos in the first three movements tend to be on the leisurely side—and on records, only George Szell conducted the second movement as a true *allegretto*—the rhythms are so firm and infectious that we scarcely notice, much less mind. The *Finale*, on the other hand, dashes off in such a good-natured jumble of barely controllable exuberance that we are reminded why Wagner called this swirling masterpiece "The Apotheosis of the Dance."

Among available tapes and LP versions of the Seventh Symphony, a scrappy yet endearing and virile performance by Pablo Casals at one of the Marlboro Festivals in the 1960s is still immensely satisfying (CBS MY-37233 [LP], MYT-37233 [T]).

Symphony No. 9 in D minor, Op. 125 "Choral"

Curtin, Kopleff, McCollum, Gramm, Chicago Symphony Chorus and Orchestra, Reiner. RCA 6532-2-RG [CD].

Shortly after he began his final season as music director of the Chicago Symphony, Fritz Reiner became so seriously ill that many feared he would never lead the orchestra again. (My father and I actually had tickets for the concert where Erich Leinsdorf stepped in at the last moment to officiate at Sviatoslav Richter's American debut.) Reiner recovered sufficiently to return for the final subscription concerts of the season with programs devoted to Beethoven's First and Ninth Symphonies, both of which he recorded in the following week.

Perhaps it is simply my vivid memory of those concerts— and for the first five years of my career as a concertgoer, Fritz Reiner's Chicago Symphony was the only professional orchestra I heard—but this recording has always seemed to me something breathlessly close to the ideal realization of Beethoven's Ninth. Brilliantly played and beautifully sung, it is a suave, rugged, polished, explosive, and inspiring performance that captures Reiner's special gifts at or very near their absolute peak. In its original 1963 incarnation, the sound— like that of most recordings made in prerenovation Orchestra Hall—was a wonder of clarity, warmth, and detail. In RCA's elegant compact disc transfer, it still rivals all but the very best on the market today.

Among that ever-shrinking collection of LPs and tapes, George Szell's electrifying interpretation from about the same period is nearly as convincing as Reiner's. There are some wonderful eccentricities in the performance (including some brass outbursts in the *Finale* that will lift you out of your chair), but essentially the recording is vintage Szell—equal parts of polish, precision, passion, and fire.

Bellini, Vincenzo
(1801–1935)

Norma

**Callas, Stignani, Filippeschi, Rossi-Lemeni, La Scala
Chorus and Orchestra, Serafin. Angel *CDC-47303*
[CD].**

**Callas, Zaccaria, Corelli, Ludwig, La Scala Chorus and
Orchestra, Serafin. Angel AVB-34062 [LP],
4AVB-34062 [T].**

Few words get the true opera lover's juices flowing more
effusively than the title of Vincenzo Bellini's masterpiece,
Norma. In one of his rare bouts of genuine humility, a celebrated opera lover named Richard Wagner said that he hoped
Tristan und Isolde would someday be seen as the German
equivalent of the opera he loved more than any other. The
celebrated Wagnerian soprano, Lilli Lehmann, insisted that a
half dozen Isoldes were far less physically and emotionally
exhausting than *one* encounter with Bellini's Druid priestess.

In this century, the great exponents of what is widely
regarded as the most brutally demanding of all soprano roles
can be counted easily on the fingers of one hand. Sixty years
ago, the matchless American soprano Rosa Ponselle began the
modern *Norma* revival with an interpretation whose sheer
vocal splendor has never been equaled. In more recent times,
the Norma of Dame Joan Sutherland was a technical wonder,

if something of a dramatic joke. And then of course, for a few brief seasons in the 1950s, there was the Norma of Maria Callas. As a vocal and theatrical experience Maria Callas' Norma ranks with Lotte Lehmann's Marschallin and Feodor Chaliapin's Boris Gudonov as one of the supreme operatic experiences of the twentieth century.

Angel was extremely wise to choose this 1954 recording for reissue as a compact disc. Unlike her much less successful, but still overwhelming stereo remake (easily the first choice among LPs and tapes), Callas' voice in the 1954 *Norma* had yet to acquire many of the hooty, wobbling eccentricities for which her admirers are always needlessly apologizing and upon which her detractors fasten like barnacles on a once-majestic ship. Here the voice is heard at its youthful best, from the velvety grace of the *Casta Diva* to the spine-tingling fireworks of *Mira, o Norma*. Even though the Pollione and Oroveso might just as well have phoned in their performances, the choice of indestructible Ebe Stignani as Adalgisa was inspired. Well past her prime at the time the recording was made, this greatest Italian mezzo of the 1930s and 1940s was still a worthy foil for perhaps the finest Norma in history.

Run, don't walk, to buy this one.

Berg, Alban (1885–1935)

Concerto for Violin and Orchestra

**Chung, Chicago Symphony, Solti. London *411804-2*
[CD], 411804-4 [T].**

**Krasner, Stockholm Philharmonic, Fritz Busch. GM
2006 [LP].**

When the history of twentieth century violin playing is
finally written, a special chapter will have to be devoted to
gentle, soft-spoken Louis Krasner. While certainly not one of
the great virtuosos of his era, his name will nevertheless be
remembered long after countless others are forgotten. For it
was Louis Krasner who commissioned two of the most important modern violin concertos: those of Alban Berg and his
teacher, Arnold Schoenberg.

The small Massachusetts-based company, GM Records,
American composer Gunther Schuller's labor of love, has
released two live Krasner performances of both those extraordinary works he helped to create. Although the performances themselves are less than perfect and the recorded sound
is of early 1930s and late 1950s aircheck variety, the living
musical history it represents (together with the violinist's
touching recollections of Berg, Schoenberg, and their turbulent times), makes the recording an absolute necessity for
anyone who is seriously interested in modern music.

Among modern versions of the Berg Concerto none is more thoroughly winning than the poetic, introspective London recording by Kyung-Wha Chung. Her basic approach has much in common with what I still consider the Concerto's greatest interpretation, the heart-rending performance by the late Arthur Grumiaux, from a Philips recording now long out of print. Unlike Itzhak Perlman, who in his sumptuous Deutsche Grammophon recording underscores the Concerto's Brahmsian grandeur and romance, Chung emphasizes the music's subtlety and almost infinite gradations of color. Her playing also has a meditative, elegiac quality, supporting Louis Krasner's contention that the already seriously ill composer consciously wrote the Violin Concerto as his own requiem.

Under Sir Georg Solti, who hasn't made a finer recording in a decade, the Chicago Symphony weaves its way through this treacherous orchestral minefield as though they were out for nothing more than a pleasant evening stroll.

Lyric Suite for String Quartet

LaSalle Quartet. Deutsche Grammophon 419994-1 [LP], *419994-2* [CD], 419994-4 [T].

This great work was already clearly established as one of the cornerstones of modern chamber music when a series of sensational discoveries proved what many listeners had long suspected: there was a bit more to the *Lyric Suite* than met the eye. The composer himself offered a key to the *Lyric Suite*'s mystery with that cryptic and, until recently, inexplicable quotation of the "Love Potion" motif from Wagner's *Tristan und Isolde* embedded in the work's final movement.

It was the brilliant American composer and Berg authority, George Perle, who finally discovered what the piece was really *about*. A score, annotated by Berg himself, and containing the startling revelation that the *Lyric Suite* had in fact been written to a secret program, came into Perle's possession. Called by the composer "A small monument to a Great Love," the work traces the events of a lengthy and passionate love affair the composer conducted with a lady who was not his wife. The final movement is in fact a wordless setting of "De Profundus Clamavi," a tortured poem about doomed, impossible love from Charles Baudelaire's *Fleurs de Mal*.

Needless to say, while the fact that the cat is finally out of the bag after a half century adds much to our understanding of Berg's motives and emotional state when he composed the *Lyric Suite*, nothing could seriously add to or detract from what has been in all that time one of the most profound and profoundly moving of all twentieth century chamber works.

The famous recording by the LaSalle Quartet is only available as part of a larger release that includes most of the major chamber works of Berg, Webern, and their teacher, Arnold Schoenberg. Though it is a considerable investment, the set is more than worth the expense. The performance of the *Lyric Suite* is especially warm and lyrical, and unlike so many performances that make the music seem far more complex and forbidding than it needs to be, their fluent, natural grasp of its language and vocabulary make it as lucid and approachable as one of the late Beethoven quartets.

Berlioz, Hector (1803–1869)

Harold in Italy, for Viola and Orchestra, Op. 16

Imai, viola; London Symphony, Davis. Philips
***416431-2* [CD].**

Ironically, the foremost champions of France's major nineteenth century composer have tended to be British. It was Sir Hamilton Harty—an Ulsterman by birth, and proud of it, thank you—who began the modern Berlioz revival through his revelatory performances with the Hallé Orchestra of Manchester in the 1920s. Sir Thomas Beecham's zany, scintillating interpretations in the middle decades of the century finally helped make the music of this strange and original composer a *bona fide* box office draw. From the mid-1960s onward, this long and fruitful tradition has been ably continued by Sir Colin Davis: in the opinion of many, the finest Berlioz conductor of this century.

Comparing his two recorded versions of *Harold in Italy* provides a fascinating glimpse at Sir Colin's growth as a Berlioz conductor. In the first recording, made with Sir Yehudi Menuhin, Davis deferred to a far more famous colleague. It was as if both the soloist and the conductor forgot that whatever else *Harold in Italy* may be, it is certainly *not* a viola concerto. (After all, Niccolo Paganini, who commissioned the work to show off his new Stradivarius viola, actually refused to play it in public, complaining that it gave him far too little to do.)

On the other hand, Sir Colin's second recording is clearly the conductor's show. As in his other Berlioz performances, the image that Davis tries to project is that of an arch-Romantic composer whose roots are firmly planted in the Classical past. While the interpretation has an appealing sweep and impulsiveness, it is also meticulously controlled. The Japanese violist Nabuko Imai plays her pivotal role with great zest and distinction, offering an unusually urbane and sensitive approach to phrasing and a physical sound whose size and beauty will make you check the record jacket to make certain she really *does* play a viola, not a cello.

As unbelievable as it may seem, not *one* of the currently available tape or LP versions of this famous work is worth a recommendation.

Overtures. (*Beatrice et Benedict, Le Carnaval romain, Le Corsair, Rob Roy, Le Roi Lear*)

Scottish National Orchestra, Gibson. Chandos 1067 [LP] or *8316* [CD].

Boston Symphony, Munch. RCA Victor AKL1-3374 [T].

London Symphony, Previn. Angel Seraphim 4XG-60424 [T].

For some mysterious reason, the three finest recorded collections of Berlioz' delightful overtures are not readily available. Sir Colin Davis' sumptuous Philips recording has vanished entirely, and those equally-valuable though vastly-different recordings by Charles Munch and André Previn can now be found only on cassette. (In their LP formats all three are definitely worth a special search, and if you're going to take the trouble to rummage through the cut-out bins, you might as well try to track down a World Record Club reissue of some spellbinding recordings made in the 1930s by Sir Hamilton Harty, performances that are guaranteed to stimulate a Berlioz lover to the very brink of a coronary.)

Until Philips, Angel, and RCA Victor bring out the Davis, Previn, and Munch recordings on compact discs, this fine Chandos recording will make an attractive stopgap. While not quite a world-caliber ensemble, the game Scottish National Orchestra plays extremely well for Gibson, who as one might expect has an especially memorable outing in *Rob Roy*. In fact, at those moments in the score when the composer actually quotes Scottish folk tunes, you can almost taste the haggis (ugh!) and smell the heather (ah!).

*R*equiem (*Grande Messe des Morts*), Op. 5

Dowd, London Symphony Orchestra and Chorus, Davis. Philips 670019 [LP], *416283-2* [CD].

Of all his major compositions, including the sprawling *La damnation de Faust*, the *Requiem* is probably Hector Berlioz' most problematic work. For just as that other great Requiem by Giuseppe Verdi is a thinly-veiled opera disguised as a sacred service, the *Grande Messe des Morts* is a dramatic symphony that almost incidentally takes as its point of departure one of the most moving texts of the Roman Catholic liturgy.

To date, it is Sir Colin Davis' 1970 recording that best reconciles the *Requiem*'s not completely resolvable sacred and secular conflicts: the *Tuba Mirum*, for once, sounds more like worship than the usual sonic sideshow, and throughout the performance Davis consistently maintains an appropriate sense of decorum without ever allowing the music to become ponderous or dull.

As an eye- and ear-opening bonus, the compact disc reissue comes with an unbelievably civilized and serious reading—and how did Davis keep a straight face?—of what is surely the most embarrassing half hour of unregenerate schlock ever perpetrated by a major composer. The brazen *Symphonie funébre et triomphale* is an utterly mindless twenty-odd minutes of musical trash that I blush to confess, I love without reservation.

While not quite in the same league as the Davis version, Charles Munch's loud and generally zany Boston Symphony recording still gives a great deal of pleasure and is easily the first choice among the slender crop of cassette tapes (RCA Victor AKL1-4984).

Roméo et Juliette, Op. 17

Quivar, Cupido, Krause, Montreal Tudor Singers,
   Montreal Symphony Orchestra and Chorus, Dutoit.
   London *417302-1* [CD], 417302-4 [T].

Chicago Symphony, Giulini. (Orchestral excerpts only).
   Angel AE-34467 [LP], 4AE-37767 [T].

In the last decade, Charles Dutoit has worked a minor miracle in Montreal by transforming a fine regional ensemble into an orchestra of international importance. On a good day—and to hear their recordings or broadcast concerts, they seem to have nothing but *very* good days—the Montreal Symphony must be considered one of the great orchestras of the world. Beginning with their intoxicating version of Ravel's *Daphnis and Chloé*, they have had such an unbroken string of recording triumphs that their gifted music director has become the first superstar conductor of the digital age.

Dutoit's recording of Berlioz' *Roméo et Juliette*—the most far-reaching and startlingly modern of all that composer's scores—has much in common with Sir Colin Davis' famous London Symphony recording for Philips, which has recently resurfaced on compact. discs. All the famous set pieces have tremendous character and individuality, while the connecting episodes refuse to sound, as they so often do, like patchwork filler in which both the composer and the performers are merely marking time. While the Dutoit performance benefits from a chorus which sings with marvelously idiomatic French inflection and feeling, to say nothing of state-of-the-art recorded sound, the real surprise is the ease with which the orchestra outplays even the great London Symphony, which on records is an all but impossible feat.

What a pity that Carlo Maria Giulini didn't record all of *Roméo et Juliette*, for his Angel recording of the orchestral music is among the supreme Berlioz interpretations of the last twenty-five years. The recording dates are from Giulini's first seasons as Principal Guest Conductor of the Chicago Symphony, a collaboration which still can be best described as an ecstatic mutual love affair. The Orchestra played for him with an affection they had not lavished on anyone since Frederick Stock. Every nuance, every subtle gradation in dynamics Giulini asked for he was given instantly, together with a rich yet translucent singing tone they have *never* given to anyone else. Every bar of the Giulini recording, as in the live concert performances which preceded it, contains some wonder of phrasing or execution. *Queen Mab*, for instance, seems to be made not of notes but of the most unimaginably-delicate fairy lace. Had Giulini chosen to record the entire score, his would undoubtedly have been the great *Roméo et Juliette* of our time.

Symphonie fantastique, Op. 14

Concertgebouw Orchestra of Amsterdam, Davis.
Philips 6500774 [LP], *411425-2*, 7300313 [T].

Boston Symphony, Munch. RCA Victor *6210-2* [CD],
ALK1-4984 [T].

In many ways, this odd and perplexing masterpiece remains the most daringly original large-scale orchestral work produced during the entire Romantic Era. Completed barely eight years after the premiere of Beethoven's Ninth, the *Symphonie fantastique* helped define an entirely new compositional aesthetic that would incalculably affect the subsequent development of nineteenth century orchestral music. For unlike the modest nature painting that Beethoven had employed in his "Pastoral" Symphony, the *Symphonie fantastique* was one of the first important orchestral works that attempted to tell a distinct and detailed story. Thus it became a seminal work in the development of Program Music, which would be further expanded in the tone poems of composers from Liszt and Smetana to Richard Strauss. And in his use of the *idée fixe*—a recurrent melody associated in the composer's mind with the heart-throb of the symphony's hero—Berlioz anticipated the use of *leitmotif* technique, the structural glue which would bind together the gargantuan music dramas of Richard Wagner.

Since the invention of electrical recording in the mid-1920s, Berlioz' bizarre, colorful, and outrageously flamboyant score has been handsomely served on records. Bruno Walter and Felix Weingartner made famous early recordings, but perhaps the greatest single recording ever made was a 1929 version by Pierre Monteux and a Parisian pickup orchestra. Long treasured by 78 collectors, this recording has never, to the best of my knowledge, surfaced as an LP.

Sir Colin Davis has recorded the *Symphonie* twice, initially with the London Symphony, and then as his first recorded work with Amsterdam's great Concertgebouw Orchestra. It is Davis' second recording that continues to offer the most balanced and exciting view in the last half century of the *Symphonie fantastique*. The playing of the Concertgebouw Orchestra is a model of modern orchestral execution, and the conception is beautifully organized and wonderfully detailed. Except for the late Jean Martinon, whose Angel recording is only a hairbreadth less effective, Davis is the only conductor (on records) to make use of the haunting cornet part in the Scene at the Ball. Similarly, he is the only conductor who sees fit to observe the all-important repeat in the opening section of the March to the Scaffold. While the first three movements are superbly disciplined and extravagantly expressive, the final two are as exciting as any Berlioz recording on the market today.

For a delightfully scatterbrained and thoroughly exhausting second opinion, consult Charles Munch's first Boston Symphony recording, recently reissued with his equally madcap performance of the *Requiem* on a pair of RCA Victor compact discs. Never one of the century's great disciplinarians—at his very first session with the orchestra, Munch cut the rehearsal short and invited such members of the orchestra who were so inclined to join him for a round of golf—Munch, like Beecham before him, believed that *under*-rehearsal was the key to excitement and spontaneity. If the menacing, insanely driven performance of the Witch's Sabbath is any indication, he certainly had a point.

Bernstein, Leonard
(1918–   )

West Side Story

Te Kanawa, Carreras, Troyanos, Ollman, Horne,
Chorus and Orchestra, Bernstein. Deutsche
Grammophon 415253/1 [LP], *414 253/2* [CD],
415963-4 [T].

If there are any lingering doubts that *West Side Story*
ranks with Gershwin's *Porgy and Bess* as one of the two
greatest works of the American musical theatre, this indispensable Deutsche Grammophon recording should dispel
them. While Bernstein may have written more important or
more obviously "serious" works— the endlessly inventive *Serenade for Violin, Strings, and Percussion* and the deeply
moving *Chichester Psalms*—this inspired transformation of
Shakespeare's *Romeo and Juliet* will probably outlast anything that any American composer, except for Gershwin, has
ever written.

One quickly gets used to the dramatic incongruity of a
Jet singing with a heavy Spanish accent, so the controversial
choice of Jose Carreras as Tony is far less problematic than the
Maria of Dame Kiri Te Kanawa. As always, listening to that
gorgeous instrument is an unalloyed pleasure, and as always
she does little with it other than make an admittedly beautiful
collection of sounds. (Compare her performance to that of the

brilliant Marni Nixon, Natalie Wood's voice in the Robert Wise film, and you'll begin to hear just how emotionally and theatrically deficient Te Kanawa's interpretation is.)

The rest of the performances, especially the sly yet earthy Anita of Tatiana Troyanos, are uniformly excellent, yet it is the composer's conducting that is the real revelation. Each of the numbers is infused with depth, tenderness, and animal excitement—from the inspired poetry of the love music to the jazzy bravado of "Cool" and the great *Quintet*. Even if you don't normally respond to Broadway musicals, don't worry: for *West Side Story* is merely a Broadway musical like the Grand Canyon is merely a large hole in the ground.

Bizet, Georges (1838–1875)

L'Arlésienne (Incidental Music); Symphony in C

Royal Philharmonic; French National Radio Orchestra,
Beecham. Angel AE-34476 [LP], *CDC-47794* [CD],
4AE-34476 [T].

After *Carmen* and the sadly neglected *The Pearl Fishers*—a most hauntingly lovely French opera that, alas, is hamstrung by its relentlessly vapid and dippy text—the incidental music Georges Bizet wrote for Alphonse Daudet's play *L'Arlésienne* is the most attractive and justly popular of all his theatrical scores.

No recording has ever made the *L'Arlésienne* music seem as colorful, original, or utterly fresh as that luminous miracle Sir Thomas Beecham taped with the Royal Philharmonic in the 1950s. As in his celebrated versions of Grieg's *Peer Gynt* and Rimsky-Korsakov's *Scheherazade*, Beecham's ability to rejuvenate and revitalize a familiar war-horse remains uncanny. Each individual section of the *L'Arlésienne* Suites emerges like a freshly restored painting; the rhythms are consistently infectious, the phrasing is pointed and always original, and as is so often the case in a Beecham recording, the solo winds are given a degree of interpretive freedom that no other major conductor would ever dare allow.

The same qualities dominate Beecham's performance of

the composer's youthful C Major Symphony. While the playing of the French National Radio Orchestra is not quite up to the standard of the Royal Philharmonic, the octogenarian conductor's obvious affection and boyish enthusiasm easily make this the preferred recording of the piece.

Carmen

> Crespin, Pilou, Py, Van Dam, Opera du Rhin Chorus, Strasbourg Philharmonic, Lombard. Erato 70900/2 [LP].
>
> Troyanos, Te Kanawa, Domingo, Van Dam, John Alldis Choir, London Philharmonic, Solti. London 414489-1 [LP], *414498-2* [CD], 414498-4 [T].

If you want to play it safe, the Solti *Carmen* has everything to recommend it: a first-rate cast of international voices (the Don Jose of Placido Domingo is especially memorable), adroit and atmospheric playing by the London Philharmonic, a famous conductor who knows the score inside out, and spectacular recorded sound. If, on the other hand, you want to hear a *Carmen* the like of which you've never heard before, snap up that wild and woolly Erato recording before someone decides to take it out of circulation.

The stars of this quirky, eccentric, but thoroughly captivating show are Régine Crespin and the conductor Alain Lombard. The most admired French soprano of her generation, Crespin's Carmen is perhaps her single greatest recorded achievement. It is a Carmen on the old-fashioned, larger-than-life scale: moody, explosive, seductive, and endlessly sexy, but one in which all the smoldering temperament is controlled by a commanding intelligence and impeccable technique.

On the other hand, the conducting of Alain Lombard is—in the most flattering possible sense of the phrase—utterly and irretrievably mad. If a single moment best sums up his wildly original approach, it is the performance of the *Gypsy*

Song. Beginning with a tempo so ridiculously slow you'll think your turntable died during the night, the music gradually but inexorably quickens until, toward the end, it seems inconceivable that anyone could play it that fast.

While this is obviously not a *Carmen* for everyone, this is the *only* one for me.

Bloch, Ernest (1880–1959)

Schelomo—Rhapsody for Cello and Orchestra

**Harrell, cello; Amsterdam Concertgebouw Orchestra,
Haitink. London 414162-1 [LP], *414162-2* [CD],
414162-4 [T].**

While Ernest Bloch's creative life spanned more than six
decades, the Swiss-born composer is best remembered for the
music he produced from about 1915 through the mid-1920s.
And rightly so, for the major works of Bloch's so-called
"Jewish Period"— when he made a conscious attempt to give
musical expression to "the complex, glowing, agitated Jewish
soul"—contain some of the most expressive and individual
music written by a twentieth century composer.

Schelomo, the Hebraic Rhapsody for Cello and Orchestra, has long remained Bloch's most popular and frequently recorded work. Gregor Piatigorsky left an impassioned account of this brooding, exotic piece in the 1950s, a
recording joined by equally distinguished interpretations
from Janos Starker and Mstislav Rostropovich.

On balance, the recent London recording by a well-
known Piatigorsky pupil, Lynn Harrell, comes closer to cap-
turing the elusive essence of this exquisite Rhapsody than any
performance has in years. Harrell, a player with vast technical
resources, has had a habit of being needlessly restrained in his

commercial recordings. In *Schelomo*, he follows the unre-
strained lead of his famous teacher with an interpretation in
which passion and discipline are joined in almost perfect
balance. As always, Bernard Haitink is an adroit and sympathetic accompanist, and as always the Concertgebouw Orchestra sounds like what it may very well be: the greatest
orchestra in the world.

Borodin, Alexander
(1833–1887)

Prince Igor: Overture, *Polovtsian Dances*

Atlanta Symphony Chorus and Orchestra, Shaw. Telarc DG-10039 [LP] or *CD-80039* [CD].

Boston Pops, Fiedler. RCA Victor AKL1-4461 [T].

The most ecstatic recording of the familiar *Polovtsian Dances* was an Angel recording from the early 1960s by the Philharmonia Orchestra conducted by Lovro von Matacic. Available for a time on the Quintessence label, it is now no longer in print. Should the performance ever resurface again, or should you come across it in the ever-expanding LP cut-out bins, buy at least a half dozen copies: three for yourself, and three to lend out to friends. (If your friends are like mine, you'll never see the records again.)

Robert Shaw's fine Telarc recording was one of the very first made with the revolutionary digital process, and the sound of both the LP and compact disc versions is still astounding. With the right playback equipment, the Atlanta Symphony's bass drummer will lift you several inches off the living room sofa. Robert Shaw's performance is stylish and enthusiastic, with some predictably full-throated and lusty singing from the impeccably trained chorus.

Among available tapes, the performances by Arthur Fiedler and the Boston Pops, in a handsome package of Russian orchestral showpieces, are more than competitive with the best on the market today.

Brahms, Johannes
(1833–1897)

Piano Concerto No. 1 in D minor, Op. 15

**R. Serkin, piano; Cleveland Orchestra, Szell. CBS
MY-37803 [LP], *MK-42261* [CD], MYT-37803 [T].**

To many, Brahms early D minor Piano Concerto has
always seemed less a concerto than a large, turbulent orchestral work with a very significant piano *obligato* appended
almost as an afterthought. The feeling, for those who have it,
is more than understandable, for the concerto actually grew
out of discarded materials for a projected D minor symphony
that the composer could not bring himself to complete.
(Brahms spent more than half his creative life looking for
ways to make symphonic noises without actually having to
produce that dreaded First Symphony. Sadly, his morbid fear
of the inevitable comparison with Beethoven delayed its composition until he was well past forty.)

For more than twenty years no recording has fought
more ferociously for the Concerto's identity *as* a concerto
than the explosive and poetic performance by Rudolf Serkin
and George Szell. Serkin's playing in this famous recording is
magisterial, delicate, and shatteringly powerful—qualities
which made him as effective in the music of Mozart as he was
in the works of Franz Liszt.

George Szell, in one of his best Cleveland recordings, provides a muscular and exciting backdrop for his old friend. The playing of the Cleveland Orchestra is above criticism, and the digitally remastered sound is superb.

*P*iano Concerto No. 2 in B-flat Major, Op. 83

Gilels, piano; Chicago Symphony, Reiner. RCA Victor AGL1-5235 [LP], *RCD1-5406* [CD], AGK1-5235 [T].

Throughout his distinguished and rewarding career, the late Emil Gilels was known unfairly as "The Other Russian," a man condemned to live out his entire professional life under the enormous shadow cast by his great contemporary, Sviatoslav Richter. While Gilels may have lacked his friend's charisma— a short, stocky, unpretentious man, he was the very image of a third assistant secretary of the Ministry of Textiles—his formidable musicianship matched Richter's in its depth and intensity, even if it lacked the last fraction of a percentage point of that unapproachable technique.

While Gilels' final recording of the Brahms B-flat Major Concerto made with Eugen Jochum and the Berlin Philharmonic in the 1970s is in every way exceptional, it is the Chicago recording, made a decade before, which captures his immense talents at their absolute best. Characteristic of his finest performances, Gilels' interpretation, while completely unmannered, is possessed of a unique power and panache. No recorded performance of the *scherzo* communicates half of this one's driven assurance or feverish pain, and the *Finale* is played with such natural and unaffected charm that for once it is not an anti-climax.

Fritz Reiner proved to be an ideal partner in this music: generous, sensitive, and deferential, yet never afraid of showing off a little power and panache of his own. And if, even in its sonic face lift, the recorded sound remains a trifle thin and shrill, this is a trivial flaw in one of the most flawless concerto recordings ever made.

Concerto in D Major for Violin and Orchestra, Op. 77

Perlman, violin; Chicago Symphony, Giulini. Angel S-37286 [LP], *CDC-47166* [CD], 4AE-47166 [T].

Kreisler, violin; Berlin Philharmonic, Blech. (Recorded 1929).
Pearl 250/1 [LP].

When I am packing up a trunk of recordings to haul off to a mythic desert island—though since my mother didn't raise a fool, the island I'll probably pack myself off to is Maui— Fritz Kreisler's 1929 version of the Brahms Concerto will be packed near the top of the stack. While not the most perfect recording the Concerto has ever received, this is far and away the noblest and most inspiring. In the sweep of its patrician phrasing, melting lyricism, and hell-bent-for-leather audacity, this is as close as we will ever come to a Brahms Violin Concerto straight from the horse's mouth. (It should be remembered that for a time in the 1880s, one of Kreisler's Viennese neighbors was the composer himself.)

Among modern recordings of the Concerto, none is more completely engaging than Itzhak Perlman's version with Carlo Maria Giulini and the Chicago Symphony. Perlman is a spiritual descendant of Fritz Kreisler: a wonderful exponent of Kreisler's own music, he also plays with that indescribable, untranslatable quality that the Viennese call, in its closest but very approximate English equivalent, "beautiful dirt." This is a dark, luxurious Brahms Concerto cut from the same cloth as Kreisler's, but one in which the modern preoccupation with technical perfection also makes itself felt. In short, it sounds very much like the kind of performance that one would give almost anything to hear—one in which Heifetz' iron fingers were guided by Kreisler's golden heart.

Concerto in A minor for Violin, Cello, and Orchestra, Op. 120

Francescatti, Fournier, Columbia Symphony, Walter.
CBS MY-37237 [LP], *MK-42024* [CD], MYT-37237
[T].

With the classic Angel recording by Oistrakh, Rostropovich, George Szell, and the Cleveland Orchestra now inexplicably out of print, the pickings among available recordings of the Brahms Double Concerto are surprisingly slim. Until that very special performance returns to the catalogue (it was one of George Szell's final commercial recordings), the Francescatti, Fournier, Walter version will have to do. In spite of occasionally wayward contributions from the violinist, the performance is actually a very strong one—the splendid Pierre Fournier is as polished and virile as always, and Bruno Walter, whose attention seems to wander from time to time, nevertheless inspires some rich and spirited playing, especially from the Columbia Symphony strings.

Ein deutsches Requiem, Op. 45

Schwarzkopf, Fischer-Dieskau, Philharmonia Chorus
and Orchestra, Klemperer. Angel *CDC-47238* [CD].

Te Kanawa, Weikl, Chicago Symphony Chorus and
Orchestra, Solti.
London 414627-1 [LP], *414627-2* [CD], 414627-4 [T].

In one of his first incontestable masterworks, Brahms produced what remains the most gently consoling of all the great Requiems: a work which seems to tell us, with the utmost civility and compassion, that dying is neither the most frightening nor the most terrible thing a human being can do.

Since its first release in the 1960s, Otto Klemperer's other-worldly recording has cast all others into the shade. Along with the characteristic breadth and depth of his interpretation, the frail but indomitable conductor also projects such a moving degree of fragile tenderness that the performance will quietly, but firmly, tear your heart out. Neither of the soloists ever made a more beautiful recording, and the singing of the Wilhelm Pitz-trained Philharmonia Chorus remains an enduring monument to the greatest choral director of his time.

From a far less elevated yet perfectly acceptable height, Sir George Solti's Chicago recording is the obvious choice for the collector of tapes or LPs.

*P*iano Quartet in G minor, Op. 25 (Orchestrated by Arnold Schoenberg)

City of Birmingham Symphony, Rattle. Angel
CDCB-47300 [CD].

Suddenly and for no apparent reason—other than the obvious explanation that conductors and recording companies are belatedly discovering what a tremendously entertaining and marketable work it is—there are now *three* excellent modern versions of Arnold Schoenberg's inspired orchestration of Brahms' G minor Piano Quartet. Arguing that, in all the performances he had ever heard, the piano part always overbalanced the strings, Schoenberg produced what has been called justifiably "The Brahms Fifth": an imaginative and singularly faithful adaption of one of Brahms' most colorful chamber works.

The recent recordings by Sergiu Commissiona and the Baltimore Symphony and by the Bavarian Radio Orchestra with Michael Tilson Thomas are exceptionally fine, but Simon Rattle's gleaming Angel performance is by far the most polished and effervescent.

For the most convincing reading of the Quartet as it was actually composed, the Philips recording by the Beaux Arts Trio and Walter Trampler (Philips 6747068) continues to lead the field. (I blush to confess that since I first learned the Quartet through Robert Craft's old Chicago Symphony recording of the Schoenberg orchestration, the original version has always seemed slightly pale. In fact, the *Finale* never sounds completely right without that wildly incongruous xylophone.)

Quintet in B minor for Clarinet and Strings, Op. 115

Hacker, clarinet; Fitzwilliam String Quartet. London 7241 [LP].

Collins, clarinet; Nash Ensemble. CRD *3345* [CD].

Zukovsky, clarinet; Sequoia String Quartet. Nonesuch T-79105 [T].

While the two great Clarinet Sonatas and the *Four Serious Songs* were Brahms' actual valedictory, no composer ever wrote a more heartbreakingly beautiful farewell than the slow movement of his B minor Clarinet Quintet. In it, Brahms' celebrated "autumnal melancholy" is burnished and memorable.

The gifted Alan Hacker—among the latest in a long line of distinguished English clarinetists descended from the legendary Reginald Kell—gives a most moving performance in the great *Adagio*. The admirable Fitzwilliam Quartet, here and in the three other movements, plays with understanding and assurance helping explain why, toward the end of Dmitri Shostakovich's life, they were the composer's favorite quartet. For those who prefer the compact disc or cassette formats, the other recordings listed above are as exceptionally fine. In fact, with any of the three, it's impossible to go wrong.

Symphony No. 1 in C minor, Op. 68

Columbia Symphony, Walter. CBS *MK-42020* [CD].

Berlin Philharmonic, Furtwängler. Deutsche Grammophon *415662-2* [CD].

Vienna Philharmonic, Bernstein. Deutsche Grammophon 410081-1 [LP], *410081-2* [CD], 410081-4 [T].

Even when Otto Klemperer's titanic recording from the early 1960s returns, as it undoubtedly will, on an Angel compact disc, Klemperer will face some formidable competition from his old friend Bruno Walter, whose final recording of the Brahms' First Symphony was made at about the same time.

Walter's 1936 Vienna Philharmonic recording was one of the great glories of the 78 era: lithe, sinewy, and intensely passionate, it was every bit the dramatic equal of Arturo Toscanini's famous interpretation, while investing the music with an expressive freedom of which the Italian maestro scarcely could have dreamed.

Although Walter was well past eighty when the Columbia Symphony recording was made, there is no hint of diminished concentration in the performance; if anything, the first movement unfolds with such searing intensity that we are almost forced to wonder what the elderly conductor had for breakfast that day. As always, Walter is without peer in the

Symphony's gentler passages; the great theme of the final movement rolls out with an unparalleled sweetness and dignity, and the performance concludes in a blaze of triumph.

While Wilhelm Furtwängler's live 1952 Berlin Philharmonic performance may not be the ideal Brahms First for daily use—the sound is both boxy and uncomfortably tubby—its energy, willfulness, and withering power have never been surpassed.

On tape and LP, Leonard Bernstein's Vienna recording, which bears a startling similarity to Furtwängler's, is my admittedly eccentric first choice in this familiar music. The distortions are many, but so too are the rewards.

Symphony No. 2 in D Major, Op. 73

Vienna Philharmonic, Bernstein. Deutsche Grammophon 410082-1 [LP], *410082-2* [CD], 410082-4 [T].

Recorded live in Vienna in 1983 as part of a larger Brahms cycle, Leonard Bernstein's performance of the composer's sunniest symphony is the most invigorating since Sir Thomas Beecham's. The general mood is one of relaxed expansiveness, and while tempos tend to be on the leisurely side, the phrasing and rhythms never even threaten to become lethargic or slack. This is not to say that the familiar Bernstein fire is not available at the flick of a baton: the *Finale* crackles with electricity and ends with a deafening roar from the incomparable Vienna Philharmonic trombones.

As a bonus, the recording includes a performance of the *Academic Festival Overture* whose sly humor and rambunctious good spirits are all but impossible to resist.

Symphony No. 3 in F Major, Op. 90

Columbia Symphony, Walter. CBS *MK-42022* [CD].

**Cleveland Orchestra, Szell. CBS MY-37778 [LP],
MYT-37778 [T].**

All the qualities that made Walter's recording of the First so special can be heard in even greater abundance in his version of Brahms' most concise and original symphony. If you have the chance to audition the recording before you buy it, listen to the last three minutes. For in this daring *coda*, which marked the first time an important symphony ended on a quiet note, Walter is so ineffably gentle that those three magical minutes should be more than sufficient to justify the purchase. An equally warm-hearted account of the *Variations on a Theme by Haydn* fills out this unusually generous and irresistibly attractive compact disc.

George Szell's stunning Cleveland Orchestra recording runs Walter's a very close second. The recorded sound and playing are both superior, making it an easy first choice among the LPs and tapes.

Symphony No. 4 in E minor, Op. 98

Royal Philharmonic, Reiner. Chesky *CD-6* [CD].

**Vienna Philharmonic, Carlos Kleiber. Deutsche
Grammophon 2532003 [LP] or *40037-2* [CD].**

**Philharmonia Orchestra, Cantelli. Seraphim
4XG-60325 [T].**

In spite of formidable competition from Bernstein, Walter, Klemperer, and the always provocative Carlos Kleiber—

whose stunning Deutsche Grammophon recording is perhaps the most impressive of those that are relatively easy to find—this recent release from the small Chesky Records label preserves one of the loveliest of all Brahms symphony recordings. Available for a time on Quintessence, the performance was originally recorded for—are you ready for this?—one of those omnibus, great-music-for-us-just-plain-folks collections produced by the *Reader's Digest.*

At the playback that followed the recording sessions, Reiner was quoted as saying "This is the most beautiful recording I have ever made," and many have been tempted to agree. Wisely, Reiner chose to capitalize on the particular strengths of the Royal Philharmonic, without trying to turn them into a British carbon copy of his own Chicago Symphony. From a string section that produced a darker and less perfectly homogenized sound than the Chicago Symphony's, Reiner coaxed the aural equivalent of a Russian sable carpet. While the string section's playing is especially memorable in the second movement, the contributions of the woodwinds and brass are equally outstanding. (At recording time, the orchestra was still, in essence, Sir Thomas Beecham's Royal Philharmonic; its individual soloists equalled those of any orchestra in Europe.)

As an interpretation, this Brahms Fourth is vintage Reiner: tautly disciplined yet paradoxically Romantic. The outer movements are brisk and wonderfully detailed, and the recording of the energetic third movement is probably the most viscerally exciting to date.

Among available tapes, the celebrated recording made by the tragically short-lived Guido Cantelli is still an immensely moving reminder of an irreplaceable loss.

*T*rio in E-flat Major for Horn, Violin and Piano, Op. 40

Tuckwell, horn; Perlman, violin; Ashkenazy, piano. London *414128-2* [CD].

Boston Symphony Chamber Players. Nonesuch 79076 [LP], T-79076 [T].

Like Aubrey Brain and his brilliant young son, who was tragically killed in his favorite sports car while rushing home from a concert at the 1957 Edinburgh Festival, Barry Tuckwell has been living proof for more than a quarter century of the unwritten law that says the world's foremost horn-player must necessarily be an Englishman—or in Tuckwell's case, a transplanted Australian. As the longtime principal horn of the London Symphony and throughout an equally distinguished solo career, Tuckwell has proven himself the only horn player of the last thirty years whose artistry compares favorably with that of the legendary Dennis Brain.

This impeccable recording of the Brahms Horn Trio dates from 1969, or roughly from that period when Tuckwell began his ascendancy to preeminent horn player of his time. From a purely technical standpoint, the playing is as flawless as horn playing can possibly be. Add to that a rich, singing tone, a musical personality which is a winning blend of sensitivity and swagger, and the immaculate performances of his two famous colleagues, and we're left with a recording of the Brahms Horn Trio that probably won't be bettered for a generation.

The fine performance on Nonesuch by members of the Boston Symphony Chamber Players can be considered competitive *only* in the absence of a compact disc player.

Triumphlied (Song of Triumph) for Chorus and Orchestra, Op. 55

Prague Philharmonic Chorus, Czech Philharmonic Orchestra, Sinopoli. Deutsche Grammophon 410864-1 [LP].

There is a variety of party record that I have never been able to resist. (A "party record," by definition, is precisely what the phrase suggests: something you whip out at a party to amuse, amaze, or completely befuddle your musical friends.) While a friend of mine in San Francisco is an enthusiastic devotee of the game in which a recording is played backward, and to win you must name not only the work but also the specific *performance*, my own, far more plebeian tastes run to the time-honored Guess Who Wrote *This* quiz.

Brahms' occasional work, *Triumphlied*—the only positive thing to have emerged from the Franco-Prussian War—is my current favorite because Arnold Schoenberg's early D Major Quartet, with its echoes of Schubert and Dvorák, is simply becoming too well known. Not only would you never guess that this buoyant, joyous, unbuttoned piece had actually been written by Johannes Brahms, but also— when its party shock value is lost —you're left with an important and engaging twenty-five minutes, for this virtually unknown choral work is a masterpiece of its kind. While Sinopoli and his forces give the work a terrific send-off in *Triumphlied*'s world premiere recording, I have the feeling that this is only the first of many fine recordings to come.

Alas, this happy nonsense has yet to find its way on to compact disc or tape.

Variations on a Theme by Haydn, Op. 56a

Columbia Symphony, Walter. CBS MP-38889 [LP],
MK-42020 [CD], YT-30851 [T].

If I've managed to talk you into buying Bruno Walter's
stellar recording of the Brahms Third Symphony, you have
this richly various version of the *Haydn Variations* already.
Wasn't that easy?

Britten, Benjamin (Lord Britten of Aldeburgh) (1913–1976)

Peter Grimes

Pears, Watson, Brannigan, Evans, Chorus and
Orchestra of the Royal Opera House, Convent
Garden, Britten. London *414577-2* [CD].

Along with *Classics Illustrated*—a collection of vivid
comic book versions of *Robinson Crusoe, Frankenstein*, and
Moby Dick that got me through many a high school book
report—and the not-to-be-missed and invariably memorized
latest issue of *Mad Magazine*, one of my most cherished bits
of boyhood reading matter was a book called *A Pictorial
History of Music*. I still own the book and leaf through it
from time to time.

The pictures are as entertaining as ever and the text,
which I never bothered to read as a boy, becomes increasingly
fascinating. In all seriousness, the author, Paul Henry Lang,
informs us that not one of Gustav Mahler's works achieves
"true symphonic greatness." (I wonder if Bernstein, Solti,
Haitink, Tennstedt and others realize they've been wasting
their time all these years.) He further explains that the symphonies of Anton Bruckner are not really symphonies at all.
Instead, they are massive "organ fantasies" (liver? pancreas?),
all of which are indistinguishable from one another. (At least
that puts Bruckner in fairly good company: except for that

"organ" business, Igor Stravinsky said almost the same thing about every concerto Antonio Vivaldi ever wrote.) Of Benjamin Britten, Dr. Lang was even less flattering. While duly noting his native facility, he eventually dismissed him as a pleasant, but shallow and irretrievably minor composer, a kind of late twentieth century English version of Camille Saint-Saëns.

These days, of course, we tend to take a decidedly different view of Lord Britten of Aldeburgh, not only as the foremost English composer of his generation, but also as the man who virtually single-handedly roused English opera from a three-century sleep. The most significant English opera since *Dido and Aeneas* by Purcell, *Peter Grimes*, which the man who commissioned it—that inveterate mauler of the English language, Serge Koussevitzky—called "Peter und Grimes" until the end of his life, is one of the handful of twentieth century operas that has found a substantial audience. And with good reason. For *Peter Grimes* is not only gripping theatre, but also a powerful and consistently rewarding musical work.

In terms of authority and understanding, the composer's own recording from the late 1950s cannot, almost by definition, be approached. The recording featured many of the singers who had created these parts, chief among them Sir Peter Pears, for whom the demanding and complex title role was written. In its compact disc reissue, this famous recording becomes more vivid and atmospheric than ever. The well-known *Sea Interludes* have an especially wonderful color and mystery, and the stature of the individual performances grows with the passage of time.

Since neither a tape nor an LP of this classic performance is presently available, the Philips recording (420975-1, 420975-4 [T]) is a very credible substitute. Vocally and dramatically, tenor Jon Vickers is overwhelming in the title role, and Sir Colin Davis conducts with an understanding and insight that nearly matches the composer's concept.

Serenade for Tenor, Horn and Strings, Op. 31

Pears, tenor; Tuckwell, horn; London Symphony,
Britten. London *417153-2* [CD].

Pears, tenor; Brain, horn; Boyd Neel Orchestra,
Britten. London 417183-1 [LP], 417183-4 [T].

With the possible exception of the marriage of Robert
and Clara Schumann, the long-time relationship of Benjamin
Britten and Peter Pears was the most productive love affair in
the history of music. It was for Pears' plaintive and eccentric
voice which Britten heard in his mind whenever he composed,
and for the great artist which possessed it, that some of the
most important vocal music of the twentieth century was
composed.

Nowhere is Pears' intimate understanding and complete
mastery of the idiom heard to greater effect than in this last of
his three recordings of the *Serenade for Tenor, Horn and
Strings*, a work that in the fullness of time may very well prove
to be Britten's masterpiece. There is no subtle inflection, no
nuance, no hidden meaning in either the words or the music
that escapes Pears' attention. The composer's conducting is as
warm and witty as can possibly be imagined, and the almost
insolent grace with which Barry Tuckwell negotiates the formidable horn part must be heard to be believed. With equally
impressive performances of two other magnificent Britten
song cycles, *Les Illuminations* and the *Nocturne*, this generously packed compact disc is not to be missed.

On LP and tape, the original 1944 recording of the
Serenade provides a fascinating contrast to the later recording.
Dennis Brain, for whom the horn part was written, is as
phenomenal as he would ever be on records, and the
smoother, steadier voice of the young Peter Pears is a delight to
hear.

Spring Symphony, Op. 44

> Armstrong, Baker, Tear, St. Clement Danes School
> Boys Choir, London Symphony Chorus and
> Orchestra, Previn. Angel *CDC-47667* [CD].

> Vyvyan, Procter, Pears, Chorus and Orchestra of the
> Royal Opera House, Covent Garden, Britten.
> London 410171-1 [LP], 410171-4 [T].

What a completely enchanting, endlessly inventive work the *Spring Symphony* is! And like the incidental music that Sir Edward Elgar composed for the *Starlight Express*—an orchestral song cycle that concludes with a richly Edwardian peroration on the familiar Christmas carol "The First Noël"—the *Spring Symphony* ends with one of the most cleverly sprung and completely appropriate surprises in English music. As the tenor soloist is busily trying to conclude a magnificent setting of Rafe's address to London from Beaumont and Fletcher's *The Night of the Burning Pestle*, the chorus and orchestra come crashing in with a lusty quotation of the bawdy Medieval lyric, "Sumer is icumin in."

Like most who love this great work, I was introduced to the *Spring Symphony* by the superb London recording made by the composer in the mid-1960s. When London issues it as a compact disc, snatch it up by all means. But don't get rid of the glowing Angel recording by the London Symphony conducted by André Previn. As fine as the Britten performance certainly is, I think Previn's performance is finer still.

The key to Previn's greatness as a Britten conductor lies in his stubborn refusal to simply present the music as Britten *the conductor* did and in his constantly finding ways to shed new light on this marvelous music, and thus, as all great interpreters must, making it wholly and unmistakably his own.

His approach in the *Spring Symphony* is altogether more relaxed and expansive than the composer's approach. In the great moments—most noticeably in the mezzo-soprano's languorous delivery of W. H. Auden's "Out on the lawn I lie in bed"— Previn tends to shy away from the faster tempos the composer favored, allowing more time for the mood and special character of each of the Symphony's individual sections to unfold. Of course, he is greatly aided, in "Out on the lawn" and elsewhere, by the ravishing work of Dame Janet Baker to whom even the admirable Norma Proctor, Britten's soloist, cannot begin to compare. The London Symphony, as usual, outdoes itself for this conductor (have they ever played as well for anyone since Pierre Monteux?), and the singing of both choirs only serves to remind us why London is, far and away, the Choral Capital of the world.

War Requiem, Op. 66

Vishnevskaya, Pears, Fischer-Dieskau, Melos Ensemble, Bach Choir, Highgate School Choir, London Symphony Chorus and Orchestra, Britten. London 414283-1 [LP] or *414283-2* [CD].

Together with Elgar's *The Dream of Gerontius* and Sir Michael Tippett's *A Child of Our Time*, Britten's *War Requiem* is one of the three most important large-scale choral works written by an English composer since the time of Handel. A poignant, dramatic, and ultimately shattering experience, the *War Requiem* is an inspired fusion of the traditional Latin mass for the dead and the poems of Wilfred Owen—those starkly horrifying visions from the trenches of the Western Front that are now regarded as the greatest poems on the subject of war yet produced in the English language.

In retrospect, it's hardly surprising that the *War Requiem*, like *The Dream of Gerontius*, was a failure at it's world premiere. Its interpretive problems are so daunting, the performing forces so enormous and complex, that only with the release of this path-breaking recording was the *War Requiem*'s deeply universal appeal properly begun.

As a performance, it remains one of Benjamin Britten's greatest achievements. The playing and singing are consistently urgent, vivid, and immediate, and the composer controls the *War Requiem*'s quickly shifting textures, from the chamber episodes to the most aggressive mass eruptions, like the undeniably great conductor he eventually trained himself to be.

The only serious flaw remains the contribution of soprano Galina Vishnevskaya. While undeniably impressive in the more declamatory moments, with repeated hearings the straining and bellowing become increasingly grating—like trying to sit still in the presence of a wobbly air raid siren with feet.

On the other hand, the interpretations of the composer's other close friends, Sir Peter Pears and Dietrich Fischer-Dieskau, will likely never be bettered. Their performance of "Strange Meeting" is more moving when we remember not only who, but also *what* the singers were: a lifelong British pacifist and a former foot soldier of the Wermacht, who actually spent time in an Allied prisoner of war camp.

Musically, emotionally, and historically, this was a milestone in the history of recording. No tape is currently available.

Young Person's Guide to the Orchestra (Variations and Fugue on a Theme of Purcell), Op. 34

Royal Philharmonic, Previn. Telarc DG 10126 [LP], *CD-80126* [CD].

From the moment it was first heard in the British documentary film, *The Instruments of the Orchestra*, Britten's *Young Person's Guide to the Orchestra* remains his most popular and frequently recorded work. Over the last forty years, there has been no dearth of first-rate recordings of the *Guide*, including the one I grew up with: a long-vanished but thoroughly electrifying performance made for one of those small music appreciation-type labels featuring an anonymous pickup orchestra conducted by George Szell. (As with my youth, I have been searching for a copy of that recording for years. To anyone who can locate it for me, I'm willing to trade any ten Herbert von Karajan recordings and what's left of my once-complete collection of 1957 Topps baseball cards.)

A narrated recording is probably redundant at this late date, unless of course you have an impressionable kid, as I once was, you'd like to hook. If so, Sean Connery's sly and slightly naughty reading with Antal Dorati and the Royal Philharmonic (London 417064-4, cassette only) is to be preferred over Leonard Bernstein's slightly condescending version for CBS.

Among the recordings in which the *Guide* is allowed to speak for itself (and of course it does with great eloquence) André Previn's recent Royal Philharmonic performance is to be preferred above all others, including, rather incredibly, the composer's own version. While Benjamin Britten brought a keen wit and insight to his famous London recording, Previn outdoes him. The personalities of the various instruments are painted in broad, yet wonderfully subtle strokes. Rarely, for instance, have the bassoons sounded quite as buffoonish, nor has anyone ever made the percussion *cadenza* seem as ingenious or as musical. The Royal Philharmonic, especially in the Fugue, plays with a hair-trigger virtuosity, and the recorded sound could not be better.

Bruch, Max (1838–1920)

Violin Concerto in G minor, Op. 55

> **Perlman, London Symphony, Previn. Angel S-36963
> [LP], 4XS-36963 [T].**
>
> **Chung, Royal Philharmonic, Kempe. London *417707-2*
> [CD].**

In 1906 toward the end of his long career, the Hungarian violinist, Joseph Joachim, for whom Brahms and Dvořák had written their violin concertos, left what still remains a fair assessment of the central European history of the form:

> The Germans have four violin concertos. The greatest, the one that makes the least concessions is Beethoven's. The one by Brahms comes closest to Beethoven's in its seriousness. Max Bruch wrote the richest and most enchanting of the four. But the dearest of them all, the heart's jewel, is Mendelssohn's.

To date, the richest and most enchanting recording of Bruch's G minor Violin Concerto is the first of two that Itzhak Perlman has made for Angel Records. Unlike Perlman's digital remake with Bernard Haitink and the Amsterdam Concertgebouw Orchestra, a strangely inert and calculated performance from two such warm-hearted musicians, the Previn recording finds Perlman at his most irresistibly boyish and romantic. An appealing improvisatory feeling prevails in the playing, and the rhapsodic support that Previn supplies could not have enhanced the interpretation more.

Kyung-Wha Chung is also very fresh and spontaneous in this music. Since Perlman's earlier version is unlikely to be remastered any time soon, the brilliant young Korean's London recording should be considered the first choice among currently available compact discs. Anne-Sophie Mutter plays astonishingly well in her Deutsche Grammophon recording (*400031-2*), but Herbert von Karajan's cloying, manipulative, utterly sterile accompaniment drowns an otherwise lovely performance in a vat of rancid strawberry jam.

Bruckner, Anton
(1824–1896)

Symphony No. 4 in E-flat Major, "Romantic;"
Symphony No. 7 in E Major; Symphony No. 8 in
C minor; Symphony No. 9 in D minor

**Berlin Philharmonic, Furtwängler. Deutsche
Grammophon 2740201 [LP].**

More than those of any other great composer (and be
assured that this squat, homely, diffident little man ranks with
the greatest composers of the Romantic era), the symphonies
of Anton Bruckner need all the help they can get. Unlike the
virtually foolproof music of Beethoven, Tchaikovsky, or
Brahms that can resist all but the most rankly incompetent
mauling, for the Bruckner symphonies to emerge as the great
works they so obviously are, nothing less than *great* performances will do. While they contain much that is immediately
appealing, including some of the most heroic brass writing in
all of music, their greatest moments tend to be private and
internal: the deeply spiritual utterances of an essentially
Medieval spirit who was completely out of step with his time.

For the interpreter, the single most pressing problem in
performing Bruckner's work is trying to maintain the level of
concentration these often mammoth outbursts require. If the
intensity relaxes for a moment, the vast but terribly fragile
structures will almost inevitably fall apart. In short, it's al-

together possible that many who are persuaded they dislike Bruckner are confusing the composer with the *performances* of his music that they've heard. Indifferent, good, or even *very* good interpretations, which in recent years are about the best the composer can expect, simply will not do.

Wilhelm Furtwängler was unquestionably the greatest Bruckner interpreter of whom we have an accurate record. All that is best and characteristic in the composer's music, its drama, grandeur, mysticism, is revealed more powerfully and clearly in Furtwängler's recordings than in those of any other conductor. Although the recorded sound in these performances from the late 1940s and early 1950s ranges only from good to barely adequate, several books could easily be written on each of the individual interpretations—from the apocalyptic holocaust that Furtwängler conjures up in the last movement of the Eighth Symphony to his unutterably beautiful performance of the Adagio from the Ninth, in which we become a party to one of the most moving spiritual journeys ever undertaken by a nineteenth century composer. While the point could be belabored indefinitely, suffice it to say that if you have yet to experience these astounding recordings, it's unlikely that you've ever really *heard* the Bruckner symphonies at all.

For collectors who are unable (or unwilling) to come to terms with Furtwängler's intensely personal conceptions or for those who grow impatient with less than state-of-the-art recorded sound, a handful of recent recordings can be recommended as reasonable, if not completely satisfying alternatives. In the "Romantic" Symphony, Eliahu Inbal's recording of the original 1874 version (Teldec 6.42921, 8.42921) is as persuasive as it is fascinating, including an entirely different *Scherzo* than the one that is usually heard. Riccardo Chailly, a gifted but terribly inconsistent conductor offers a superbly played, brilliantly recorded version of the Seventh Symphony for London (414290-1 [LP], 414290-2 [CD], 414290-4 [T]). Of all modern recordings of the Eighth, none has yet to surpass either the warmth or virtuosity of Bernard Haitink's Philips recording with the Amsterdam Concertgebouw Orchestra (6725014 [LP], *412465-2* [CD]). For a Furtwängler Ninth in up-to-date sound, Bruno Walter's handsomely remastered recording from the early 1960s comes surprisingly close to filling the bill. (CBS MP-39129 [LP], *MK-42037* [CD], MPT-39129 [T]).

Canteloube, Joseph
(1879–1957)

Songs of the Auvergne

Gomez, soprano; Royal Liverpool Philharmonic,
Handley. Angel AE-34471 [LP], *CDM-62010* [CD].

Te Kanawa, soprano; English Chamber Orchestra,
Tate. Volume 1: London 410004-1 [LP], *410004-2*
[CD], 410004-4 [T]. Volume 2: London 411730-1
[LP], *411730-2* [CD], 411730-4 [T].

For much of his life, the indefatigable French composer
Joseph Canteloube devoted himself to collecting and arrang-
ing the charming, haunting, and frequently scintillating folk
songs of the Auvergne region of central France. Although
none of his original works ever succeeded in making much of
an impression, the four-volume *Songs of the Auvergne* are
well on their way to becoming modern classics. Beginning
with the pioneering recordings of Natania Davrath and Victoria de los Angeles in the late 1950s and early 60s, famous
singers have been drawn almost irresistibly to these minor
masterworks, not only because they are so vocally and musically rewarding, but also because any album with "Songs of
the Auvergne" on its cover is almost guaranteed to sell.

The most rewarding single collection to have appeared
so far features the radiant singing of Jill Gomez, whose name
may not be as familiar as those of other singers who have

made *Auvergne* recordings, but whose fresh, girlish voice and keen understanding of the texts (along with what is reputed to be an absolute mastery of the Provençal dialect) make her Angel recording all but impossible to equal, much less surpass.

Dame Kiri Te Kanawa, in some of her finest work in the recording studio to date, has so far recorded two excellent collections. While the interpretations can't quite match the charm or the insight of the Gomez performances, her ravishing, peaches-and-cream instrument serves the music very well. Both recordings, especially Te Kanawa's, are wonderfully warm and detailed, though it is Gomez' promised second volume—to say nothing of Volumes 10 through 20—that we died-in-the-wool *Auvergne* junkies await with the greatest pleasure and anticipation.

Chausson, Ernest
(1855–1899)

Poème for Violin and Orchestra, Op. 25

**Chung, violin; Royal Philharmonic, Dutoit. London
417118-2 [CD].**

One of the most provocative of all "What if?" musical
speculations concerns the effect on the subsequent development of French music had Ernest Chausson been as accomplished a bicyclist as he was a composer. His premature death,
from injuries sustained when he drove his bicycle into a brick
wall in 1899, robbed French music of the most distinct and
original voice between those of Hector Berlioz and Claude
Debussy.

Together with the Symphony in B-flat—which can be
heard to memorable effect in a recording by José Serebrier
and the Belgian Radio Symphony for Chandos (1135 [LP],
CD-8369 [CD], or 1135 [T])—and the sumptuous orchestral
song cycle *Poème de l'amour et de la mer*, the *Poème* for
Violin and Orchestra is a finished, justly popular masterpiece
by an already established master and a tantalizing, heartbreaking suggestion of what might have been.

The greatest performance the *Poème* has ever received
on, or probably off, records was that rich and passionate
recording the tragically short-lived French violinist Ginette
Neveu made in the late 1940s. Kyung-Wha Chung's London

recording resembles Neveu's in its emotional depth and technical facility. Only Itzhak Perlman, on a superb Angel cassette (4XS-37118), can create the similar illusion that this extremely thorny work is so childishly simple to play. As usual, the support that Charles Dutoit gives Ms. Chung is as imaginative as it is sensitive, not only in the *Poème*, but also in Saint-Saëns' *Habañera* and *Introduction and Rondo Capriccioso*, and Ravel's *Tzigane*, the other popular violin showpieces that round out this extremely appealing release.

While none of the currently available LPs can be recommended, a superb tape featuring Itzhak Perlman at his absolute best is available from Angel (4XS-37118).

Chopin, Frédéric
(1810–1849)

Piano Concerto No. 1 in E minor, Op. 11; Piano Concerto No. 2 in F minor, Op. 2l

Zimmerman, piano; Los Angeles Philharmonic, Giulini.
Deutsche Grammophon 2531125 [LP], *415970-2* [CD],
3301125 [T] (Op. 11); Deutsche Grammophon 2531126
[LP], *415971-2,* [CD] 3301126 [T] (Op. 21).

In addition to being the central works in concerto literature for the instrument, the Chopin piano concertos dispel several myths that continue to cling to one of history's most popular composers. There are those who still insist that Chopin was essentially an incomparable miniaturist who was uncomfortable with and, indeed, incapable of sustaining larger-scaled forms. The same people, no doubt, are convinced that this first important composer to write piano music constructed entirely in *pianistic* terms was thoroughly incapable of writing gracefully and idiomatically for other instruments, that is, for the nineteenth century orchestra. Hogwash. Both as larger forms and as concerted works for piano and orchestra, these two concertos are as masterful as those that any composer of the Romantic era produced.

One or the other of these two exceptional Deutsche Grammophon recordings probably introduced most of the world to the great young Polish pianist, Krystian Zimmerman. As a general rule, I am extremely suspicious of the phrase "great young" when applied to anyone, but in Zimmerman's case, it most assuredly *does* apply. He has instinct, technique, and temperament to burn, together with a maturity and insight that many pianists twice his age would be hard pressed to match. (Compare his playing with that of his highly touted near-contemporary, Ivo Pogorelich. The difference is one between a precocious, yet very nearly finished artist and a precocious, but unruly and self-indulgent child.)

Zimmerman's performances of the Chopin concertos are as nearly perfect as any that have been heard in a generation. In them, poetry and youthful impetuosity are combined with a highly disciplined musical intelligence, and the results are an unalloyed delight for both the heart and the mind. The backdrops provided by Giulini and the Los Angeles Philharmonic could not have been more suave or sympathetic, and the recorded sound has a warm and natural bloom.

Vigorously recommended.

Solo Piano Works

Ballades (4); Scherzos (4). Rubinstein, piano. RCA Victor LSC 2370 [LP], *RCD1-7156*[CD], CRK2-5460 [T].

Mazurkas (35). Rubinstein, piano. RCA Victor ARL3-5171 [LP], *5614-2-RC*[CD], CRK-2-5171 [T].

Nocturnes (21). Rubinstein, piano. RCA Victor LSC-7050 [LP], *5613-2-RC*[CD], CRK2-5018 [T].

Polonaises (17). Rubinstein, piano. RCA Victor *5615-2-RC* [CD], CRK2-7026 [T].

Waltzes (19). Rubinstein, piano. RCA Victor LSC-2726 [LP], *RCD1-5492*[CD], RK-1071 [T].

Although this phenomenally popular body of music has attracted almost every important pianist of the last 150 years, it's unlikely that Frédéric Chopin ever found, or ever will find, a more ideal interpreter than Artur Rubinstein. To be sure, pianists like Joseph Hoffman, Leopold Godowsky, and Vladimir Horowitz gave infinitely more brilliant performances of the music. Even some brighter lights of the younger generation, Dinu Lipatti in the 1950s and Maurizio Pollini in our time, managed to find an intellectual and spiritual depth in Chopin that Rubinstein, for much of his career, never did. Yet on balance, these remain the definitive recordings of Chopin's piano music, as authoritative and unapproachable in their way as Furtwängler's recordings of the Bruckner symphonies, or the music of Frederick Delius led by Sir Thomas Beecham.

The key to Rubinstein's greatness as a Chopin interpreter is his combination of utter naturalness as a performer and his enormously sophisticated musical mind. Nothing ever seems forced or premeditated; there are no sharp edges or sudden flashes of insight. In fact, the illusion that the performances create is one of the music flowing, without benefit of a human intermediary, directly from the printed page to the listener's heart. Of course, only the greatest artists are able to create such illusions, and then only after a lifetime of study, experience, self-examination, and backbreaking work.

At almost every moment in these classic recordings, Rubinstein discovers some wonder of color or phrasing. He brings out a beautiful inner voice that it seems we've never heard before, and in general creates the impression of a man for whom playing this often fiendishly difficult music is no more difficult than breathing or making love. In short, Rubinstein's great and completely unaffected humanity breathes such life into these performances that they will always move, enlighten, and inspire perceptive listeners.

Copland, Aaron (1900–)

Appalachian Spring

Los Angeles Philharmonic, Bernstein. Deutsche
   Grammophon 2532084 [LP], *413324-4* [CD], 423168-4
   [T].
St. Paul Chamber Orchestra, Davies. Pro Arte PAD-140 [LP],
   CDD-149 [CD], PCD-140 [T].

In many ways, Aaron Copland remains the most dramatic musical manifestation of the "melting pot" genesis of
American history. For the composer who, in his most popular
works, seemed to capture the very essence of Middle America
and the Western frontier, was in fact born in a working-class
Jewish neighborhood of Brooklyn, and received his principal
musical training with Nadia Boulanger in Paris.

Appalachian Spring, a ballet composed for the celebrated American dancer Martha Graham, is probably the
composer's masterpiece. All the best qualities of Copland's
"Enlightened Populist" style are heard to their best advantage.
Bracing, wide-open harmonies, folksy and unforgettable melodies, are bound together with Copland's expressive idiom
that mixes tenderness, exuberance, sentimentality, and sophistication in roughly equal amounts.

Like the exhilarating recording that Leonard Bernstein
made with the New York Philharmonic in the 1960s, this

newer version with the Los Angeles Philharmonic is an unqualified triumph. The orchestra plays with great delicacy and
conviction, and the special excitement that all of Bernstein's
live performances generate can be felt throughout.

For a somewhat less compelling, but thoroughly satisfying look at the ballet in its original version for chamber
orchestra, the performance led by Dennis Russell Davies
handily defeats all other contenders, including the composer's
own recording.

Billy the Kid; *Rodeo*. (Complete)

**St. Louis Symphony, Slatkin. Angel DS-37357 [LP],
CDC-47382 [CD], CDC-47382 [T].**

For more years than anyone can remember, Leonard
Bernstein, one of the composer's oldest and closest friends,
has virtually owned this music. For nearly a quarter century
his CBS recordings of Copland's immensely appealing Cow-
boy ballets— both of which quote more actual frontier tunes
than a typical Zane Grey novel—have been all but unapproachable in their dramatic flair and authority. That is, at
least, until now.

Leonard Slatkin, who in the last decade has galvanized
the St. Louis Symphony into one of America's finest orchestras, leads a pair of performances that are even more
successful than Bernstein's are. The rhythms are tighter and
more infectious, the phrasing is consistently more alert and
imaginative, and the playing of this great young ensemble
sounds every bit the equal of any orchestra in the world.
Together with demonstration-quality sound, the recording
presents both ballets note-complete. While this represents
only a few extra minutes of actual music, it makes what is
already an immensely attractive recording virtually irresistible.

Debussy, Claude
(1862–1918)

Images for Orchestra; *Prelude to the Afternoon of a Faun*

London Symphony, Previn. Angel *CDC-47001* [CD], 4DS-37674 [T].

Boston Symphony, Thomas. Deutsche Grammophon 415916 [LP].

Claude Debussy despised the term "Impressionism" whenever it was applied to his own music, largely because he did not want anyone to think that he had merely created a slavish aural imitation of the paintings of Monet and the poetry of Stéphane Mallarmé. The composer had a point. Actually, his music represents one of the great turning points in music history: a complete re-thinking of musical color and texture whose influence would rival that of Wagner's harmonic upheaval or the rhythmic revolution that began in Igor Stravinsky's *The Rite of Spring*.

This spectacularly fine-sounding Angel recording (the very first digital recording released by the company) conveniently brings together two of the composer's most important scores: the *Prelude to the Afternoon of a Faun*, with which Debussy launched his gentle revolution in 1892, and the *Images for Orchestra*, one of his final and most ambitious orchestral works.

While there have been more vivid interpretations of *Im-ages*, and recordings of the *Prelude* that capture more of its tenderness and mystery, no Debussy recording on the market today is more brilliant or revealing. The recorded sound captures every nuance of these tremendously adroit and po-etic performances. In the final few minutes of *Iberia*, for instance, we seem able to hear more notes (and even more instruments) than we have ever heard. If you have just bitten the bullet and bought a compact disc player, this is an ideal vehicle for showing off your new toy.

Among the ever-shrinking LP versions of these popular works, the Deutsche Grammophon recording by Michael Tilson Thomas and the Boston Symphony is easily the one to own. Recorded at the very beginning of Thomas' career, the performances project a youthful enthusiasm, coupled with an interpretive maturity and brilliance of execution that continue to make them unique.

La Mer

Chicago Symphony, Reiner. RCA Victor AGL-1-5285 [LP], *RCD1-7018* [CD], AGL-1-5285 [T].

New Philharmonia Orchestra, Boulez. CBS MY-37261 [LP].

When Pierre Boulez' recording of Debussy's most evoca-tive work was first released two decades ago, it was widely hailed as a major revelation, and to be fair no other recording has ever succeeded in presenting this stunning, magically at-mospheric work with greater precision and clarity. Still, the final test of any performance of *La Mer* is the extent to which it makes you see, taste, and smell the sights and sounds of the sea.

The wonderful recording that Fritz Reiner made with the Chicago Symphony in the late 1950s still passes that test most effectively. In compact disc reissue, the range of color in this virtuoso performance is incredibly rich and varied, and the drama that Boulez' otherwise fine interpretation lacks, Reiner finds in abundance. Listen, for instance, to the electrifying playing in *La Mer*'s final bars, where the conductor whips up such visceral excitement that you almost suspect you're listening to the finale of a Tchaikovsky symphony.

Originally and incongruously coupled with Reiner's final and finest recording of Strauss' *Don Juan*, the digitally remastered record and tape now offer gleaming performances of Ravel's *Alborada del Gracioso* and *Rhapsodie espagnol*, while the compact disc adds the sexiest commercial recording of Rimsky-Korsakov's *Scheherazade* (see below).

Nocturnes for Orchestra; *Jeux*

Concertgebouw Orchestra of Amsterdam, Haitink. Philips 6768284 [LP] or *400023-2* [CD].
Boston Symphony, Munch. RCA Victor 6719-4 [T].

I blush to confess that I was far too long in seeing the light on the subject of Bernard Haitink. As an ardent admirer of his great predecessor in Amsterdam, Eduard van Beinum, and as an absolute *fanatic* on the subject of van Beinum's predecessor, Willem Mengelberg, Haitink seemed, in contrast, little more than a competent journeyman. He represented to me a talented, but rather anonymous figure who could be relied upon for little more than polite and handsomely organized performances. Throughout the last decade, with the release of every new Haitink recording, I have eaten what amounts to Brobdingnagian helpings of crow. In almost every recording that Haitink has made, recordings which cover an unusually broad range of repertoire, he combines intelligence, passion, craftsmanship, and utter professionalism more thoroughly than any other contemporary conductor. If Haitink, like Felix Weingartner and Pierre Monteux before him, is not the most glamorous conductor of his generation, he is usually the most consistently satisfying.

Haitink faces formidable competition in this most popular of all Debussy's major works, yet no other modern recording of the *Nocturnes* begins to match this one's effortless perfection. The interpretation of "Nuages" is a masterpiece of mood and texture, "Fetes" crackles with electric excitement, and "Sirens" is so seductively alluring that we understand why countless ancient mariners cracked up on these dangerous ladies' reefs. On the other hand, Haitink's interpretation of *Jeux* is nothing less than a major revelation. Whereas other conductors have made this strange, tennis court ballet seem an interesting work at best, Haitink dares to suggest that it may actually be an unjustly neglected masterpiece. Note: The current LP edition is available exclusively as part of a three-record set featuring only slightly less successful versions of Debussy's other major orchestral works.

Charles Munch's Boston Symphony recording is one of his very best: an engaging mixture of color, brilliance, and panache make it the first choice among currently available tapes.

Quartet in G minor, Op. 10

Melos Quartet of Stuttgart. Deutsche Grammophon *419750-2* [CD].

Juilliard Quartet. RCA Victor AGL1-5290 [LP], ATP1-5390 [T].

The G minor String Quartet is the finest of Debussy's chamber works and a cornerstone of modern quartet literature. While a relatively early work, it was the last piece he would compose in an identified key and to which he assigned an opus number.

For years, the most meltingly beautiful of all its many recordings was the Guarneri Quartet's version, now temporarily out of print, for RCA Victor. While the Guarneri has been perhaps the most maddeningly inconsistent of the world's great quartets, they were at their absolute best in both the Debussy and its inevitable companion piece, the F Major Quartet of Maurice Ravel. The playing has such a natural ease, sensitivity, and unanimity of frankly Romantic purpose, that Victor would be well advised not to waste time in returning these lovely performances on compact disc.

Until RCA's executives get off their duffs and do the same, the Melos Quartet's superb Deutsche Grammophon compact disc recording will fill the gap quite handsomely, just as an early version by the Juilliard Quartet will have to perform the same function among available tapes and LPs. While their physical sound lacks the last measure of the Guarneri's character and individuality, both groups play with great polish and feeling, and perhaps with a finer, more finished technique. Yet in the acid test—the Quartet's ravishing slow movement—the performances are merely overwhelmingly moving, as opposed to the Guarneri interpretation, which with tremendous skill and deliberation, calmly proceeds to yank out the listener's heart.

Suite bergamasque; Estampes; Images oubliees; Pour le Piano

Zoltán Kocsis, piano. Philips 412 118-1 [LP], *412-118-2*, [CD] 412 118-4 [T].

Given the fact that he was largely responsible for the most original and popular piano music produced after Chopin, there exists a surprising, one is tempted to say *scandalous*, dearth of first-rate Debussy recordings. (Perhaps we are simply going through one of those predictable droughts, during which the major recording companies are gearing up to reissue the Debussy piano treasures in their vaults as compact discs.) Whatever the explanation, virtually none of the definitive recordings made by that arch-poet Walter Gieseking are readily available, and Debussy's living interpreter, the

Czech pianist Ivan Moravec, is currently represented by only a few tantalizing bits and pieces.

This generous and brilliantly played collection by the young Hungarian pianist Zoltán Kocsis is one of the few genuine treasures in a shockingly barren field. Kocsis, who obviously possesses an important technique, plays with great subtlety and refinement. The *Suite bergamasque* is particularly successful, offering considerable wit, admirable control, and an attractively understated account of the famous *Clair de Lune* (which the incomparable Victor Borge, before all of his inimitable performances, invariably introduced by saying, "English translation: Clear the saloon"). The recorded sound, especially in compact disc format, offers one the most realistic recreations of piano timbre in recent memory.

Delius, Frederick
(1862–1934)

Over the Hills and Far Away; Sleigh Ride, Marche caprice; Brigg Fair—An English Rhapsody; *Florida Suite; Dance Rhapsody No. 2; Summer Evening; On Hearing the First Cuckoo in Spring, Summer Night on the River; A Song Before Sunrise;* Intermezzo from *Fennimore and Gerda;* Prelude to *Irmelin; Songs of Sunset*

Forrester, contralto; Cameron, baritone; Beecham Choral Society, Royal Philharmonic Orchestra, Beecham. Angel *CDCB-47509*[CD].

With the possible exception of the amoral, egomaniacal, virulently anti-Semitic, and treacherous Richard Wagner who repaid the unswerving loyalty of at least two of his most ardent supporters by sleeping with their wives, Frederick Delius, of all the great composers, was probably the most thoroughly unpleasant human being. Cruel, ruthless, pathologically self-ish, and a self-styled reincarnation of Nietzsche's idealized Nordic superman, Delius fought his long, lonely struggle for recognition while making the lives of everyone around him (especially that of his devoted, long-suffering wife Jelka) abso-lutely miserable. As much as his apologists, his amanuensis Eric Fenby, and the Australian composer Percy Grainger have tried to pardon his unpardonable behavior, Delius, to the day he died—a blind and paralyzed victim of tertiary neurosyphilis—was a complete and thoroughgoing beast.

And yet contained within this difficult, often despicable man was one of the most original and rarified talents in musical history. At its best, Delius' music is among the most delicate and ineffably gentle ever produced by an English composer, and as one of the last late-Romantic nature-poets, he remains unique.

For those of us who are hopelessly addicted to his admittedly limited, but irresistibly appealing art, or even for those perfectly sensible, though sadly misguided souls who gag at the very mention of his name, this recent Angel recording represents the most valuable single release since the introduction of compact discs. For contained on these two tightly packed and handsomely remastered discs are all the stereo recordings of Delius' music that his greatest champion, Sir Thomas Beecham, ever made.

In Beecham's hands—though, alas, in few others' since the conductor's death—the music of Delius clearly emerges as that of a major composer. Almost every bar of these famous performances is shot through with Beecham's special interpretive wizardry. *On Hearing the First Cuckoo in Spring* very nearly says as much as the whole of Beethoven's "Pastoral" Symphony, and the legendary version of *Bring Fair* sounds not only like the finest Delius recording ever made, but also precariously close to the most magical fifteen minutes in recording history.

For dyed-in-the-wool Delians, this is an invaluable release; for the unconverted, an ideal invitation to join us.

Dohnányi, Ernst von
(1877–1960)

Variations on a Nursery Song, Op. 25

Katchen, piano; London Philharmonic, Boult. London
417052-4 [T].

Schiff, piano; Chicago Symphony, Solti. London 417294-1
[LP], *417294-2* [CD], 417294-4 [T].

Until relatively recent times, the smart money insisted
that Ernst von Dohnányi was the twentieth century's greatest
Hungarian composer. A late-Romantic whose painstaking
craftsmanship earned him the sobriquet "The Hungarian
Brahms'" Dohnányi would eventually be overtaken and almost completely overshadowed by his younger, more radical
contemporaries, Béla Bartók and Zoltán Kodály. In fact, the
extent to which Dohnányi's reputation is now in eclipse may
be gathered from the fact that there are only three available
recordings of his most popular piece, the witty and ingratiating *Variations on a Nursery Song*. Until Angel reissues that
immensely impressive interpretation by the Brazilian pianist,
Christina Ortiz, collectors face a painful quandary: the finest
single performance is available solely on cassette, and the only
acceptable compact disc version is certainly nothing to write
home about.

Andras Schiff, in his recording with Sir Georg Solti and
the Chicago Symphony, has many fine moments, but the

conductor, lamentably, is well off his form. In fact, for much of the time, Sir Georg seems to be leafing through yesterday's newspaper, instead of a singly delightful early twentieth century score.

The late Julius Katchen, on the other hand, gives a performance that overflows with wit, romance, and high spirits and is supported by one of Sir Adrian Boult's most alert and amusing accompaniments. The way Sir Adrian builds that portentous and shaggiest of shaggy-dog introductions leading up to the soloist's two-fingered announcement of "Twinkle, Twinkle, Little Star" is itself worth the price of the recording. Unfortunately, the LP version of this delectable interpretation has recently disappeared, and the compact disc is not yet in sight. On the brighter side, those who spend a good deal of time listening to tapes while jogging or in their cars are decidedly in luck.

Donizetti, Gaetano
(1797–1848)

Lucia di Lammermoor

Callas, Tagliavini, Cappuccilli, Ladysz, Philharmonia
Orchestra and Chorus, Serafin. Angel *CDCB-47440*[CD],
4AV-34066[T].

More than any other of Gaetano Donizetti's sixty-odd
operas, which were often produced at the mind-boggling rate
of eight to ten per year—a contemporary caricature shows the
composer seated at a desk, his famous mop of hair askew,
writing with two hands simultaneously—*Lucia di Lammermoor* is the archetypal representative of all that is best *and*
most ridiculous in *Bel Canto* opera. As theatre, it is both
grippingly effective and utterly absurd. The famous *Sextet* is a
high water mark of nineteenth century ensemble writing and
the long, demanding *Mad Scene* is a silly and thinly veiled
excuse for a twenty minute coloratura concert. (Of course it
could be argued that Lucia's lengthy conversation with an
equally energetic flute is no more preposterous than that
goofy scene the recently stabbed Gilda, fresh from her gunny
sack, is asked to deliver at the end of Verdi's *Rigoletto*, or that
equally exhausting vocal and dramatic *tour de force* the con-
sumptive Violetta uses to conclude that same composer's *La
Traviata*.) But then again, loving opera has always been de-
pendent on a healthy disregard for common sense. And *Lucia*

di Lammermoor, with the proper attitude, and more importantly the proper cast, can be as rewarding an experience as the opera house has to offer.

Vocally, the most impressive Lucia of modern times was the young Joan Sutherland, whose 1959 London recording recalled the exploits of the almost mythic Luisa Tettrazini, the great turn-of-the-century diva who is best remembered today for the chicken and spaghetti recipe which still bears her name. Dramatically and emotionally, Sutherland's Lucia was a rather different matter, but in her far less impressive remake with her husband Richard Bonynge, what were once merely Sutherland eccentricities become annoying cliches. Her diction makes almost every word completely incomprehensible, and that droopy, sad-little-girl delivery tempts you to throw her down the nearest open manhole.

What the opera *should* be, as both a dramatic and a vocal experience, is still best suggested by the classic recording made by Maria Callas. Like the Callas *Norma*, it is an exceedingly rich and beautiful characterization. It contains some of the finest singing that Callas would ever deliver in a recording studio. The famous *Mad Scene*, for once, is not the unintentionally uproarious joke it usually is, but a riveting piece of theater cut from the same cloth as Shakespeare's scene on the blasted heath from *King Lear*. The rest of the cast, even the aging tenor, Ferrucio Tagliavini, is more than adequate. And the veteran Tulio Serafin gives us countless thrilling moments which confirm his reputation as one of the last great blood-and-thunder opera conductors. For Callas fans, or for anyone interested in making the rare acquaintance of *Lucia di Lammermoor* as convincing musical drama, this recording is an absolute must.

Given the opera's popularity, the absence of an acceptable LP version is scandalous.

Dukas, Paul (1865–1935)

The Sorcerer's Apprentice

Orchestre de Paris, Jacquillat. Angel S-35618 [LP].

New York Philharmonic, Bernstein. CBS MY-37769
[LP], *MYK-37769* [CD], MTY-37769 [T].

Don't let any of those slightly smug and self-important music lovers who are going through that inevitable, pseudo-sophisticated "Trashing the Warhorses" phase of their development fool you. In spite of the fact that *The Sorcerer's Apprentice,* in that otherwise turgid and self-conscious classic, *Fantasia, did* serve as the backdrop for one of Mickey Mouse's greatest performances, it is still one of the most dazzlingly inventive tone poems in the history of music.

Of the twenty or so recordings that are currently available, the most thoroughly appealing are those by Jean-Pierre Jacquillat and Leonard Bernstein. Jacquillat's is a typically French interpretation, which means, unfortunately, that along with an appealing slyness and elan, we are treated to a group of solo voices that sound more like adenoidal saxophones than bassoons. Nonetheless, the Orchestre de Paris, in its first commercial recording responds quickly and effortlessly to Jacquillat's colorful and dramatic approach.

Predictably, the Bernstein recording also leans heavily on

wit and drama, together with a visual acuity that makes the playing extremely cinematic in the best possible sense of the word. While both conductors offer a handsome collection of other French showpieces as filler (Chabrier's *España*, Saint-Saëns' *Danse macabre*, and so on), the real show-stopper is Jacquillat's performance of Hector Berlioz' stupefying setting of Roget de Lisle's *La Marseillaise*, in which the French national anthem is magically transformed into a glorious seven minute scene from the grandest of all imaginable French grand operas.

Dvořák, Antonín
(1841–1904)

Concerto in B minor for Cello and Orchestra, Op. 104

Fournier, cello; Berlin Philharmonic, Szell. Deutsche
Grammophon 415330-4 [T].

Feuermann, cello; Berlin State Opera Orchestra, Taube
(Recorded 1929). Opal 809 [LP].

Du Pré, cello; Chicago Symphony, Barenboim. Angel
CDC-47614 [CD].

The events which led to the composition of this greatest
of all cello concertos are movingly documented in Josef
Škvorecký's magnificent 1987 novel *Dvořák in Love* (Knopf),
probably the finest fictional treatment of the life of any composer. The concerto's second movement was written as an
elegy for the composer's sister-in-law, the only woman with
whom Dvořák was ever in love. In fact, embedded in this
poignant outpouring of grief is a quotation from an early song
that Dvořák wrote for Josephine Cermaková a few years before he married her sister, Anna.

For more than a half century, the Dvořák Cello Concerto has been brilliantly served in the recording studio, beginning in 1929 with what remains the most spellbinding realization of the solo part. In that classic recording by cellist Emanuel Feuermann, the recorded sound is fairly dismal even by standards of the time, and the Berlin State Opera Orchestra under Michael Taube is barely equal to the task. Still, it is this recording, more than any other, that demonstrates conclusively why Feuermann, not Pablo Casals, was the great cellist of the twentieth century. The combination of bravado, patrician phrasing, and flawless technique that Feuermann brought to the Concerto has never been duplicated. Hearing this superb Opal restoration makes us realize anew what the world lost when Emanuel Feuermann died during a routine operation in 1942, a few months short of what would have been his fortieth birthday.

The modern recording that comes closest to approaching the brilliance and passion of Feuermann's is that pointedly dramatic interpretation by Pierre Fournier and George Szell, recorded in Berlin in the 1960s and now available on a Deutsche Grammophon cassette. Fournier plays the solo part with fire, subtlety, and conviction, and Szell, who led the Czech Philharmonic in Casals' famous recording from the 1930s, gives what is arguably his most intense and involving recorded performance. (Now, for a Feuermann-Szell recording in up-to-date sound, I would willingly trade my priceless baseball autographed by Mickey Mantle, ten percent of my annual income, and my firstborn male child.)

The late Jacqueline Du Pré's Angel recording with Daniel Barenboim and the Chicago Symphony is also very special. It is a red-blooded, slightly (but always persuasively) wayward interpretation in which the playing may owe something to that of her teacher, Mstislav Rostropovich, but which fortunately lacks his tendency to vulgarity and self-indulgence. The cellist's husband, Daniel Barenboim, offers a sweepingly romantic yet sensitive accompaniment, and both the orchestra and recorded sound are absolutely first rate.

String Quartet in F Major, Op. 96 "American"

Talich String Quartet. Calliope 1617 [LP], *CAL 9617*[CD], 4617 [T].

Dvořák wrote the "American" Quartet during a few days' summer vacation spent in the amiable, hard-drinking Czech colony of Spillville, Iowa, where he also completed the "New World" Symphony. His "American" Quartet is only the most famous and colorful of those fourteen works that, taken together, constitute the most important contribution a nineteenth century composer made to the form after the death of Franz Schubert. Like the "New World" Symphony, the "American" Quartet was inspired by Dvořák's passionate love affair with the sights and sounds of America, although like the Symphony it does not contain, as has been so frequently suggested, a *single* American folk tune. (The subtitle, incidentally, was not the composer's, but the idea of a discreet publisher who sought to correct the brazen stupidity of an unforgivably insensitive time. Shamefully, on the original title page, the F Major Quartet was called "The Nigger.")

Until the warmly appealing Deutsche Grammophon recording by the Prague String Quartet is returned to circulation, this handsome Calliope recording by the Talich Quartet is recommended without hesitation. Founded by a nephew of the great Czech conductor Václav Talich, the group plays with an engaging mixture of polish and youthful enthusiasm. Like the Prague and Smetana Quartets, they have this music in their bones, and unlike other non-Czech groups which tend to overemphasize the music's "New World" color, they never forget that this great work is first and foremost an intensely Bohemian score. Also, their performance of the Op. 61 Quartet is so engaging that if you haven't begun to explore Dvořák's lesser-known chamber works, the urge to do so will probably be overwhelming.

Serenade for Strings in E Major, Op. 22; Serenade in D minor, Op. 44

Academy of St. Martin-in-the-Fields, Marriner. Philips
400020[CD].

English Chamber Orchestra, Mackerras. Angel AE-34448
[LP].

There has never been a day so wretched, a problem so insoluble, a night so long, a winter so bleak, a toothache so painful, that one or the other of these enchanting works couldn't cure. On those days when I walk in the door exhausted, disgruntled, disillusioned, full of contempt for all things human, and beating down an insane desire to kick the cat, I put on one of the Dvořák Serenades, make for the nearest chair, and within a few minutes a dippy grin—the external manifestation of a mood of avuncular forgiveness and beatific peace—invariably steals over my face. If only this inexhaustibly charming music were a little better known, many of the nation's psychiatrists would have to start looking for honest work.

Sir Neville Marriner's glowing Philips recording contains the most radiant performances of both Serenades on the market today. The string tone in the Op. 22 is the aural equivalent of a morning in early June, while the wind playing in the Op. 44 is a marvel of individuality and character. (The thin, nasal twang of English oboes has never been one of my favorite sounds; here, I hardly notice.)

For those who have yet to make the leap of faith into compact discs, the recording by Sir Charles Mackerras is exceptionally fine. While not quite as spontaneous-sounding as the Marriner interpretations, Sir Charles, who was once a pupil of the great Václav himself, performs with an instinctive, authoritative grasp of the idiom that have made his old teacher proud.

Slavonic Dances, Op. 46 and 72

Cleveland Orchestra, Szell. Odyssey Y2-33524 [LP],
YT-34626/7 [T].
Royal Philharmonic, Dorati. London *411735-2* [CD].

Once, during the interval of a Cleveland Orchestra rehearsal at Severance Hall, a member of the orchestra greeted a
visiting friend by saying, after carefully looking over his shoul-
der to see who might be listening, "Welcome to the American
home of Bohemian Culture." And throughout his tenure with
the orchestra, George Szell was an enthusiastic champion of
the music of Dvořák, Smetana, and that Moravian giant, Leoš
Janácek. Although born in Budapest, Szell had considerable
Czech blood in his veins; he studied in Prague and early in his
conducting career was a familiar fixture in the Bohemian
capital.

Szell's recordings of Dvořák's most popular works, the
Slavonic Dances, are the only ones that bear favorable comparison with Václav Talich's unsurpassable versions from the
late 1940s. The Cleveland Orchestra's playing is a wonder of
brilliance and flexibility, and the conductor, while demanding
the last word in virtuoso execution, never overlooks the music's wealth of subtle color and irrepressible charm. Even
though a single-disc reissue from CBS is currently available, it
is certainly no bargain. The physical sound is considerably
compressed and, far worse, the remastered tapes cut out
virtually all the repeats.

From a somewhat less dizzying, but perfectly respectable
height, Antal Dorati's recent London recording is also very
satisfying, especially if nearly flawless recorded sound or the
compact disc format are absolute musts.

Symphony No. 7 in D minor, Op. 70

Cleveland Orchestra, Dohnányi. London *417564-2* [CD].

For the first time in nearly thirty years, the darkest and, many would insist, the greatest of the Dvořák symphonies is without an incontestably great recorded performance. For decades, the very different but equally devastating interpretations by Carlo Maria Giulini and George Szell towered over the competition. Their withdrawal has created a vacuum that none of the current crop of Dvořák's Sevenths has been able to fill.

With Rafael Kubelik's excellent Berlin Philharmonic recording now available only as a Deutsche Grammophon tape (419088-4), Christoph von Dohnányi's competent, professional, and intermittently exciting London recording must be declared the winner by default. Certainly, the performance has much to recommend it. The playing of the orchestra is rich and authoritative, but the interpretation, while serious and dedicated, never quite succeeds in scaling the work's precipitous heights or plumbing its even more profound and moving depths. In sum, this is a perfectly acceptable way of marking time until either Angel or CBS send Giulini or Szell riding to the rescue.

None of the currently available tapes or LPs are worth bothering about.

Symphony No. 8 in G Major, Op. 88

Cleveland Orchestra, Dohnányi. London 414422-1 [LP], *414422-2* [CD], 414422-4 [T].

Unlike their recording of the Dvořák Seventh—which, admittedly, has been enthusiastically, even ecstatically praised elsewhere—it is this recording, more than any other, that confirms the Cleveland's reemergence as one of the world's great orchestras. Although during Lorin Maazel's unsettled and unsettling tenure as the orchestra's music director, standards were never allowed to slip, the orchestra nevertheless played as though their hearts weren't quite in it. At very least, the old Szell electricity was clearly gone.

If this splendid recording of the most amiable and open-hearted of Dvořák's mature symphonies is any indication, the Cleveland Orchestra's spirit, under Christoph von Dohnányi, has been thoroughly revived. Not since Szell has the orchestra given another conductor such awesome precision. But the healthiest indication that Dohnányi's is not a caretaker regime can be heard in the work of the middle and lower strings, who play with an even darker, more burnished quality than they did under Szell. The interpretation itself reminds me more than anything of Bruno Walter's immensely rewarding CBS recording, though one in which the Walter charm is matched by a Szell-like bite and point. For instance, in the rousing *coda* of the final movement, Dohnányi makes a point that many conductors seem to miss: namely, that this three minutes of unbridled enthusiasm is nothing more than a thinly-veiled *Slavonic Dance*.

Symphony No. 9 in E minor, Op. 95 "From the New World"

Chicago Symphony, Reiner. RCA Victor 5606-2 [CD].

Many conductors have approached this justly popular symphony as though it were utterly fool proof. For the most part, they're absolutely right. The "New World" Symphony *is* virtually fool proof; *idiot*-proof, however, it's *not*. While there is nothing overtly idiotic in any of Herbert von Karajan's several recordings of the symphony, the idiocy lies in assuming that anyone could muster the slightest interest in the vapid, arrogant, smooth-shod mockery he makes of the piece. (What did poor Dvořák ever do to him?) For the *truly* masochistic, there is even a video accompanying his latest unprovoked attack, so we can both hear and *see* him nearly destroy what everyone innocently assumed was a completely indestructible work.

If Karajan is almost alone at the bottom of the "New World" Symphony barrel, the competition for the top slot is unusually keen. In spite of inspired challenges from Kiril Kondrashin, Sir Colin Davis, Klaus Tennstedt, and from Bruno Walter's recently issued CBS compact disc, Fritz Reiner's craggy yet affectionate early stereo recording remains in a class by itself. With wonderfully warm and responsive playing from the Chicago Symphony, Reiner makes the most of both the elegant simplicity and the complex drama of the work. The *Scherzo* bustles with high-spirited humor. The opening movement and the *finale* are especially lean and taut, and aided by Lawrence Thorstenberg, the finest English horn player of his generation, the famous *Largo* has never seemed more profoundly gentle, or more gently profound.

As a bonus, the compact disc reissue contains three other Reiner gems: the most electrifying of all recordings of Dvořák's *Carnival Overture*, a performance of Smetana's *Bartered Bride* Overture in which the furious string articulation must be heard to be believed, and last, but far from least, a glorious performance of the brash and brassy Polka and Fugue from Jaromir Weinberger's *Schwanda the Bagpiper*.

Given the paucity of worthwhile LPs, George Szell's crisp and dramatic Cleveland Orchestra recording for CBS (MY-37763) stands like a rock in a raging torrent of mediocrity.

Elgar, Sir Edward
(1857–1934)

Concerto in E minor for Cello and Orchestra,
Op. 65; *Sea Pictures*, Op. 37

> DuPré, cello; Baker, mezzo-soprano; London Symphony,
> Barbirolli. Angel S-36338 [LP] (Concerto only),
> *CDC-47239*[CD].

Anyone who has ever been sprung from an institution of
higher learning has understandable feelings of affection and
gratitude toward Sir Edward Elgar for his best known work. It
is usually to the stirring strains of the *Pomp and Circumstance March* No. 1 in D Major, also known in England as
"Land of Hope and Glory," that most high school and college
inmates make their final, glorious escape. While the average
music lover still persists in thinking of him as little more than
the stuffy, official musical voice of Edwardian England, Sir
Edward Elgar was one of the last incontestably great Romantic composers. Finding one's way into Elgar's rich and occasionally overripe world certainly isn't easy. I should know. For
it was only after years of mulish resistance that Elgar finally
became one of my greatest musical passions.

I can't think of a better way of introducing Elgar to
People Who Think They Don't Like Elgar than this hauntingly beautiful Angel recording of two of the composer's
loveliest and most important works. The Cello Concerto, the

only work in the literature which can be compared favorably with Dvořák's, has never been better served than by the young Jacqueline Du Pré, who made this ardent, rhapsodic recording at the beginning of her fame in 1965. Sir John Barbirolli, the most impassioned Elgarian of his generation, captures both the aching melancholy and searing tragedy of this great work more convincingly than any other conductor. In the *Sea Pictures*, among the most ravishing of all orchestral song cycles, he lays down a thrillingly sumptuous carpet of sound for the wonderful Dame Janet Baker, who here gives one of her finest and most memorable performances.

Concerto in B minor for Violin and Orchestra, Op. 61

Kennedy, violin; London Philharmonic, Handley. Angel *CDC-47210*[CD].

Like the symphonies of Anton Bruckner, this longest, and many would say *noblest*, of all violin concertos has one minor flaw. In spite of its incomparably majestic length, it is still *much* too short. Originally composed for the Viennese violinist Fritz Kreisler, the Concerto dates from a very fertile period in Elgar's creative life. Written during the waning years of the Edwardian era—a period which also saw the composition of the composer's two symphonies—the Violin Concerto is one of several key works in which Elgar tried to confine his flood of melodic invention and naturally expansive temperament within the limits of more rigid musical forms.

Apart from the work's sheer enormity—in most performances the Concerto requires nearly fifty minutes to play—it presents other challenging interpretive problems, chief among which is an immense (and immensely original) accompanied *cadenza* in the final movement. In his 1932 recording with the sixteen-year-old Yehudi Menuhin, the composer demonstrated that the Concerto's difficulties are trivial when compared to its enormous rewards, and fortunately, after years of neglect, a new generation of violinists is beginning to agree.

The modern performance which most closely approximates the depth and authority of Sir Edward's classic interpretation can be found on a recent Angel recording by the admirable English violinist, Nigel Kennedy. With a purity of tone and entrancing sweetness of spirit, Kennedy surmounts the Concerto's formidable problems in much the same way the teenage Yehudi Menuhin had before him: by tossing them off as though they were, quite literally, child's play. Yet the real star of the show is the conductor, Vernon Handley, whose ability to highlight a wealth of striking local detail without ever losing sight of the work's overall sweep and architecture only confirms his reputation as one of the preeminent Elgarians of our time.

While no acceptable LP version of the Concerto is currently in print, there is a fine tape by Itzhak Perlman (Deutsche Grammophon 413312-4), which also makes much of the grandeur and nobility of the piece.

Enigma Variations, Op. 36

Royal Philharmonic, Previn. Philips *416813-2* [CD].

BBC Symphony, Bernstein. Deutsche Grammophon 2532067 [LP], *413490-2* [CD], 3302067 [T].

With the passing of Sir John Barbirolli and Sir Adrian Boult, many admirers of Elgar's music feared that it would suffer the same fate that Frederick Delius' did following the death of Sir Thomas Beecham. Of course, there was never any serious danger of that: unlike the rarified, specialized genius of his younger contemporary, Elgar was always the far more important and universal composer. Alas, while no major Delius conductor has emerged to take the place of the inimitable Baronet, the Elgar tradition continues to grow and flourish in the hands of a brilliant new guard of sympathetic advocates, whose brightest light is clearly André Previn.

As in his superlative recordings of the symphonies of Ralph Vaughan Williams (see below), Previn not only speaks the traditional Elgarian language as though it were his native tongue, but also—and wisely—has never resisted the temptation to throw in a few new accents of his own. While his early Angel recording of the *Enigma Variations* was characterized by a refreshing openness and spontaneity, this new version with the Royal Philharmonic is clearly the work of a mature master. The vibrancy and sense of discovery have certainly not vanished, but along with the still-youthful enthusiasm we can hear a far more confident grasp of the larger ebb and flow of the piece. Each of these inspired and inventive variations has great individual character and identity, yet that episodic quality which sabotages so many performances is nowhere to be found. In short, this is the one *Enigma* on the market today in which the whole adds up to considerably more than the sum of the admittedly striking individual parts.

Unfortunately, since the annual Grammy Awards ceremony is something of a joke as far as classical recordings are concerned, and since the prestigious *Grand Prix du Disc* competition does not have a category for "Wackiest Recording of the Decade," I hereby announce the winner of the first (and possibly annual) "Jimmy" Prize to Leonard Bernstein for the most insanely self-indulgent Elgar recording ever made. Tempos, especially in the *Nimrod* variation, tend to be preposterously slow, and rhythms are hauled around so arbitrarily that even Willem Mengelberg, King of the Score Maulers, would have blushed. Predictably, this live BBC performance of the *Enigma Variations* left the generally cheerless English critical establishment either totally befuddled or fit to be tied. And in truth, whatever else the goofy thing might be, it is certainly *not* the *Enigma Variations*. Perhaps it is a measure of the work's indestructible greatness or the force of

Leonard Bernstein's hypnotic personality, but I treasure this delightful madness almost more than any other Elgar recording I own.

Symphony No. 2 in E-flat Major, Op. 63

London Philharmonic, Boult. Angel *CDC-47205* [CD].

Together with the dark and dramatic Symphony No. 1 in A-flat—which is now best represented by André Previn's powerful new recording with the Royal Philharmonic (Philips 416612-1, *416612-2,* 416612-4 [T])—Elgar's E-flat Major Symphony is one of the absolute summits of late-Romantic symphonic thought. Like *The Dream of Gerontius,* it represents much of what is best in Elgar: from the striding confidence of the opening movement through the ineffably poignant closing bars of the *Finale,* the Symphony is a sort of gentlemanly and gently refined *Götterdämmerung* of the entire Edwardian era. As a matter of fact, the composer was already at work on the Symphony's emotional heart, the devastating *Largo,* when word reached him that the man who gave the age its name had died. This long, beautifully painful, inexpressibly moving elegy for Edward VII is one of the great farewells in all of music.

Sir Adrian Boult recorded the Elgar Second at least a half dozen times, and his final recording is easily his best. Boult invests the music with a dignity and significance that no other conductor equalled, and there is no hint of the stodgy standoffishness that occasionally marred his later work. The interpretation is powerful yet proper, dramatic and colorful yet beautifully shaped. The only other comparable modern recording was that feverish, tempestuous outburst by Sir John Barbirolli, a performance that, with Sir John's incomparable version of *The Dream of Gerontius,* is shamefully now out of print.

For those who *must* have the piece on LP or tape, only the stately, and occasionally stuffy Chandos recording by Bryden Thomson and the London Philharmonic (ARBD-1161, ABTD-1161 [T]), begins to approach Boult's finish and nobility.

Falla, Manuel de
(1876–1946)

Nights in the Gardens of Spain

De Larrocha, piano; London Philharmonic, Frühbeck de
Burgos. London *410289-2* [CD], 410289-4 [T].

Rubenstein, piano; Philadelphia Orchestra, Ormandy. RCA
Victor AGL1-5205 [LP].

When she first walks out on stage, Alicia de Larrocha
looks exactly like the slightly plump but demurely elegant
Barcelona housewife she happens to be when she is not off on
one of her concert tours. Yet the moment she begins to play
we are instantly ushered into the presence of a great modern
pianist. Her Mozart shimmers with crystalline purity and
inner strength; and her Liszt is an exhilarating amalgam of
volcanic intensity and urbane sophistication. However, De
Larrocha remains unique for the colorful, evocative music of
her fellow countrymen. It's unlikely that Isaac Albéniz, Enrique Granados, or Manuel de Falla ever had a more sympathetic or persuasive interpreter of their piano music, and
barring some unforseen miracle they will probably never have
one of this quality again.

In her most recent recording of de Falla's exquisitely
dreamy *Nights in the Gardens of Spain*, De Larrocha plays
with all the sensitivity and profound understanding that made
her now-deleted London version of Albéniz' *Iberia* a classic of

recent recording history. (That London saw fit to withdraw that indispensable recording was an act of insensitivity bordering on criminal negligence; one can only hope that plans for a compact disc reissue are currently in the works.) Unlike many pianists who cheapen the *Nights* by flooding it with too much local Spanish color, De Larrocha approaches it with the ease and assurance of one who speaks its musical language fluently. Never has the music seemed more natural or more naturally indebted to the piano music of Ravel and Debussy, nor has there ever been another performance so utterly spontaneous that it creates the illusion of improvisation. Rafael Frühbeck de Burgos provides De Larrocha with some richly idiomatic support, and the recorded sound is breathtaking in its dynamic range and presence. Clearly, this is the recording of the *Nights* that will dominate catalogues for years to come.

Artur Rubenstein's RCA Victor recording from the early 1960s was one of the best of his later efforts and is the finest LP version of the work currently available. The playing has a wonderful and easy grace, and is supported admirably by Ormandy's evocative accompaniment.

The Three-Cornered Hat; El Amor Brujo.

Boky, mezzo-soprano; Montreal Symphony, Dutoit. London 410008-1 [LP], *410008-2* [CD], 410008-4 [T].

With its intoxicating rhythms, harmonic language, color, wit, and distinctively original use of the modern orchestra's resources, Manuel de Falla's *The Three Cornered Hat* —originally composed for Sergei Diaghilev's Ballets Russes—is the most important large-scale orchestral work ever written by a Spanish composer. All of its freshness and overt, provocative sensuality have remained intact for nearly seventy years, and with Bizet's *Carmen*, that masterpiece by a great French tourist, the ballet remains one of the most vivid of all musical distillations of Spanish sights and sounds.

The Three-Cornered Hat has never gone begging for first-rate recorded performances. Ernest Ansermet gave the work its world premiere in 1919 and left a commandingly vivid interpretation in 1961, only to have it superceded by an even finer Angel recording by André Previn and the Pittsburgh Symphony two decades later. However, Charles Dutoit's recent effort for London captures more of the ballet's drama and atmosphere than has any other recording.

The secret of the Dutoit performance lies in the fact that it projects a perfect balance between the sophistication and studied sensuality that are both so explicit in de Falla's score. The rhythmic vitality that Dutoit breathes into the more famous dances gives them a freshness that has probably not been heard since *The Three Cornered Hat* was new. But it is in the less familiar music, which so often can seem like padding, that the performance *really* comes to life. For instance, the ballet's opening bars, with those relentless tympani, castanets, and repeated cries of *Ole!*, seem, in this performance, like some of the most inspired opening minutes any composer has ever written.

As always, the Montreal Symphony plays with tremendous dash and precision, and London's engineers, as they usually seem to do for Dutoit, set new standards for brilliance, warmth, and razor-sharp clarity of detail.

Fauré, Gabriel (1845–1924)

Requiem, Op. 48

> Ashton, Varcoe, Cambridge Singers, City of London Sinfonia,
> Rutter (1893 version). Collegium COL-101 [LP],
> *COLCD-101* [CD], COLC-101 [T].

> Battle, Schmidt, Philharmonia Orchestra and Chorus, Giulini
> (1900 fully orchestrated version). Deutsche Grammophon
> 419243-1 [LP], *419243-2*, 419243-41 [T].

While the French consider Gabriel Fauré the consummate musical embodiment of their culture—and certainly no French composer ever produced a more cultivated body of chamber music, piano works, and songs—for most non-French ears, Fauré, to use the tired metaphor, is the classic example of a rare, virtually priceless wine that simply refuses to travel. Outside his native country, his discretion, restraint, and natural reticence are still insufficiently appreciated. But then again, expecting any but an educated Gallic audience to enjoy the subtle delicacies of a song cycle like *La Bonne Chanson*, is a little like expecting a non-German listener to fully grasp the more thorny *lieder* of Hugo Wolf.

Together with the melancholy and sinuously beautiful pops concert staple, the *Pavane*, one of the rare Fauré works that has enjoyed considerable worldwide popularity is that gentlest and most reserved of the great nineteenth century

Requiems. As in all his important music, the Fauré *Requiem* makes its subdued points without so much as wrinkling an inch of its immaculately polished surface. From first note to last, the music flows in an inevitable, unhurried way, offering not only quiet spiritual consolation, but also an extraordinary and original sonic beauty.

The recent Collegium recording—the first to present the composer's work in its original chamber music instrumentation—makes the strongest case yet for the *Requiem*. In fact, the reduced scale of the performing forces is such a perfect complement to the music's intimate nature that one wonders why no one ever thought of recording it this way before. Both the singing and playing are engagingly fresh and youthful, and Collegium's spacious but detailed recording captures every nuance of an extremely subtle interpretation.

For those who prefer a Fauré *Requiem* with a little more meat on its bones, Carlo Maria Giulini's iridescent Angel recording of the 1900 orchestration, while maintaining the restrained poise of a fine chamber music performance, still overflows with old-fashioned romanticism and warmth.

Franck, César (1822–1900)

Sonata in A Major for Violin and Piano

Perlman, violin; Ashkenazy, piano. London *414128-2*[CD].

Mintz, violin; Bronfman, piano. Deutsche Grammophon
415683-1[LP], *415683-2*[CD], 415683-4[T].

Like the Moravian composer Leos Janácek, who did not
begin to produce his greatest music until he entered his seventh decade of life, the Belgian-born César Franck was a
classic late bloomer among the major composers. He produced some shockingly dreadful music early in his career—
Hulda, for instance, has a better than average claim to being
the worst French opera of the nineteenth century, and *that's*
saying something—and yet, toward the end of his life, he
found his own distinct voice in a tiny handful of masterworks
that will probably endure forever.

Franck's Violin Sonata in A Major—known in some
irreverent corners of the classical music radio trade as "The
Frank Sinatra"—stands with those of Brahms and Schumann
as one of the finest violin sonatas after those of Beethoven. As
in all of Franck's most powerful and characteristic music, the
Sonata represents a conscious attempt to contain Romantic
sentiment within formal classical structures, a tendency
which his French critics lambasted mercilessly, charging the
composer with an unseemly and almost treasonous fondness

for German formalism. (As preposterous as it might seem, many of those same critics took George Bizet's *Carmen* to task for being so obviously and slavishly "Wagnerian".)

While I still have the fondest memories of a long-vanished Decca interpretation by the fabulously musical Viennese violinist, Erica Morini, Itzhak Perlman's London recording from the mid-1970s easily surpasses all currently available recordings of the work. While poised and elegant throughout, the playing of both violinist and pianist is also shot through with a wonderful sense of dramatic urgency and immediacy. In their hands, for instance, the turbulent second movement emerges as one of the composer's greatest creations.

On a somewhat more reserved, but no less compelling level, the recent recording by Schlomo Mintz and Yefim Bronfman has much to recommend it, including youthful ardor, meticulous execution, and more up-to-date recorded sound.

Symphony in D minor

Chicago Symphony, Monteux. RCA Victor AGL1-5261 [LP], 6805-2-RG [CD], ART-4443 [CD].

There are people whose friendship I value and whose musical opinions I respect who absolutely cannot *abide* Franck's D minor Symphony. (Curiously enough, they tend to be the same people who have an inexplicable revulsion for the music of Frederick Delius. Consequently, I never argue either subject with them, but instead tend to look their way with a mixture of benign sorrow and genuine confusion.) For if truth be told, what's *not* to like in this tuneful, brilliant, melancholy, triumphant work? It has something for everyone: despair, adventure, exuberance, romance, and an English horn solo in the second movement for which anyone who ever played the instrument, myself included, would cheerfully sell his grandmother to the gypsies.

For students of English horn playing, the legendary Lawrence Thorstenberg gives one of the greatest performances of his incomparable career in this 1961 RCA Victor recording. For those whose interests are a bit less parochial, Larry's luscious playing can be heard in what also happens to be the greatest recorded performance that the Franck D minor Symphony has ever been given.

If further proof was needed that Pierre Monteux was one of the most consistently satisfying conductors of the twentieth century, this stunning performance goes a long way to underscore the point. With a youthful impetuosity that only this ageless octogenarian could muster, he levitates Franck's often problematical symphony almost to the level of Johannes Brahms'. The first movement seethes with a barely containable intensity, the slow movement is a seamless, diaphanous love song, while the *Finale* becomes a Tchaikovskian explosion of exuberance and romance. With his London Symphony *Daphnis and Chloé*, and Boston Symphony version of Stravinsky's *Rite of Spring*—two works that Pierre Monteux introduced to the world—this is a principal monument of a unique and irreplaceable talent.

Gabrieli, Giovanni
(c.1555–1612)

Canzona for Brass Choirs

Chicago, Cleveland and Philadelphia Brass Ensembles. CBS
MP-38759 [LP], MP-38759 [T].

When this stunning recording was originally released in
the late 1960s, a respected English magazine's review insisted
it was a great pity that no one who really knew about the
"proper" way of playing this music was present at the recording sessions. By " proper," I suppose the reviewer meant one
of those deadly serious period-instrument types who would
have found the lush and full-throated excitement generated by
some of the world's finest brass players a trifle *too* exciting for
his refined and etiolated tastes. Thank goodness no such
creature could be found.

No doubt the performances contained on this famous
recording are woefully anachronistic: imagine the gall of playing older music on modern instruments, *and* playing it in such
a way that the magnificent music of a sixteenth century composer becomes instantly, and irresistibly accessible to twentieth century ears. Tsk. Tsk. It's a pity that after releasing a
recording containing some of the most thrilling brass playing
ever captured, CBS didn't follow it up with another dozen
volumes.

Gershwin, George
(1898–1937)

*An American in Paris; Concerto in F; Rhapsody in
Blue*

**Golub, piano; London Symphony, Miller. Arabesque Z 6587
[CD], ABQC 6587 [T].**

At very *least*, this is the greatest single Gershwin recording ever made. Where it ranks among the great classical
recordings of the last twenty-five years only time will tell,
though my suspicion is that it will rank very high. Among so
many other things—peerless oboist, television star, and recording executive whose list of discoveries reads like a Who's
Who of American popular music—Mitch Miller is also one of
the most revealing and exciting conductors in the world today.
This recent Arabesque recording of music by his friend
George Gershwin may well be the crowning achievement to
date in a long and colorful career.

What Miller brings to Gershwin's music is an unusual
combination of freshness and authority. But paradoxically, the
freshness comes from simply playing the music as the composer intended: intentions that Miller discovered firsthand
while playing in the orchestra for the composer's 1934 American tour and in the original production of *Porgy and Bess*.
Working from scores that Miller carefully marked according

to Gershwin's own interpretations and instructions, the performances emerge out of this astonishing Arabesque recording sounding like no others you've ever heard before. While infinitely more lyrical, expansive, and direct in their emotional expression, they are also more intricate and subtle than any other Gershwin recording on the market today. The important, but rarely heard inner voices are coaxed out of the background with a startling clarity, and the jazz inflections, for once, are not simply tossed in as cheap effects, but can clearly be heard for what they were all along: part of the natural organic structure of the music itself.

The playing of the London Symphony ranges from the merely sensational to the absolutely terrifying—at times, the LSO brass section wails with the electrifying unanimity of purpose of the old Count Basie Band—and the technically spellbinding, but intelligent and poetic playing of David Golub suggests that he is one of the finest pianists before the public today. For Gershwin lovers, the recording is an obvious necessity; for those who have never been able to warm to the composer's more obviously "serious" music, this is an excellent opportunity to hear it, quite literally, for the very first time.

Among the handful of LPs that remain in print, the best are the CBS recording by Leonard Bernstein and the New York Philharmonic (MY-37242) and the Philips version (412661-1) by André Previn and the Pittsburgh Symphony.

Porgy and Bess

Albert, Dale, Smith, Shakesnider, Marshall, Houston Grand Opera Chorus and Orchestra, DeMain. RCA Victor ARL1-4680 [LP], *RCD3-2109* [CD], ARK3-2109.

Although many of its arias have long since become popular standards—is there anyone who can forget their first encounter with "Summertime"?—Gershwin's last great achievement, *Porgy and Bess*, remains a neglected classic. Its initial run, while more than respectable for an opera, was disastrous by the standards of a broadway musical, and ever since its ill-fated first production, *Porgy and Bess* has had the undeserved reputation of being a hard-luck show.

This handsome RCA Victor recording by the Houston Grand Opera (the same adventurous company that recently brought us John Adams' *Nixon in China*, whether we wanted it or not) proves conclusively that Gershwin knew precisely what he was about. For with the proper care and dedication— which does not necessarily mean the services of world class voices or an internationally famous conductor—*Porgy and Bess* can clearly be heard as the closest thing we have to The Great American Opera.

Not since the trailblazing Columbia recording that Goddard Lieberson produced in 1950, has any recorded version of the opera made such a convincing case for *Porgy and Bess'* greatness. The entire cast is uniformly distinguished and enthusiastic, especially the bewitching Clama Dale, and under John DeMain's precise but free-wheeling and expressive direction, this *Porgy* adds up to a very convincing musical and dramatic whole. If DeMain misses the occasional inflection or the wonderfully sexy phrasing that made Lehman Engel's conducting such a joy on the old Columbia set, his vigorous sincerity is certainly to be preferred to Lorin Maazel's impeccably played and sung, but rather cold and calculated run-through for London.

Gilbert, Sir William S.
(1836–1911)

and

Sullivan, Sir Arthur
(1842–1900)

H. M. S. Pinafore

D'Oyle Carte Opera Company, Sargent (Recorded 1930).
Arabesque 8052 [LP], *Z-8052* [CD], 9052 [T].

The Mikado

D'Oyle Carte Opera Company, Nash. London *417296-2*
[CD].

The Pirates of Penzance

D'Oyle Carte Opera Company, Godfrey. London *414286-2*
[CD], 414286-4 [T].

Like their inedible cuisine (and who, but they, would even consider *looking* at such emetic delights as "Steak and Kidney Pie" and "Beans on Toast"?) or their public monuments (are there any structures in the civilized world quite as ugly as the Albert Memorial or the facade of Euston Station?), another of the great and presumably imperishable English National Monuments are those fourteen operas written by two of the strangest and most unlikely bedfellows in theatrical history, W. S. Gilbert and Arthur Sullivan. (By the way, the myth that the two were close, inseparable friends is precisely that. From beginning to end, the relationship was characterized by mild mutual respect tempered by constant suspicion, distrust, and frequently open, albeit gentlemanly, contempt. In fact, all the two men had in common was an unshakable belief that each was prostituting his sacred talent for the sake of making money.)

Those of us who are hopelessly drawn to the Gilbert and Sullivan operas tend to treat our affliction as we would any other incurable disease. Except among ourselves, admitting to a passion for Gilbert and Sullivan is a bit like admitting to something of which one should be slightly ashamed. For instance, that we might be, to quote Sheridan Whiteside in *The Man Who Came to Dinner*, "the sole support of a two-headed brother."

For anyone similarly smitten, or for those who are thinking of taking the ghastly plunge for the very first time, the recordings listed above represent a fair cross-section of the D'Oyle Carte Opera Company's finest achievements. While the *Mikado* and *Pirates* recordings are among the very best that the late and greatly lamented company founded by Gilbert and Sullivan themselves would ever make—John Reed, the last in the unbroken line of Savoy patter comics is especially delightful—the 1930 *Pinafore* remains in a class by itself. The principal attraction here, aside from the buoyant conducting of the young Malcolm Sargent, is one of the few complete recorded performances left by the greatest Savoyard of all. After a career spanning more than fifty years, Sir Henry Lytton was the only Gilbert and Sullivan performer ever knighted for his services. Even the great Martyn Green could not approach the horrible perfection of Lytton's Sir Joseph Porter, K.C.B. Dramatically, it is a triumph of bumbling incompetence and unbridled lechery. Musically, it is absolutely glorious, thanks in no small part to an inimitable "voice" which can best be described as a cross between a soggy Yorkshire pudding and a badly opened beer can.

Glass, Philip (1937–)

While I continue to be amazed at the success of the Minimalist movement, one does well to remember H. L. Mencken's chilling but prophetic observation: "Nobody ever went broke underestimating the intelligence of the American people." Philip Glass is a very nice man who has gotten very rich not by underestimating, but by completely *ignoring* his audience's intelligence. With a perfectly straight face—and presumably a perfectly clear conscience—he has built a formidable career by purporting to have discovered the triad and the C Major scale and then proceeding to do precious little with either. In short, Minimalism is a not especially funny Emperor's-New-Clothes kind of joke that really has gone on long enough. Whenever I hear this mindless drivel, I am reminded of something John Simon once said of the pre-Minimalist poetry of Robert Creeley: "There are two things to be said about Creeley's poems: they are short; they are not short enough."

Gluck, Christoph Willibald (1717–1787)

Orfeo ed Euridice

Speiser, Gale, Baker, Glyndebourne Festival Chorus, London
Philharmonic, Leppard. Erato 75042 [LP].

Listening to this best-known of Gluck's "Reform"
Operas today, it is all but impossible to understand the violent
passions it unleashed more than two centuries ago. In Paris,
where Gluck had set up shop in 1773, the composer's in-
sistence that drama, instead of florid singing, should be the
true focus of the operatic stage generated heated public debates. As a matter of fact, it even provoked a number of private
duels in which many of his partisans and those of his principal
rival, Nicola Piccinni, were killed. Today, of course, Gluck's
revolutionary operas seem rather tame and timid stuff, largely
because the reforms he inaugurated have long been accepted as
elementary tenets of how opera should behave.

After Purcell's *Dido and Aeneas*, *Orfeo ed Euridice* is
the earliest extant opera which is performed with any frequency today. While the action is generally static, and the
characters are little more than cardboard cutouts, *Orfeo* has
some beautiful moments that still have the power to move us
deeply, including the celebrated "Dance of the Blessed Spirits"
and the haunting aria, "Che, faro senza Euridice."

"Moving" is certainly an apt description of this molten

and limpid recording, based on a now-historic production mounted at the Glyndebourne Festival. Raymond Leppard leads a superb cast in a measured, affectionate performance whose chief glory is the Orfeo of Dame Janet Baker, who chose this role for her official farewell to the operatic stage. Unlike a host of great divas from Adelina Patti to Zinka Milanov who went on singing long after common sense—and common decency—should have told them to stop, Dame Janet, as she sounds here, may have been one of those rarest of singers who actually retired far too soon.

No suitable tape or compact disc has yet to appear.

Gounod, Charles
(1818–1893)

Roméo et Juliette

Malfitano, Kraus, Quilico, Van Dam, Bacquier, Capitole de
Toulouse Chorus and Orchestra, Plasson. Angel
CDCC-47365[CD], 4D3X-3960[T].

Poor Charles Gounod has fallen on decidedly hard
times. But then again, it's rather difficult to work up any real
sympathy for one of the luckiest musicians who ever lived. It
was a major miracle that a man who was perhaps the tenth
best French composer of his generation parlayed a gift for
sugary melody into one of the greatest successes in operatic
history. His opera *Faust* was once performed with such mo-
notonous frequency that a turn-of-the-century wag once recommended the Metropolitan in New York be renamed the
"Faustspielhaus."

That *Faust* may finally be losing its vicelike grip on the
world's affections is suggested by the fact that currently there
are only a handful of available recordings of the opera, and
the best of those is a turkey. The finest thing in the London
version of Gounod's syrupy classic is the surprisingly adept
conducting of Richard Bonynge. The conductor's wife, Joan
Sutherland, is caught in one of her droopiest moods, and
Franco Corelli is badly miscast in the title role. While he sings
well enough, the characterization is fairly gruesome. Whoever

coached Corelli in his French diction and pronunciation must have been the same person who taught English to Desi Arnaz.

In marked contrast to the composer's immensely lucrative Goethe travesty, his setting of Shakespeare's *Romeo and Juliet* is a far less presumptuous, and probably far finer work. With the proper cast, this genuinely touching, but sadly neglected opera can make a very moving impression, as this superb Angel recording easily proves. While the two principals don't exactly efface the memory of the legendary performances that Jussi Bjorling and the Brazilian soprano Bidu Sayao gave at the Metropolitan Opera shortly after the end of the War, both are exceptionally fine: Catherine Malfitano is a melting, delectably innocent Juliette, and the Romeo of the aging but always canny Alfredo Kraus is a triumph of interpretive savvy and consummate musicianship over a voice which has clearly lost its bloom.

Michel Plasson's conducting is consistently sensitive, supportive, and richly romantic. The orchestra plays wonderfully, and the recorded sound, especially in the compact disc transfer, is first-rate. Had these same forces turned their attention to *Faust*, that sadly shopworn opera might have been given, at least on records, another of its innumerable new leases on life.

Grieg, Edvard (1843–1907)

Piano Concerto in A minor, Op. 16

Richter, piano; Monte Carlo Opera Orchestra, Matacic.
Angel *CDC-47164* [CD], 4AM-34702 [T].

Fleisher, piano; Cleveland Orchestra, Szell. CBS MP-38757
[LP].

One of the most apt but not completely flattering de-
scriptions of the music of Edvard Grieg came from Claude
Debussy, who called the diminutive Norwegian composer "A
bon-bon filled with snow." The implication, of course, is that
along with the bracing Nordic freshness of his music, Grieg
was essentially a miniaturist, a composer of delicious little
trifles and nothing more. For more than a century this most
popular of all Romantic piano concertos has given the lie to
the suggestion that Grieg was only at his best when he was
thinking small. True, his finest work *does* tend to come in
smaller packages, but this enduring classic also demonstrates
that he was perfectly comfortable in large-scale forms as well.

While some superb straightforward versions of the Concerto are currently available—the poetic, introspective Radu
Lupu/André Previn London recording, and the fresh and
lightly-sprung Bishop-Kovacevich/Colin Davis interpretation
for Philips are both unusually appealing—it is the controversial madhouse thrown together by Sviatoslav Richter and

Lovro von Matacic that remains the most electric recording the piece has ever received.

With an arrogant bravado recalling turn-of-the-century barnstorming virtuosos, Richter all but rewrites this familiar music. Lyrical passages are drawn out to, and sometimes *beyond* the breaking point, while the more dramatic episodes are throttled with a demonic fury and horrifying accuracy. The always-fascinating Yugoslavian conductor Lovro von Matacic—who was certainly no shrinking violet when it came to turning a well-known score on its ear—proves a perfect accomplice, matching Richter insight for insight and outrage for outrage every step along the way. With artists of lesser stature, such a performance would be little more than a bizarre and inexplicable practical joke; from artists of *this* stature, it is among the most original and exciting commercial recordings ever made.

The Fleisher/Szell recording for CBS is also tremendously exciting, although both soloist and conductor are far better mannered and burn a much lower flame. Still, with the dearth of available LPs, this fine performance easily sweeps the field.

Peer Gynt (Incidental Music), Op. 23

> Hollweg, soprano; Beecham Choral Society, Royal Philharmonic, Beecham. Angel *CDM-69039* [CD], 4XSS-32813.
>
> Carlsen, Hanssen, Bjorkoy, Hansli, Oslo Philharmonic Chorus, London Symphony, Drier. Unicorn *UKCD-2003/04* [CD].

Like Tchaikovsky who thoroughly despised his *Nutcracker* Suite, and Sergei Rachmaninoff who often became violently nauseous at the prospect of having to give yet another performance of his C-sharp minor Prelude, Edvard Grieg was not especially fond of his most frequently performed work. In a famous letter written to the playwrite Henrik Ibsen, he had this to say of the soon to be world-famous *In the Hall of the Mountain King*: "I have written something for the hall of the Troll king which smacks of so much cow dung, ultra-Norwegianism and self-satisfaction that I literally cannot bear to listen to it." In that opinion, of course, Grieg has always been a minority of one. The score he composed for a production of Ibsen's poetic drama *Peer Gynt* contains some of the best-loved moments in all of music.

For anyone who cut their musical teeth on the evergreen chestnuts from the two *Peer Gynt* Suites, Unicorn's world premiere recording of the complete incidental music will come as major and unfailingly delightful surprise. (Incidentally, all other recordings that claim to contain the "complete" incidental music are stretching the laws of truth in advertising. With Neemi Järvi's recent, and slightly less successful Deutsche Grammophon recording, there are now precisely *two*.) Containing nearly an hour of unknown *Peer Gynt* music, this performance led by the fine Norwegian conductor Per Drier makes for an enlightening experience, to say the very least. While the "heavy hits" are all done to near-perfection, it is the cumulative impact of the other, completely unfamiliar episodes that creates the more indelible impression. Far from being the lightweight collection of saccharine lollipops it can often become, the *Peer Gynt* music for once emerges as vivid and powerful drama. Drier leads his forces with great individuality, charm and authority; the Norwegian cast and chorus are consistently brilliant and idiomatic, and the London Symphony's playing is above reproach.

The only serious flaw in this otherwise flawless recording is one which none of these dedicated performers could possibly control. For all its professionalism and devotion, it is simply *not* in the same stratospheric league with that vocally klutzy, harshly recorded source of wonder and despair that Sir Thomas Beecham perpetrated a generation ago. In its new compact disc incarnation, this ageless performance seems even more magnetic and unsurpassable than ever. *Anitra's Dance* contains some of the most graceful playing ever captured in a recording studio, the *Death of Aase* becomes a muffled outcry of insupportable grief, and *Morning* dawns with a sylvan freshness that suggests the very first morning of the world. Yet it is in *The Hall of the Mountain King* that Beecham really makes us wonder what the composer's whining "cow dung" letter was all about. Unless, of course, Beecham read it too and took that as his cue to do his best, in this macabre and terrifying performance, to scare a similar substance out of his listeners.

Speaking of unmitigated horrors, not a *single* worthwhile LP version of the *Peer Gynt* music can be found on the market today.

Handel, George Frideric (1685–1759)

Concerti Grossi (12), Op. 6

Academy of St. Martin-in-the-Fields, Brown. Philips *410048*
[CD].

English Concert, Pinnock. Deutsche Grammophon
ARC-2742002 [LP], *ARC-410897-9-1* [CD], 410897-9-4
[T].

I somehow manage to shock people when I tell them I
have always preferred the music of George Frideric Handel to
that of Johann Sebastian Bach. I find Handel not only a far
more appealing composer, but also a far more interesting
man. Aside from assiduously devoting his energies to prayer,
the production of music, and twenty-odd children, Bach seems
to have been a classic seventeenth century Lutheran home-
body whose life story makes for singularly boring reading.
Handel, who was an internationally famous figure while Bach
was still a provincial *Kapellmeister*, was a mass of fascinating

contradictions. In spite of his many physical and psychological afflictions—he was nearly felled by several major strokes, went blind at the end of his career, and for more than sixty years exhibited many of the classic symptoms of manic depression—Handel was nevertheless one of the healthiest composers in the history of music, a man whose many enthusiasms and vigorous love of life can be heard in virtually every bar of music he ever wrote.

Nowhere is the essence of Handelian exuberance and inventiveness more clearly in evidence than in these dozen concerti grossi he composed, largely for money, in 1749. (Dr. Johnson may have actually had Handel in mind when he framed one of the most irrefutable of all his aphorisms: "No man but a blockhead ever wrote, *except* for money.") While much of the thematic material was purloined from the works of other composers—and Handel never stole more imaginatively than from Handel—the collection is full of an utterly original and irresistible beauty. The dance movements are as infectious as any written by a baroque composer, the slow movements are often poignant and invariably memorable, and the slapdash, good-natured fugues remain as impressive as any that Bach ever wrote.

Of all the fine recordings currently available, pride of place clearly goes to the elegant Philips set by the Academy of St. Martin-in-the-Fields led by Iona Brown. While detailed and scholarly, these non-Period-Instrument performances have none of that musty, stuffy, academic quality that has marred so many recent Handel recordings. Under Iona Brown, as they had for years under Sir Neville Marriner, the St. Martin's Academy plays with an appealing combination of bravado and finesse, and the Philips engineers have provided a warm but lively acoustic that is the perfect mirror of the performances themselves.

For the Baroque Authenticity Purists, Trevor Pinnock's only slightly less desirable Deutsche Grammophon recording offers a fine period instrument alternative, which has the further advantage of also being available on LP and tape.

Coronation Anthems (4)

**Academy and Chorus of St. Martin-in-the-Fields, Marriner.
Philips 412733-2 [CD], 412733-4 [T].**

If until very recently the House of Windsor has seemed one of the least interesting and most dim-witted of Britain's royal families, the Windsors have been like rocket scientists compared to the ill-starred and unlamented Hanoverian kings. George I, the founder of the line, not only refused to learn English during his reign, but also succeeded in enraging his British subjects further by refusing to trade in his German mistresses for English ones. His unstable Grandson, George III, who suffered from recurrent bouts of madness throughout his life, was responsible for the loss of the nation's American colonies. In fact, the only significant accomplishment the entire dynasty can point to with pride was its employment of the Saxon composer George Frideric Handel, who produced for them some of the greatest ceremonial and occasional music ever written.

The magnificent *Coronation Anthems* are all that survive from the thoroughly bungled coronation of George II in 1727. At their first performance, the sequence of the hymns together with most of the actual ceremony was somehow thrown completely out of whack, thereby making it a typically Georgian event. Still, the anthems that Handel provided are so stirring in their grandeur, so rich in their invention and execution, that upon hearing them, even the most tenaciously republican of her former colonists might almost be tempted to ask Her Majesty to take us back.

Neville Marriner's Philips recording offers suitably grand, though never grandiose, performances of these imposingly noble works. The interpretation of the seven-minute *Zadok the Priest*, with its mysteriously hushed opening and thundering final fugue on the word "Alleluia," is in itself worth more than the price of the recording. For anyone addicted to eighteenth century pomp and circumstance, or who simply wants to be convinced that there *will* always be an England, this is a recording which cannot be passed up.

On LP, Trevor Pinnock leads the English Concert and Westminster Abbey Choir in a fine, if rather boomy, recording for Deutsche Grammophon (2534005).

Messiah

Marshall, Robbin, Rolfe-Johnson, Hale, Brett, Quirke, Monteverdi Choir, English Baroque Soloists, Gardiner. Philips 414041-1 [LP], *411041-2* [CD], 411041-4 [T].

While his dramatic oratorios *Jeptha* and *Theodora* are probably finer works—Handel considered the chorus "He Saw the Lovely Youth" from *Theodora* his absolute masterpiece—*Messiah* has more than earned its status as the best-loved sacred work of all time. Its level of inspiration is astronomically high, and its musical values are phenomenally impressive, given the fact that the whole of the oratorio was dashed off in something under three weeks.

Although there are nearly two dozen *Messiah* recordings currently available, the catalogue could easily stand to make room for three more that are no longer in print. Perhaps the most beautifully played and sung of all *Messiahs* was Sir Colin Davis' Philips recording with the London Symphony, which is not to be confused with his disappointing digital remake with the Bavarian Radio Orchestra. Sir Thomas Beecham's famous recording of the stunning arrangement by Sir Eugene Goossens certainly deserves a compact disc face-lift. And until you've heard *Messiah* with Jon Vickers' singing, Beecham's racy tempos, and an orchestra which includes trombones, tubas, tam-tams, cymbals, snare drums, and gong, you haven't *really* lived. For a time, there was also a wonderful version of that greatest *Messiah* arrangement of all: Sir Charles Mackerras' loving interpretation of Mozart's German edition, in which the ingenious wind parts that were grafted onto Handel's string torso make for such an intoxicating amalgam of Christ and *Don Giovanni*.

John Elliot Gardiner's triumphant period-instrument version can be confidently mentioned in the same breath with any great *Messiah* recordings of the past. In fact, in many ways it is the most completely satisfying *Messiah* ever released. Using the reduced performing forces and older instruments common to almost every *Messiah* recording of the last decade, Gardiner nevertheless succeeds in projecting almost all of the oratorio's size and significance in a performance that is still very intimate in its physical dimension and sound. The soloists are all intelligent and musical, the chorus—in which Gardiner has wisely opted for sopranos instead of the more "authentic" choice of boys—sings with joy and devotion, and the English Baroque Soloists, while they play with great precision and high-minded intensity, still give the unmistakable impression that they're all having an enormous amount of fun. While nothing will ever make me part with my well-worn copies of the Davis, Beecham, and Mackerras recordings, the exultant new Gardiner version now joins that select circle of *Messiahs* I cannot do without.

*M*usic For the Royal Fireworks

Cleveland Symphony Winds, Fennell. Telarc DG-10038, *CD 80038* [CD].

London Symphony, Szell. London 411854-1 [LP], 411854-4 [T].

It was through an arrangement for modern orchestra by the gifted Ulster composer and conductor Sir Hamilton Harty that Handel's *Music for the Royal Fireworks* and *Water Music* first became accessible to twentieth century audiences. And although that curious hybrid composer Handel/Harty is now *persona non grata* in most musical circles, George Szell's gorgeous London recording from the mid-1960s proves just how ridiculous such snobbery is. The arrangements, while admittedly anachronistic, are as tasteful as they are exciting, and if you can bear the scorn of the baroque purist crowd, this recording will offer you countless hours of undiluted pleasure and delight.

Thanks to the classic series of recordings he made with the Eastman Wind Ensemble for Mercury, the name of Frederick Fennell is far more closely associated with Sousa Marches than with Baroque Authenticity. Nevertheless, on this brilliant Telarc recording he leads the finest "authentic" performance of the *Royal Fireworks Music* currently available. Since, as its title implies, the work was originally intended for performance in the open and soon-to-be sulfur-clogged air, Handel's original scoring called for instruments that had a fighting chance of making themselves heard above the ruckus: a huge wind band dominated by oboes and bassoons. Fennell's forces make a spectacular noise on this high-tech Telarc recording. You can almost hear every buzzing vibration in that forest of double reeds, and the brass are so emphatic and lively you can nearly smell the valve oil. For audiophiles, Handel lovers, and anyone who has ever spent time in a high school band, this is an absolutely essential recording.

The Water Music

Los Angeles Chamber Orchestra, Schwarz. Delos *DCD-3010* [CD].

English Baroque Soloists, Gardiner. Erato 71461 [LP], *EDC-88005* [CD].

My unremitting enthusiasm for the Los Angeles Chamber Orchestra's recording has absolutely nothing to do with civic pride. The only Southern California cultural institutions for which I have a blind and uncontrollable passion are the Dodgers and Disneyland. This is, quite simply the most thrillingly played of all recorded performances of Handel's popular score and, by a comfortable margin, the craziest. The insanity here consists largely of what might best be described as virtuosity gone berserk. In a performance that features nearly as many added ornaments as notes in the score, Gerard Schwarz leads his brilliant ensemble through one of the last decade's great recorded bravura exercises. The playing is dumfounding in its swaggering effortlessness: listen especially to the LACO oboes and horns for some of the most breathtaking technical legerdemain to be heard on a recording.

For a somewhat less exhausting period-instrument performance, John Elliot Gardiner's Erato recording is as impeccable and entertaining as any that this greatest living antiquarian has made. While there are few musicians who are so consistently brilliant that I could make such a sweeping recommendation, make it I will because I have learned to trust this man implicitly and so, for that matter, can you. Any recording you see that has Gardiner's name attached, *buy* it. You won't be disappointed.

Among available tapes of the complete *Water Music*, Trevor Pinnock's affable period-instrument recording for Deutsche Grammophon (410525-4) is to be preferred over Christopher Hogwood's imaginative, but occasionally harsh and insensitive recording for Oiseau Lyre (KDSLC 543).

Hanson, Howard
(1896–1981)

Symphony No. 2, Op. 30 "Romantic"

Eastman-Rochester Orchestra, Hanson. Mercury 420806-1 [LP], 420806-4 [T].

One of the most embarrassing of the numerous embarrassing moments I have suffered during my radio career occurred at a small station in upstate New York, shortly after I introduced this moltenly beautiful symphony as being a work by "the late Howard Hanson." Midway through the first movement, the "late" Dr. Hanson phoned the station and proceeded to point out, in the most unimaginably charming way, that my information was not entirely accurate.

For anyone who attended the National Music Camp at Interlochen, Michigan, the principal theme of the "Romantic" Symphony has many powerful associations. Since the late 1930s it has served to conclude every concert as the "Interlochen Theme" and was, for years, the signature theme of the camp's weekly NBC broadcasts. (More recently, Jerry Goldsmith used it to memorable effect at the end of his score for Ridley Scott's Sci-fi thriller, *Alien*.)

Since we have needed a recording of this great American symphony in up-to-date sound for more than a quarter century, Leonard Slatkin's eagerly anticipated Angel compact disc with the St. Louis Symphony came as a major disappointment. While full of fine moments, the interpretation remains strangely uninvolved and limp. For instance, one would have thought that the jazzy, brassy passage leading to the great theme's final peroration in the *finale* might have been tailor-made to Slatkin's talents and specifications. Alas, no such luck.

Until a suitable compact disc edition of this national treasure becomes available, the composer's own Mercury recording, faded acoustics and all, is still warmly recommended. As always, the Eastman-Rochester Orchestra plays with enormous enthusiasm and conviction, and Hanson's interpretation, needless to say, is definitive.

Harris, Roy (1898–1979)
and
Schuman, William
(1910–)

Symphony No. 3

New York Philharmonic, Bernstein. Deutsche Grammophon 419780-2[CD].

If the late Roy Harris was not the most original and important symphonist America has produced, the only other possible candidate for that distinction is the still vigorously active William Schuman. This superb recording of two live New York Philharmonic performances featuring probably the finest symphonies of both composers affords us an excellent opportunity to make up our minds.

On balance, the Harris Third, which enjoyed a tremendous vogue during the 1930s and 1940s, still seems the fresher and more startling work. In its day, this concise, dramatic, and often soaringly lyrical work attracted more than the usual New Music Crowd audience, and Harris regularly received fan mail from all sorts of people, including cab drivers, politicians, and baseball managers. The Schuman Third, while it may lack the Harris Symphony's apparent ease of inspiration, is nonetheless a starkly proud and powerful statement by a keen and frequently astringent musical mind. It may also be the better-made of the two works, which given Harris' fanatical approach to craftsmanship, is saying a very great deal.

Leonard Bernstein's invigorating interpretations of both symphonies will provide an ideal introduction to anyone who is not yet familiar with these seminal works of American symphonic thought. While Berstein made some very fine studio recordings of both symphonies during his years with Columbia, the excitement of these concert performances easily outstrips the earlier versions. The LP version of the Harris is no longer in print, but the Schuman—coupled with an even more persuasive version of that composer's Symphony No. 5—can still be found on CBS MS-7442.

Haydn, Franz Joseph
(1732–1809)

Concerto for Trumpet and Orchestra in E-flat
Major

**Marsalis, trumpet; English Chamber Orchestra, Leppard.
CBS IM-37846 [LP], *MK-37846* [CD], IMT-37846 [T].**

While he was the literal father of the Classical symphony
and string quartet (the nineteenth century didn't call him
"Papa" for nothing), few of the numerous operas, keyboard
sonatas, or instrumental concertos that Haydn composed
throughout his life have ever been very popular, with the
exception of the delightful and justly famous Trumpet Concerto. Along with its abundance of memorable melody and
virtuoso fireworks, the E-flat Major Concerto is also a work
of considerable historical significance. It was the first work by
a major composer written for a new-fangled contraption that
was several generations ahead of its time: the first, but not
completely practical incarnation of the *valved* trumpet.

When Wynton Marsalis' now famous recording was released a few years ago, it was accompanied by an enormous
amount of ballyhoo and hype. As the first Classical recording
by one of the finest jazz musicians of the younger generation,
it promised little more than Barbra Streisand's ill-starred
venture into art song, or the wonderful Cleo Lane's horren-
dous Frankenstein-Meets-the-Wolfman encounter with

Schoenberg's *Pierrot Lunaire*. What it delivered, on the other hand, was one of the most stylish and spellbindingly brilliant recordings that this popular work has ever received.

While Marsalis faces formidable competition from Gerard Schwarz on Delos and a majestic Deutsche Grammophon recording by the recently retired principal trumpet of the Chicago Symphony, Adolf Herseth, this CBS recording continues to set the standard for both lyric expressiveness and bravura display. In fact, the cadenzas that Marsalis supplies are so electrifying that the playing would make the hair on a bald man's head stand on end.

The Creation (Die Schöpfung)

Mathis, Baldin, Fischer-Dieskau, Academy and Chorus of St. Martin-in-the-Fields, Marriner. Philips 6769047 [LP], *416449-2* [CD], *416449-4* [T].

One of the absolute high water marks in the sacred music of the Age of Enlightenment, *The Creation* is an innocent, dramatic, unaffected, and beautifully made celebration of the God of whom Haydn said so frequently, "When I think of Him, my heart leaps with joy." Even for those who do not typically respond to lengthy religious works, *The Creation* overflows with such a wealth of inspired melodic and theatrical invention that only the most adamant of pagans are able to resist its glories. For instance, the choral outburst on the words "Let there be light" must certainly rank with the most exultant moments in all of music.

For the last thirty years, *The Creation* has led a charmed life on records. With the exception of Herbert von Karajan's most recent effort—a performance recorded at the 1982 Salzburg Festival so sinister in its calculation that it would warm the cockles of an atheist's heart—there has really never been a *bad* recording of *The Creation*. Even Karajan's 1969 Deutsche Grammophon version has much to recommend it, especially the unbelievably moving singing of tragically short-lived Fritz Wunderlich, captured in one of the final commercial recordings made by that incomparable tenor.

The most consistently rewarding version of the oratorio currently available is Sir Neville Marriner's masterful interpretation for Philips. While the performance is essentially one of chamber proportions, the big moments still have a tremendous punch and weight. The Academy's playing is as alert and full of character as it has ever been on records, the singing of the three superb soloists, especially Dietrich Fischer-Dieskau, is refined without ever becoming precious or cute, and Philips' engineers have wrapped it all in warm, yet brilliantly focused recorded sound. In short, if you have the most latent of missionary tendencies, this is the recording of *The Creation* that you might want to try on your favorite unbeliever.

Mass No. 9 in D minor, "Nelson Mass"

Blegen, Killibrew, Riegel, Estes, Westminster Choir, New York Philharmonic, Bernstein. CBS MP-39759 [LP], MT-39759 [T].

Most of the dozen great masses that Haydn composed date from the final years of his extraordinarily productive career. The fact that they contain some of the most wonderful music Haydn, or anyone else for that matter, would ever write bears eloquent testimony to his willingness to learn and grow.

For some peculiar reason, this phenomenal series of masterworks is currently badly under-represented in the catalogue. What I have always considered the most inspired of the series, the "Harmoniemesse," has no adequate commercial recording, and even the popular "Nelson Mass" has yet to be captured successfully on compact disc. (Sir Colin Davis' Philips version is strangely unsatisfying from a Haydn conductor of his stature, and a Swiss performance—names withheld to protect the guilty—from the small Claves label has all the energy of an overcooked string bean.)

Leonard Bernstein's powerful CBS recording from the 1970s is one that certainly deserves immediate transfer to compact disc. The interpretation is both sensitive and highly charged, with brilliant singing and playing from everyone involved. As a matter of fact, CBS should also consider reissuing Bernstein's scintillating version of the "Harmoniemesse" before Philips or Deutsche Grammophon persuade him to make a new recording for them. Philips, by the way, has already issued an electrifying live performance of the "Mass in Time of War" (Philips 412734-1, *412734-2*, 412734-4 [T]), further persuasive evidence for the argument that Bernstein is the finest Haydn conductor of our time.

String Quartets (6), Op. 76

Tátrai Quartet. Hungaroton *HCD-12812/3* [CD].
Tokyo Quartet. CBS M3-35879 [LP].

With that historic collection published as his Opus 20, Haydn, in effect, invented the single most important vehicle of Western chamber music, the modern string quartet. In all the works he had written previously, the function of the viola, second violin, and cello was to support and embellish the first violin's solo line; with Opus 20, all four instruments began to become the equal partners that they have remained ever since.

Of the eighty-two string quartets—from many of his earliest published compositions to the unfinished D minor fragment he was working on at the time of his death—none have proven to be more popular than the Op. 76 collection, which contains the "Quinten," the "Sunrise," and the "Emperor", three of the most familiar of all string quartets.

A choice between the Tátrai and Tokyo Quartets in this

music will be largely one of personal taste or your preference for the LP or compact disc format, since both versions of the complete cycle are superb. While the Hungarian ensemble may play with a warmer idiomatic grasp of the material, the precision and infectious vitality of the gifted Japanese musicians is also very hard to resist.

Symphony No. 88 in G Major; Symphony No. 92 in G Major, "Oxford"

Vienna Philharmonic, Bernstein. Deutsche Grammophon 413777-1, [LP] *413777-2* [CD], 413777-4 [T].

Listening to any of Haydn's 107 works in the form (in addition to the 104 numbered pieces, there are three others which we now know for certain were his) one is invariably tempted to paraphrase Will Rogers: "I never heard a Haydn symphony I didn't like." In no other body of work can one hear such a consistently high level of invention and craftsmanship or take greater delight in the sheer act of creativity than in the marvelous series of symphonies that history's finest professional composer produced throughout his career.

Leonard Bernstein's Vienna recording of these two popular G Major symphonies is among the most desirable Haydn recordings of the last decade. The interpretations are warm, witty, and in the slow movements unabashedly and unashamedly romantic. The "Oxford" Symphony has never sounded more lively or luxuriant on records, and this unbuttoned, brilliantly executed yet meltingly tender performance of the 88th is the only one that can be mentioned in the same breath with Wilhelm Furtwängler's famous, wonderfully screwball 1951 recording, which is currently available on compact disc coupled with Schumann's Fourth Symphony (Deutsche Grammophon *415661-2*).

Symphonies 93–98

Royal Philharmonic, Beecham. Arabesque 8024, 9024 [T].

If you can get past the relatively dingy mid-1950s monaural sound, this handsome Arabesque release is a priceless souvenir of one of history's greatest Haydn conductors. As in his equally revolutionary Mozart interpretations, it was Beecham more than anyone who introduced modern audiences to the passionate, frequently uproarious, always intensely human, flesh-and-blood composer who had always lurked beneath the surface of those flawless ink strokes and that immaculately powdered wig. Whether captivated by the special drama of the opening movements, the charmingly sprung rhythms and inimitable phrasing of the minuets, or the headlong forward propulsion in the *finales*, these classic performances are a source of perpetual wonder and delight.

Symphony No. 94 in G Major, "Surprise"; Symphony No. 96 in D Major, "Miracle"

Academy of Ancient Music, Hogwood. Oiseau-Lyre 414330-1 [LP], *414330-2* [CD], 414330-4 [T].

While the story of how the "Miracle" Symphony earned its name is probably apocryphal—allegedly the audience that heard the world premiere in London was so moved by the music that it rushed up *en masse* to congratulate the composer a few seconds before a massive chandelier crashed into their recently vacated seats—and while every Haydn symphony is a "surprise" symphony in one way or another, in this delicious Oiseau-Lyre recording two of the composer's most popular works more than earn their subtitles. The playing of Christopher Hogwood's spirited Academy of Ancient music really *is* quite miraculous in both symphonies, and the revelations in texture and balance that these period-instrument performances afford *are* a source of endless surprise. The winds play with such individuality and character that we suspect the conductor must have swallowed an entire bottle of Sir Thomas Beecham pills, and Hogwood himself provides innumerable subtle comments from his chair at the forte-piano. The familiar slow movement of the 94th Symphony has rarely seemed as sly or tensely dramatic as this, and the *Finale* of the "Miracle" Symphony rushes off with such a flurry of unbridled high spirits and good humor that we can easily believe the old chandelier story might, after all, have been true.

Symphony No. 100 in G Major, "Military"; Symphony No. 104 in D Major, "London"

Amsterdam Concertgebouw Orchestra, Davis. Philips
411449-2 [CD], 7300670 [T].

Academy of Ancient Music, Hogwood. Oiseau-Lyre
411833-1 [LP], *411833-2* [CD], 411833-4 [T].

Here is some persuasive evidence for the argument that Sir Colin Davis, with Leonard Bernstein and Sir Neville Marriner, is one of today's finest Haydn conductors. These beautifully crafted, brilliantly executed performances of two highly popular later symphonies rank with the very best Haydn recordings of the last twenty years. The playing of the great Concertgebouw Orchestra is as suave as it is polished, and their seriousness of purpose and interpretive strength are matched by their amiability and humor.

For anyone interested in a period-instrument approach or who belongs, with me, to that ever-shrinking minority of diehards who refuse to accept the death of the LP, Christopher Hogwood's sparkling Oiseau-Lyre recording is also highly recommended.

Hindemith, Paul
(1895–1963)

Concerto for Violin and Orchestra; *Symphonic Metamorphosis of Themes by Carl Maria von Weber*

Oistrakh, violin; London Symphony, Hindemith, Abbado. London 414437-1 [LP], 414437-4 [T].

In the quarter century since his death, German-born Paul Hindemith's reputation has declined alarmingly. Once a leading voice of the twentieth century *avant garde*, a composer whose thorny, elegantly crafted experiments in dissonant counterpoint caused many to liken him to a modern Bach, Hindemith has now been unfairly dismissed as a stuffy "academic" composer who has little to say to a generation brought up on the mindless delights of Minimalism.

While much of his music *can* seem rather dry and forbidding—although musicians love Hindemith, because he never wrote a piece that wasn't at least as much fun to play as it was to hear—the two works that London has brought together in this immensely attractive package should go a long way to transforming even the most dyed-in-the-wool Hindemith-haters into enthusiastic fans. David Oistrakh's performance of the 1940 Violin Concerto makes it seem like one of the most richly lyrical and romantically expressive such works of modern times, along with being one of the most ingeniously made.

Oistrakh plays with his typical combination of sweeping passion and refined poetry, and the accompaniment that the composer provided in one of his last commercial recordings could not have been more sensitive, polished, or intense.

While Hindemith's most popular work, the stirring and unspeakably clever *Symphonic Metamorphosis*, has had many superb recordings—including that classic, now out of print version by the Cleveland Orchestra and George Szell that was nearly perfect—Abbado's elegant version with the London Symphony is the strongest entry in a distressingly empty field. While it is primarily the conductor's precision and lack of mannerisms that make the performance so attractive, the playing also has abundant color and excitement. The *Turandot Scherzo* has rarely seemed more vivid or amusing, and the final movement crackles with electricity.

Until CBS decides to reissue the Szell recording, as they inevitably must, there is no acceptable version of the *Symphonic Metamorphosis* available on compact disc.

Holst, Gustav (1894–1934)

The Planets (Suite for Large Orchestra), Op. 32

London Philharmonic, Boult. Angel *CDM-69045* [CD].

**Toronto Symphony, A. Davis. Angel DS-37362 [LP],
CDC-47417 [CD], 4SX-37362 [T].**

Every conductor who has ever tried to come to terms
with this phenomenally popular score has had to do so under
an enormous shadow. Even the composer himself, who made
his own recordings during the 78 era, was no match for the
man who led the world premiere of *The Planets* in 1918.
During the next six decades, Sir Adrian Boult would record
the work no fewer than *seven* times.

Over the years, the legendary Boult interpretation
changed very little. In fact, the tempos remained so consistent
that the variance in timings from one recording to another
amounted to no more than a few seconds—except, that is, in
his final version, which the conductor recorded in his nine-
tieth year.

The conductor's last look at *The Planets* is a great modern orchestral recording. Beginning with a *Mars* of such
weight and menace that all other performances seem
positively pacifist in comparison, Boult somehow manages to
find new expressive possibilities even *he* had previously overlooked. *Venus* is more subtle and dreamy, *Jupiter* roars with a

Falstaffian good humor, and *Uranus* lumbers along with a wit and rhythmic point that no other recording can really begin to match.

While any of the fine alternative interpretations by André Previn, Sir Georg Solti, or Charles Dutoit would be the preferred recording of *The Planets* were it not for Boult's astounding and unapproachable achievement, the most interesting of that large and impressive crop of also-rans is Andrew Davis' excellent Toronto Symphony recording for Angel. Along with brilliant orchestral execution and recorded sound, there is a novel device in the concluding *Neptune* that is so strikingly effective you wonder why no one ever thought of it before. Instead of the usual wordless women's chorus, Davis opts instead for a children's choir. Their singing has such an unearthly purity about it that as this version of *The Planets* fades into nothingness, it does so on a suitably otherworldly note.

Suites (2) for Military Band

Cleveland Symphonic Winds, Fennell. TelarcDG-10038 [LP], *CD-80038* [CD].

Among old bandsmen (and whether or not they give it the more snooty name of "Wind Ensemble," a band is still a band) the name of Frederick Fennell has been the stuff of legend for more than thirty years. An old bandsman himself whose principal instrument, believe it or not, was the bass drum, Fennell's classic series of Mercury records with the Eastman Wind Ensemble were probably the finest band recordings ever made. They not only forced the classical music establishment to take the "Wind Ensemble" more seriously, but also, along with their celebrated, spit-and-polish Sousa albums, gave many premiere recorded performances of some absolutely wonderful music.

While Fennell's Eastman versions of these first great classics of the modern band repertoire were indispensable in their day, his latest recording of Holst's magnificent Suites for Military Band is even finer still. The Cleveland Symphonic Winds play with the same gusto and precision as the old Eastman crowd, and Fennell's interpretations, if anything, have become even more suave and energetic with the passage of time. If these marvelous performances fail to raise the hair on the back of your arms (or possibly even a lump in your throat), all it proves is that you've never experienced the indescribable thrill of sidestepping horse droppings at a brutal 120-beat-per-minute cadence during a Memorial Day parade.

On tape, an Angel recording by the Royal Air Force Central Band (4AE-34477), while pleasant enough, never really gets off the ground.

Honegger, Arthur
(1892–1955)

Pacific 231; Pastorale d'été; Rugby; Symphony No. 1

Bavarian Radio Symphony, Dutoit. Erato NUM-75254 [LP], *EDC-88171* [CD], MCE-75254 [T].

With the mercurial Jean Cocteau as their spokesman, a half dozen rebellious young French composers banded together into a loose but like-minded confederation called *Les Six* in the 1920's. Of the six, only three went on to achieve lasting recognition as major twentieth century composers. If Darius Milhaud possessed the most robust and prolific talent, and Francis Poulenc the most rarified and individual gifts, then the most powerful and versatile voice in the group belonged to Arthur Honegger.

His best music is characterized by a neoclassical formal economy in which driving rhythms, astringent harmonies, and a facile, often very moving Gallic lyricism are thrown together in a heady and original brew. His oratorio *Le Roi David* is among the most significant twentieth century sacred works, and his five symphonies constitute one of the last largely undiscovered treasure troves of modern orchestral thought.

This brilliant Erato recording provides an excellent introduction to Honegger's fresh and exhilarating First Symphony and offers the finest available performances of his three most popular shorter works: *Pastorale d'été*, *Rugby*, and the delightfully graphic *Pacific 231*, the tone poem about an American locomotive that caused a near-riot at its scandalous premiere in 1924. Charles Dutoit is a perceptive and sympathetic interpreter of Honegger's music, and the fine Bavarian Radio Symphony here plays well above its recorded average. As this is clearly one of the most satisfying recordings of Honegger's music on the market today, satisfied customers might also want to explore another superb Erato recording by the same forces (NUM-75117, *ECD-88045*, MCE-75117 [T]) that features equally persuasive interpretations of the composer's Third and Fifth Symphonies.

Humperdinck, Engelbert (1854–1921)

Hänsel und Gretel

**Schwarzkopf, Grümmer, Felbermeyer, Ilosvay,
Philharmonia Orchestra, Karajan. Angel
CDMB-69293 [CD].**

Now that this best-loved of all children's operas has
finally made its debut on compact disc, how appropriate that
it should be in that magical recording from 1953 that captures more of *Hänsel und Gretel's* wonder and wide-eyed
innocence than any other performance ever has. Elisabeth
Schwarzkopf and Elisabeth Grümmer are unsurpassable as
Humperdinck's immortal tykes, and Herbert von Karajan's
warm, glowing conducting provides a depressing reminder of
what a chilling, arrogant wretch that once superlative musician has become. The supporting cast sings with immense
character and devotion, and the original recorded sound has
been made to seem extraordinarily fresh and alive.

At present, no LP or cassette version can be recommended with any conviction—especially in the face of one of
the greatest operatic recordings ever made.

Husa, Karel (1921–)

Apotheosis of This Earth; Music for Prague 1968

University of Michigan Symphony Band, Husa. Golden Crest GC 4134 [LP].

If you've become convinced that Contemporary Music now means either minimalist drivel or incomprehensible noise, you have yet to hear the music of Karel Husa. He is the major musical voice to have emerged from Czechoslovakia since Bohuslav Martinü, and one of the most powerful and original composers of our time. While his idiom is thoroughly and often aggressively modern, Husa is essentially a conservative: a composer who believes that music must carry enormous emotional and expressive burdens above and beyond the notes on the printed page. With his String Quartet No. 3—which won the 1969 Pulitzer Prize—Husa's most celebrated work to date has been *Music for Prague 1968*, which has so far amassed the astonishing total of more than seven thousand performances.

Written in reaction to the tragic events that engulfed the Czech capital in the Fall of that year, *Music for Prague 1968* is a furious, brutally dramatic, and hauntingly beautiful evocation of a city and a people who, in the last ten centuries, have known precisely twenty years of political freedom. This Golden Crest recording of a live performance led by the composer himself clearly demonstrates why *Music for Prague 1968*, with its vivid colors, brilliant craftsmanship, and searing intensity is one of a handful of authentic large-scale masterworks of modern times. Equally gripping is the performance of *Apotheosis of This Earth*, a scathing, overwhelming indictment of an even larger injustice: the wholesale devastation of the planet's natural resources, or in Husa's own words, "Man's brutal possession and misuse of nature's beauty."

I once devoted a program to Husa's music which bore the purposefully provocative title, "The Greatest Living Composer?" I should now confess what I *really* think. Lose the question mark.

Ives, Charles (1874–1954)

Symphony No. 2; Symphony No. 3, "The Camp Meeting"; *The Unanswered Question*

New York Philharmonic, Bernstein. CBS *MK-42407*[CD].

Amsterdam Concertgebouw Orchestra, Thomas. (Second Symphony only) CBS IM-37300 [LP], IMT-37300.

It was Leonard Bernstein's famous Columbia recording of the Second Symphony that almost single-handedly sparked the Ives revival of the 1960s. Prior to the release of that classic recording by the man who had led the work's world premiere more than a half century after it had been composed, Ives had been an obscure figure with a small but knowledgeable following. Within a few years, he was to become an American Original, a cult phenomenon, a composer who, in Bernstein's words, was "the Washington, Jefferson, and Lincoln of our music."

Now that the hoopla surrounding the Ives centennial in 1974 has begun to fade into the distance like one of those crack-brained parades that haunt his music, a more balanced guess at the importance of his achievement can finally begin to be made. Like the Hartford poet Wallace Stevens, another insurance executive who was also a diligent weekend artist, Ives possessed an important, original, and peculiarly American talent. And if, as his admirers claim, he was one of the most forward-looking composers of his generation (he *did* anticipate many of the most important trends in twentieth century music years and often decades before anyone else) there was also, in Ives, a good deal of the archetypal American Crank, a kind of musical Rube Goldberg raised to the Nth degree.

The Second Symphony remains his most approachable and instantly likeable work. In fact, it's difficult *not* to like a work whose principal themes include "Bringing in the Sheaves" and "Where, O Where, Are the Pea Green Freshman?"—a Yale student song that sounds like an impossibly civilized version of "Dixie"—and that concludes with a fabulous peroration on "Columbia, Gem of the Ocean," flanked by the cavalry charge and the most spectacular orchestral raspberry (an eleven-note chord cluster) that anyone ever wrote.

In its compact disc reissue, Bernstein's performance sounds more joyous, committed, and spirited than ever, and his versions of the "Camp Meeting" Symphony and the intriguing *The Unanswered Question* should still be considered the definitive performances of both works.

Michael Tilson Thomas' more recent digital recording is also a tremendous amount of fun. While the performance may lack the last measure of Bernstein's savvy and gusto, this is the first commercial recording of the critical edition of the Symphony, and the playing of the Concertgebouw Orchestra, as playing *per se*, can't really be approached.

Janáček, Leoš (1854–1928)

The Cunning Little Vixen

Popp, Jedlicka, Randová, Vienna Philharmonic,
Mackerras. London *417129* [CD].

Had Leoš Janáček died at the same age as Beethoven, he
would be remembered today—if at all—as a very minor late
Romantic composer, conductor, and organist whose name
would occasionally turn up in the more complete biographies
of his friend, Antonín Dvořák. It was not until 1904, at the
age of fifty, that he began to produce, apparently from out of
nowhere, that startling series of works upon which his reputation as one of the most powerfully original twentieth century
composers now rests. Janáček's sudden and mysterious transformation from a provincial nobody into a modern giant is
without precedent in the history of music. In the other arts,
only William Butler Yeats' relatively late emergence as the
great English language poet of the twentieth century offers a
similar example of such mysterious and wonderful growth.

The cornerstone of Janáček's achievement is that series of
nine operas that are slowly being recognized as some of the
most important works of the modern operatic stage. Their
general acceptance was understandably delayed by the difficult Czech language itself, and because they are by definition
untranslatable, since Janáček's musical language was inti-

mately connected with the rhythms and inflections of Czech speech. And then, too, their subject matter is often so peculiar that theatres outside Czechoslovakia once thought them to be all but impossible to produce. For instance, the heroine of *Več Makropulos* (*The Makropulos Case*—though a more correct translation would be *The Makropulos Thing*) is a 300-year-old opera singer; *Z mrtveho domu* (*From the House of the Dead*) is set in a Tsarist prison camp, and the cast of characters in *Přihody lišky Bystroušky* includes a dog, a badger, a cricket, a grasshopper, and a group described simply as "the various vermin." In spite of its profound and delightful eccentricity, *The Cunning Little Vixen* is neither nonsense, nor simply another children's story, but one of the most bewitching and enchantingly beautiful operas ever composed.

Sir Charles Mackerras' grasp of the special power, charm, and expressive potential of Janáček's music is without equal in the world today. As a student he studied the scores with the man who gave many of them their world premieres, the composer's friend, Václav Talich. At this late date it is absurd to ask if Mackerras, an American-born Englishman of Australian parentage can possibly speak Janáček's language as idiomatically as a native; it is doubtful that any Czech conductor, except for Talich, has ever begun to speak it half as well.

Sir Charles' version of *The Cunning Little Vixen* is one of the greatest in an already triumphant series of Janáček recordings. He leads the Vienna Philharmonic through the difficult, delicate score as though it were no more challenging than an early Haydn symphony. The predominantly Czech cast is largely wonderful, especially since most of them drop the wobbly, intrusive vibrato that so many Eastern European singers are apparently taught from birth. Most wonderful of all, however, is the exquisite Vixen of Lucia Popp, one of the most hugely gifted sopranos of the last half century. Her passion, precision, and the extraterrestrial beauty of her physical sound make this one of the great characterizations of the last twenty years, and renders an already invaluable recording a completely indispensable one.

Unfortunately, neither an LP nor a tape version is currently available.

Jenůfa

Söderström, Popp, Randová, Dvořsky, Ochman, Vienna Philharmonic, Mackerras. London 414483-2 [CD].

Jenůfa was the first of Janáček's great operas and it remains the most popular and instantly approachable. It is also, by a comfortable margin, the most conventional of all his works for the stage. Set in a sleepy Czech village, the direct but not-so-simple story of jealousy, vengeance, violence, and redemption is a dramatic amalgam of Smetana's *The Bartered Bride* and Mascagni's *Cavelleria Rusticana*. Musically, however, *Jenůfa* is an entirely different matter—a fresh, tuneful, and powerfully dramatic score in which one of history's major operatic composers first found his distinct and utterly original voice.

Like all the recordings in Sir Charles Mackerras' historic cycle of Janáček operas, this is the *Jenůfa* that will probably dominate the catalogues until well into the next century. It is also one of those rare studio recordings which has all the immediacy and excitement of a live performance. Elisabeth Söderström—is there a finer Janáček heroine in the world today? —is both ineffably tender and witheringly powerful in the title role, and the rest of the cast, together with the orchestra and conductor, are all captured at the very top of their forms.

If you are one of those people who are convinced, perhaps with good reason, that Opera came to a screeching halt with the death of Giacomo Puccini, give *Jenůfa*—especially this *Jenůfa*—a try. At present, neither an LP nor a tape version is available.

Sinfonietta; Taras Bulba

Vienna Philharmonic, Mackerras. London 410138-2 [CD].

Beginning with George Szell's stunning Cleveland Orchestra version from the 1960s, Janáček's most popular orchestral work, the blazingly heroic *Sinfonietta*, has had some wonderful recordings. Currently, the piece is ably represented by Simon Rattle's cultivated but immensely stirring Angel recording, and a slightly scrappy but powerfully compelling Supraphon recording featuring Václav Neumann and the Czech Philharmonic.

As both an interpretation and a recording of demonstration quality, Sir Charles Mackerras' Vienna Philharmonic performance will be difficult to better for the foreseeable future. As usual, not even the most subtle detail of Janáček's complex language escapes this conductor's attention. The occasionally intricate rhythms and always complicated inner voicing are invested with a drive and clarity they have never been given before. The last time that the Vienna Philharmonic brass, augmented for the occasion by a dozen extra players, were heard to play with such ferocious bite and mind-boggling unanimity was in Sir Georg Solti's famous recording of Wagner's *Ring*, made two decades ago.

The *Sinfonietta*'s inevitable companion work, the orchestral rhapsody *Taras Bulba*, is given an equally memorable performance. In fact, Mackerras invests it with such surging life and drama that some will be persuaded—as I must admit I always *have* been —that *Taras* may in fact be the more important and rewarding piece. At last check, there were no suitable disc or tape versions of either work in the catalogue.

Slavonic Mass (M'ša Glagolskaja)

Söderström, Drobková, Livora, Novák, Czech
Philharmonic Chorus and Orchestra, Mackerras.
Supraphon C37-7448 [CD].

Lear, Rössel-Majdan, Haeflinger, Crass, Bavarian
Radio Symphony Chorus and Orchestra, Kubelik.
Deutsche Grammophon 413652-1 [LP].

To call Janáček's Slavonic Mass one of the great sacred
works of twentieth century music is as accurate as it is slightly
misleading. Written in the composer's seventy-second year, the
Slavonic Mass was originally thought to be a final act of
contrition by a lifelong agnostic. When a Prague music critic
described it as being the work of a "pious old man," the
composer immediately shot back a postcard with the single
line, "Neither old nor pious, young man."

The unshakable faith the Slavonic Mass expresses with
such moving tenderness and Medieval grandeur has to do less
with the composer's religious convictions, which were all but
non-existent, than with his almost Messianic belief in the
survival of the Czechoslovak Republic, whose tenth anniver-
sary in 1928 M'ša Glagolskaja was written to celebrate.

The Mackerras recording is one of the most successful in
his brilliant Janáček series: the playing of the Czech Philharmonic is as vivid and emphatic as it has ever been on records;
the soloists are exceptional, the chorus alert and powerful,
and the recorded sound is shattering in its realism and impact.
Rafael Kubelik's older Deutsche Grammophon recording still
holds up remarkably well. Less driven and more gently lyrical
than the Mackerras version, it nevertheless has more than its
share of electrifying moments. Bedrich Janáček—who I believe is no relation—is spellbinding in the titanic organ inter-
lude; in the Mass's brazen postlude, the Bavarian Radio Symphony trumpets play with such wild abandon that you can
almost see the musicians' tongues popping out of their instruments' bells.

Joplin, Scott (1868–1917)

Rags

Rifkin, piano. Nonesuch 73026 [LP], 71263 [LP],
 71248 [LP], 71305 [LP], *79159-2* [CD], NS-1264
 [T].

Perlman, violin; Previn, piano. Angel S-37113 [LP],
 CDC-47170 [CD], 4XS-37113 [T].

Well before the composer's music was belatedly made
into a national institution in the hit movie *The Sting*, I had
already become hopelessly addicted to Scott Joplin's piano
rags thanks entirely to Joshua Rifkin. It was primarily Rifkin's
path-breaking series of Nonesuch recordings that introduced
the world to the subtle, infectious, endlessly inventive music
of a man who, in essence, transformed the musical wallpaper
of turn-of-the-century bordellos into a high and distinctively
American art. In any of his several recordings, Rifkin's self-
effacing yet enormously colorful and individual interpretations are still the definitive solo piano versions of these works.

No less delightful is the Angel recording of the arrangements for violin and piano, played with tremendous bite and
enthusiasm by Itzhak Perlman and André Previn. For the
serious Joplin lover, the Houston Opera production of the
composer's rather quaint but utterly engaging Ragtime opera
Treemonisha, in a warm and thoroughly captivating performance led by Gunther Schuller (Deutsche Grammophon
423308-1), is also highly recommended.

Kodály, Zoltán (1882–1967)

Dances of Galanta; Dances of Marósszek; Variations on a Hungarian Folksong (Peacock Variations)

Hungarian Radio Orchestra, Lehel. Hungaroton
SLPX-12252 [LP], *HCD-12252* [CD], MK-12252
[T].

Philadelphia Orchestra, Ormandy. CBS MP-38762
[LP].

After his friend and near contemporary, Béla Bartók, Zoltán Kodály was the most significant composer Hungary had produced since the death of Franz Liszt. While he began his career as a composer of serious and politely ignored chamber works, it was Kodály's discovery of Hungarian folk music in the early 1920s which transformed him into an internationally famous composer. Beginning with the folk opera *Háry János*, Kodály combined the unmistakable flavors of Hungarian folk song with a technique that owed much to Debussy and Ravel and created some of the most refreshingly distinctive and original music of the twentieth century.

György Lehel leads some exceptionally fine and warmly idiomatic performances of the *Galanta* and *Marósszek Dances*. If his performance of Kodály's masterpiece, the *Peacock Variations*, is not quite a match for Istvan Kertesz' brilliant but now withdrawn London recording, it is easily the best available LP version in a shockingly uncrowded field.

Eugene Ormandy's performances of both sets of *Dances*, together with the familiar *Háry János* Suite, is easily one of the best recordings that dedicated, but rather shallow and vulgar musician ever made. The Philadelphia Orchestra plays with a virtuosity that was probably unequaled by any other orchestra of its time, and the conductor, one of Kodály's former students, is content to let the music unfold simply and naturally instead of drowning it, as he so often did, in the famous "Philadelphia Sound."

Háry János

> Takács, Sólyom-Nagy, Gregor, Hungarian State Opera
> Chorus and Orchestra, Ferencsik. Hungaroton
> SLPX-12187/89 [LP], *HVD-12837/38* [CD],
> MK-12187/89 [T].

Háry János Suite

> Cleveland Orchestra, Szell. CBS MY-38527 [LP],
> *MYK-38527* [CD], MYT-38527 [T].

While the Suite that Zoltán Kodály extracted from his 1925 folk opera *Háry János* remains his most universally loved and frequently recorded work, the opera itself is one of the treasures of the modern lyric theatre. Its fantastic plot is a series of tall tales told by a retired Hussar from the village of Abony Magna—the irrepressible Háry János—who after defeating Napoleon and his legions single-handedly has nearly as much trouble fending off the attentions of Napoleon's ardent wife.

Fortunately, the only recorded performance of the complete opera is an extremely attractive one. Beautifully played and, for the most part, beautifully sung, the performance projects much of the opera's unique and unmistakable color. Since much of the humor is lost on non-Hungarian listeners, one can only hope that London will some day reissue Istvan Kertesz' dazzling recording from the early 1970s, which not only included all of the opera's musical numbers, but also featured the inspired Peter Ustinov in all the speaking roles.

For those who feel they don't really need to go beyond the popular *Háry János Suite*, George Szell's tender, flamboyant, meticulous, and uproarious CBS recording has never been equalled.

Korngold, Erich Wolfgang (1897–1957)

Concerto in D Major for Violin and Orchestra, Op. 35

Heifetz, violin; Los Angeles Philharmonic, Wallenstein.
RCA Victor AGM1-4902 [LP].

Perlman, violin; Pittsburgh Symphony, Previn. Angel
CDC-47846 [CD].

As a child prodigy whose accomplishments were compared by no less an authority than Gustav Mahler to those of Mozart, or as the man who first brought genuine symphonic music to Hollywood films, Erich Wolfgang Korngold was one of the most fascinating musical figures of the twentieth century. His opera *Die tote Stadt*, begun when he was only nineteen, made him world famous, and his frightening abilities even convinced Richard Strauss that Korngold would inevitably supplant him as the century's foremost composer of German opera. Forced to flee Europe after Hitler's annexation of Austria, Korngold eventually settled in Hollywood. There, with the scores for *Anthony Adverse*, *King's Row*, *The Adventures of Robin Hood*, *The Sea Hawk* and other classic Warner Brothers films of the 1930s and 1940s, he established the grammar and syntax of an entirely new musical language whose influence can still be clearly and distinctly heard in the scores of John Williams and countless other film composers.

The Korngold Violin Concerto, whose thematic material was derived from several of his movie themes, is one of the most startlingly beautiful works in the instrument's repertoire. Sentimental, exciting, and unabashedly Romantic, it is as instantly approachable as it is impossible to forget. Although written for the Polish violinist Bronislaw Huberman, it was Jascha Heifetz who gave the work its world premiere and made the first commercial recording. Technically, of course, the playing is flawless; yet here, Heifetz invests the music with a warmth and humanity that almost none of his other recordings possess. Itzhak Perlman's Angel recording is also exceptionally lovely. If in the quicksilver *Finale* the violinist lacks the last measure of Heifetz' dizzying abandon, he milks the molten slow movement like the wonderfully shameless Romantic he has always been.

Unfortunately for tape collectors, neither performance is currently being offered on cassette.

Lalo, Edouard (1823–1892)

Symphonie espagnole for Violin and Orchestra, Op. 21

Perlman, violin; Orchestre de Paris, Barenboim.
Deutsche Grammophon 2532001 [LP], 400032-2
[CD], 3302011 [T].

One of the most individual and restlessly inventive of all nineteenth century French composers, Edouard Lalo is now known for only two apparently indestructible works: the D minor Cello Concerto and the *Symphonie espagnole*, which is not, in fact, a "symphony" at all, but rather a form of the composer's own devising that incorporates the structural elements of the concerto and the suite. As one of the most inspired of all French musical tourist works, *Symphonie espagnole* is to the brighter elements of Spanish musical culture what Bizet's *Carmen* is to the darker side: a virtuoso evocation of a specific time and place that few other works can match.

With some vivid, expressive support from Daniel Barenboim and the Orchestre de Paris, Itzhak Perlman here gives one of his most buoyant and colorful recorded performances. Along with its fabulous dexterity, the playing combines a bracing rhythmic vitality with tasteful schmaltziness in a way that only Perlman, these days, seems able to do.

Lehár, Franz (1870–1948)

The Merry Widow

Schwarzkopf, Steffek, Gedda, Wächter, Philharmonia
Orchestra and Chorus, Matacic. Angel AV-34044
[LP], *CDCB-47177* [CD], 4AV-34044 [T].

While he never quite scaled the golden heights of Strauss'
Die Fledermaus, *The Gypsy Baron*, or *A Night in Venice*—
the primary reason why his music has since been designated
the summit of the Viennese operetta's "Silver Age"—Franz
Lehár was a charming and entirely individual composer
whose stage works represented the final, bittersweet sunset of
one of the most endearing of all musical forms. While
Giuditta and *The Land of Smiles* are probably finer works, it
was the effervescent and eternally glamorous *Die lustige
Witwe* that became the only operetta in history, short of the
Savoy Operas of Gilbert and Sullivan, to mount a serious
popular challenge to the absolute supremacy of *Die Fledermaus*.

Even if Viennese operetta in general, or Lehár operettas
in particular, are not exactly your cup of *kaffee mit schlag*, I
guarantee you will find this ageless recording one of the most
thrilling musical experiences of your life. Elisabeth Schwarzkopf, the greatest Marschallin and Mozart singer of her time,
gives what may well be the performance of her career as

Hanna: regal, witty, sentimental, and unbelievably sexy, the characterization all but leaps into your living room. As a matter of fact, there have been only two or three other operatic recordings in history that begin to match the uncanny sense of presence this one generates from its very first notes. The admirable Nicolai Gedda and Eberhard Wächter also turn in something close to the performances of *their* careers, and under the inspired leadership of Lovro von Matacic, who casts what amounts to a magical spell over the proceedings, this *Merry Widow* effortlessly swirls its way into the ranks of the greatest recordings of all time.

Note: While the tape and LP versions offer only excerpts from the operetta, the selection is as intelligent as it is generous.

Leoncavallo, Ruggiero
(1857–1919)

I Pagliacci

Callas, Di Stefano, Gobbi, Panerai, La Scala Chorus
and Orchestra, Serafin. Angel *CDCC-47981* [CD].

Caballé, Domingo, Milnes, McDaniel, John Alldis
Choir, London Symphony, Santi. RCA Victor
LSC-7090 [LP].

Since the days that Enrico Caruso virtually adopted
Canio's histrionic Act I aria "Vesti la Giubba" as his signature
tune, Leoncavallo's *I Pagliacci*, with its inseparable companion piece, Mascagni's *Cavalleria Rusticana*, has remained a
staple of the operatic repertoire. Based on an actual case that
the composer's father, a local magistrate, tried when Leoncavallo was a boy, *I Pagliacci* is one of two quintessential
works of the slice-of-life *verismo* school of Italian opera: a
work in which the uncontrollable passions of ordinary people
result in a delightful mosaic of jealousy, betrayal, and violent
death.

The famous La Scala recording from the early 1950s is
more earthy and blood-curdling than ever in its recent compact disc reincarnation. Titto Gobbi is a wonderfully sly and
malevolent Tonio, and the Nedda of Maria Callas is unapproachable in its vulgar animal magnetism and dramatic intensity. Still, *I Pagliacci* has always been the tenor's show, and

it is this recording, perhaps more than any other, which demonstrates what Giuseppe di Stefano *might* have been. As it stood, his career was probably the most brilliant of any of the post-War Italian tenors; had it been managed with greater intelligence and care, it might have been *the* career since Caruso's. His Canio is painted in very primary colors and for the most part is very beautifully sung; still, for all its power, we can hear the unmistakable signs that his incredible instrument had already seen its best days.

The finest Canio of our time, Placido Domingo, is even more impressive in his RCA Victor recording. Predictably, the characterization has both intensity and intelligence to burn, and the singing is as musical as it is undeniably exciting. In other words, it is one of countless performances suggesting rather conclusively that Domingo, not Luciano Pavarotti, is the preeminent tenor of modern times. While Monserrat Caballé's overly-civilized Nedda is no match for Callas', Sherill Milnes is an imposing Tonio and Nello Santi's conducting is first-rate. For those who need *I Pagliacci* in more up-to-date sound, this version is the obvious choice; for those who simply want a blood-curdling demonstration of what the old warhorse can do when it's given its head, the La Scala production remains in a class by itself.

While none of the available tapes merits a serious recommendation, the strongest is probably the London performance (414590-4), which has Luciano Pavarotti sweating bullets, but offers the charming Nedda of Mirella Freni and some very fine conducting from Giuseppe Patané.

Liszt, Franz (1811–1886)

Piano Concerto No. 1 in E-flat Major; Piano
Concerto No. 2 in A Major

**Richter, piano; London Symphony, Kondrashin. Philips
412006-2 [CD].**

**Arrau, piano; London Symphony, Davis. Philips
412926-1 [LP], 412926-4 [T].**

Composer, conductor, philosopher, ascetic, charlatan,
religious mystic, prodigious sexual athlete, and, in all probability, the greatest pianist who has ever lived, Franz Liszt was
the epitome of the Romantic musician: a restless bundle of
ambition, nervous energy, and insatiable appetites whose influence on the development of nineteenth century music was
so enormous that it is still difficult to assess. As a composer he
all but invented the tone poem, one of musical Romanticism's
most enduringly popular forms. His experiments in thematic
transformation were decisive in the *Leitmotif* technique per-
fected by his son-in-law, Richard Wagner. And in churning
out endless reams of fiendishly difficult piano music for use
on his innumerable concert tours, he bequeathed gainful employment to virtuoso pianists in perpetuity.

Liszt's Piano Concertos have long been staples of the
concert repertoire, and each is a revealing glimpse at the two

mutually complimentary and often contradictory sides of the composer's essential makeup: the brash, outgoing, self-indulgent E-flat Major Concerto, and the moody, poetic, introspective Concerto No. 2 in A Major.

No modern interpretations have ever captured more of the Concertos' poetry and barnstorming excitement than that sensational Philips recording by Sviatoslav Richter. On a purely technical level, they are among the most hair-raising piano recordings ever made. Yet along with phenomenal virtuosity, Richter brings so much grandeur and profundity to the music that those who are tempted to dismiss it as empty-headed bombast will never be tempted to do so again.

For record and tape collectors, Claudio Arrau's often odd, but always deeply personal interpretations are also very desirable. While the playing is not on Richter's level, the performances have an easy, quirky authority. As a matter of fact, the pianist's wayward, rhapsodic approach serves what is often some extremely wayward and rhapsodic *music* exceptionally well.

A Faust Symphony

> Young, tenor; Beecham Choral Society, Royal Philharmonic Orchestra, Beecham. Angel *CDC-49260* [CD].
>
> Riegel, tenor; Tanglewood Festival Chorus, Boston Symphony Orchestra, Bernstein. Deutsche Grammophon 415009-1 [LP], 415009-4 [T].

A *Faust Symphony* is probably the most inspired musical treatment of Goethe's great philosophical poem. It may also be Franz Liszt's masterpiece. Each of its three movements is an elaborate character sketch of the play's three central figures: a brooding, heroic, poetic movement devoted to Faust himself, a lyrical second movement called "Gretchen," and a *Finale* devoted to Mephistopheles in which Liszt, like Milton before him, could not resist giving the Devil all the best lines. One of the lengthiest and most challenging symphonies written up to that time, *A Faust Symphony* still makes tremendous demands on its interpreters. The two recordings that are most successful in solving the work's innumerable problems are those by Sir Thomas Beecham and Leonard Bernstein.

Originally released in the mid-1950s, the Beecham *Faust Symphony* was among the conductor's finest recorded performances. Lyrical, pensive, impetuous, and shot through with a genuinely demoniacal wit, its only serious drawback was the rather shrill and harsh recorded sound, which the compact disc remastering has brilliantly managed to correct. Bernstein's recording with the Boston Symphony is no less appealing, especially since it is imaginatively coupled with a most eloquent modern recording of the spectacular Prologue from Boito's *Mefistofele*. If in the outer movements, Bernstein yields a few points to Beecham in terms of heroism and devilish humor, his version of the "Gretchen" movement is tenderly beautiful. While a clear-cut choice between these two superlative recordings is all but impossible to make, Bernstein's will be more appealing to the audiophiles, while the Beecham is the only great performance currently available on compact disc.

*P*iano Sonata in B minor

Brendel, piano. Philips *410115-2* [CD].

Wild, piano. Etcetera ETC-2010.

Richard Wagner was especially fond of his father-in-law's only piano sonata. Shortly after Liszt sent him the manuscript, Wagner wrote back, saying, "It is sublime, even as yourself." Johannes Brahms was also particularly keen to hear it performed, but at the private concert Liszt arranged in his honor, Brahms showed his gratitude by falling asleep. While much of Liszt's piano music is little more than gaudy ephemera, his B minor Sonata, with those of Schubert and Chopin remains the Romantic Era's most enduring contribution to the form. It is among that tiny handful of nineteenth century piano sonatas that are every bit the equal of any Beethoven sonata.

Until London Records returns Sir Clifford Curzon's homeric and inspired interpretation on a compact disc, the choice among available recordings of the work lies between the studied introspection of Alfred Brendel and the flamboyant virtuosity of Earl Wild. Brendel, whose link to the composer is a direct one—his teacher, Edwin Fischer, was a pupil of the Liszt pupil, Eugen D'Albert—gives an immensely intelligent performance on this Philips compact disc. If Brendel's playing is not the last word in individuality or animal excitement, he nevertheless reveals the Sonata's complex structure with a disarming lucidity and ease. Earl Wild, while a bit less thoughtful than Brendel, makes the music flash and thunder like one of those hell-bent-for-leather virtuosos of the past. Now, the ideal recording of the Liszt Sonata would be a combination of Wild's fire with Brendel's brains—which is *precisely* what Sir Clifford Curzon gave us two decades ago. (Got the message, London?)

On tape, the strongest performance comes from Tamás Vásáry on Deutsche Grammophon (415918-4).

Les Préludes (Symphonic Poem No. 3)

London Philharmonic, Solti. London *417513-2* [CD].

Chicago Symphony, Barenboim. Deutsche Grammophon 415851-1 [LP], *415851-2* [CD], 415851-4 [T].

Of the thirteen works with which Franz Liszt all but invented the tone poem, only *Les Préludes* is heard with any frequency today. Listening to Bernard Haitink's heroically ambitious cycle for Philips (6709005) will quickly show you why. For in spite of the best of intentions and some of the best recorded performances that any of these works are ever likely to receive, most of the Liszt tone poems are unmitigated junk. (It *is* difficult to think of another great composer whose ratio of trash to masterworks was quite as high as his.) While often as schlocky and bombastic as the rest, *Les Préludes* is saved in the end by its grandiose gestures, flood of memorable melody, and utter sincerity. Schlock it most certainly *is*, but of a wonderfully urgent and lovable variety.

Although Daniel Barenboim is extremely ardent in his version with the Chicago Symphony, Sir Georg Solti's recording with the London Philharmonic is probably more valuable. While the playing is undeniably exciting, rarely has *Les Préludes* been invested with such power and genuine nobility. Coupled with equally riveting and dignified performances of the rarely-heard *Tasso* and *Prometheus*, this is probably the strongest case for the Liszt tone poems that any single recording has ever made.

Mahler, Gustav (1660–1911)

Das Lied von der Erde

Patzak, tenor; Ferrier, contralto; Vienna Philharmonic,
Walter. London 414194-1 [LP], *414194-2* [CD],
414914-4 [T].

The popularity that Gustav Mahler's music now enjoys
would have been all but unthinkable a generation ago. Most
of the symphonies remained unrecorded, and of those that
were recorded, many featured mediocre to wretched performances that could only begin to hint at the greatness contained
in these noble, neurotic, enervating, and uplifting works. Today, recordings of the Mahler symphonies are nearly as common as those of Beethoven's, which is as it should be. For just
as the Romantic symphony was born in that series of nine
works that Beethoven produced at the beginning of the nineteenth century, its convulsive, extravagantly beautiful death
can be heard in the works that Mahler wrote at the beginning
of our own century.

For most of his eighty-five years, Bruno Walter, Mahler's
disciple and protege, was the composer's most impassioned

and indefatigable champion. It was Walter who led the world premieres of the Ninth Symphony and *Das Lied von der Erde* and left what remain some of the most telling and authoritative of all Mahler recordings.

This famous 1952 version of the great symphonic song cycle *Das Lied von der Erde* is not only one of Walter's greatest recorded performances, but also one of the most intensely moving Mahler recordings ever made. While the credit for this must be shared with the incomparable Kathleen Ferrier, whose haunting, richly sabled singing of the concluding "Abschied" has never been matched, and with the superb Viennese tenor Julius Patzak— whose thin, leathery voice and consummate musicianship recalls the art of another leather-voiced Viennese magician, Richard Tauber—it is the conductor's gentle intensity that makes this one of the major triumphs in the history of the gramophone. All the passion and subtlety of this brilliantly executed interpretation can be heard with remarkable clarity in London's remastered recording. The compact disc is especially miraculous in the way it makes the original 1952 recording seem as though it were made the day before yesterday.

Symphony No. 1 in D Major

Chicago Symphony, Solti. London 411731-1 [LP],
411731-2 **[CD], 411731-4 [T].**

Few composers reach maturity in their first major orchestral works like Gustav Mahler did with his First Symphony. Completed when Mahler was only twenty-eight, the D Major Symphony—still known, in spite of the composer's violent objections as the "Titan"—contains many of the key compositional ingredients of the seasoned Mahler style. Its olympian length, the sheer size of the performing forces, the gentle Viennese charm, the obsession with death in the gallows humor of the funeral march, and the ecstatic, almost

hysterical triumph of its closing bars are all significant por-
tents of what was to come.

While there are nearly two dozen versions of the D
Major Symphony currently in print, none comes within
shouting distance of that overwhelming and endlessly inventive recording Jascha Horenstein made with the London
Symphony in the late 1960s. Originally released by Unicorn
and available for a time on the Nonesuch label, it was one of a
few studio recordings that managed to convey an on-the-spot
sense of creation that we encounter in only the most gripping
live performances. A triumph of excess, exaggeration, and
personality—certainly no conductor ever made the final ten
minutes seem more exultant or monumental—it was the Mahler First of a lifetime, and one we should not expect to be
bettered any time soon.

Among available recordings, Sir Georg Solti's Chicago
Symphony version is the most exciting and thrillingly played.
While Solti's more recent interpretation has lost some mystery
and moodiness from his earlier London Symphony performance, the recorded sound and orchestral execution are both in
a class by themselves. Nevertheless, the Horenstein recording,
by hook or by crook, must be returned to circulation, as
should his even more impressive version of the Mahler Third.

Symphony No. 2 in C minor, "Resurrection"

**Armstrong, soprano; Baker, mezzo-soprano;
Edinburgh Festival Chorus, London Symphony
Orchestra, Bernstein. CBS M2-32681 [LP],
M2K-42195 [CD].**

When Leonard Bernstein's second stereo recording of the
"Resurrection" Symphony was first released, most critics
pounced all over it for its alleged self-indulgence and exag-
gerations. Of course, to say that of *any* performance of this
inherently self-indulgent and exaggerated work would have

been a bit like busting a Sodom-and-Gomorrah city councilman for indecent exposure. In fact, the recordings of the "Resurrection" that fail most decisively—those by Kubelik, Maazel, and Sinopoli, for example—are those that try to make the Symphony more polite, coherent, and civilized than it can possibly be. To his great credit, Bernstein simply yanks out all the stops and allows this paradoxical hodgepodge of pathos, bathos, banality, and nobility to speak eloquently and unforgettably for itself.

On cassette, a vastly moving, surprisingly straightforward RCA Victor recording (ALK2-5392) by Leopold Stokowski is one of that always unpredictable magician's finest efforts.

Symphony No. 3 in D minor

Horne, mezzo-soprano; Glen Ellyn Children's Chorus,
Chicago Symphony Chorus and Orchestra, Levine.
RCA Victor ARL-2-1757 [LP], *RCD2-1757* [CD],
CRK2-1757 [T].

The longest symphony ever written by a major composer—and because of that fact, one of the few classical works that earns a place in *The Guinness Book of World Records*—the Third is obviously among the most challenging of Mahler symphonies to perform. In concert, it can make for a long and uncomfortable evening if the conductor has not done his homework; in the living room, it can offer countless excuses to turn off the receiver and see what's on TV.

Like Jascha Horenstein in his daring and temporarily unavailable Unicorn recording, James Levine assumes that his listeners are willing to give him nearly two hours of their undivided attention in exchange for the real, and frequently incomparable rewards that this vast and sprawling work offers in return. The result is one of the most adult and uncompromising of all Mahler symphony recordings. While the first five movements present certain difficulties, Levine overcomes them magnificently. But the Third, like the Seventh, contains a problematic final movement, and Levine's solution to this endless elegy is to adopt a tempo so dangerously slow that the movement sounds even longer than it actually is. The results of Levine's courage are admirable, for instead of anti-climax, the *Finale* becomes genuine catharsis: a tender and inexpressibly moving conclusion to a difficult but towering masterwork.

Symphony No. 4 in G Major

Raskin, soprano; Cleveland Orchestra, Szell. CBS MY-37225 [LP], *MK-42416* [CD]. MYT-37225 [T].

It is with this most concise, charming, and popular Mahler symphony that most people find their way into the composer's music: the Mahlerian equivalent of Bruckner's "Romantic" Symphony. Yet like that other Fourth Symphony, the Mahler G Major is probably the composer's least characteristic work. Genial, untroubled, and—except for a few dark moments in the third movement—completely lacking in any neurotic symptoms, the Fourth is as happy as Mahler can become and still remain Mahler. Even the inevitable presentment of death in the *Finale* is a singularly trusting and innocent vision of heaven provided through the eyes of a child.

George Szell's classic 1965 interpretation remains one of the most completely successful Mahler recordings ever made. With a charm and glowing humanity that many of his enemies rarely accused him of possessing, Szell handles the music with a deceptively relaxed, but always exceedingly firm grip. Climaxes, even the shattering one at the end of the third movement, merely seem to happen; and in fact, the entire performance creates the illusion of unfolding by itself without the intervention of human will.

The late Judith Raskin gives one of the most engrossingly spontaneous performances of her brilliant career in the final movement; the Cleveland Orchestra has never been better, and in spite of some slightly intrusive hiss from the original analogue tapes, the compact disc restoration is remarkably fine.

Symphony No. 5 in C-sharp minor

Chicago Symphony, Solti. London 414321-1 [LP],
414321-2 [CD], 414321-4 [T].

Chicago is still a town that suffers from its age-old "Second City" complex and is hence a place where superlatives tend to get thrown around more casually than anywhere else. The local Republican newspaper, the Chicago Tribune, calls itself "The World's Greatest Newspaper" on its masthead, therefore the call letters of its television and radio stations are WGN. WLS, its Sears-owned competitor, is a reminder of "The World's Largest Store." Only in Chicago would things like the World's Tallest Building (the Sears Tower) or the World's Busiest Airport (O'Hare International) be pointed to as objects of civic pride, and only in Chicago would the city's orchestra, fresh from its first European tour, be cheered by a crowd who rarely ever set foot in a concert hall and with banners proclaiming it as (what else?) the World's Greatest Orchestra.

I was there in Orchestra Hall when Sir Georg Solti led an absolutely spellbinding performance of the Mahler Fifth during his first season as music director of the Chicago Symphony. The recording made several weeks later not only captures much of the overwhelming excitement of that interpretation, but also served to announce that the orchestra, after its stormy association with Solti's predecessor Jean Martinon, was at last back on form. They *do* sound very much like The World's Greatest Orchestra in this early recording with their new music director. The woodwinds and brass negotiate this difficult music with supreme confidence and bravado, and the strings—both in the famous, gentle *Adagietto* and in the whirlwind *Finale*—give Solti everything he asks for, which here amounts to the last word in excitement and finesse. This is, by a comfortable margin, the best-played Mahler Fifth ever released—Solti's interpretation is a subtle, yet powerfully dramatic one, and the somewhat harsh sound of the original recording has been improved considerably.

Symphony No. 6 in A minor, "Tragic"

London Philharmonic, Tennstedt. Angel DS-3945 [LP], *CDC-47049* [CD], 4X2S-3945 [T].

The Sixth Symphony occupies a unique position in Mahler's output as perhaps the most paradoxical work that this endlessly paradoxical composer would ever produce. It is simultaneously the most objective and deeply personal of all his symphonies, the most rigorous in its formal organization, and the most devastating in its emotional effect. It is the only one of his ten completed works in the form—including *Das Lied von der Erde*—that in its original version adhered to the traditional format of the classical symphony, and the only one that ends on a note of catastrophic, inconsolable despair.

While the recordings by Solti, Bernstein, Levine, and Abbado all have much to recommend them, it is Klaus Tennstedt's combination of turbulent fury and arching lyricism that in the end proves most effective. If in the opening movement and *Scherzo*, the conductor doesn't quite whip up the level of manic intensity that some of his rivals do, his reading of the sinuous *Andante* is wonderfully unaffected in its simplicity and beauty. In the massively complicated *Finale*, Tennstedt gives us both more structural coherence and less hysteria than any other recorded performance has been able to do previously. That is not to say that the movement fails to communicate its full measure of anguish and terror; it simply does so with an unusually adult combination of iron control and impeccable taste.

Symphony No. 7 in E minor

Chicago Symphony, Abbado. Deutsche Grammophon 413773-1 [LP], *413773-2* [CD], 413773-4 [T].

The Seventh is easily the most difficult of all the Mahler symphonies to approach, and finally to love. In the mysterious *Scherzo*, flanked by two movements called *Nachtmusik*, the composer wrote some of his most harmonically adventurous, forward-looking music. And if the opening movement presents more than its share of structural problems, the *Finale* has always seemed, in comparison, utterly fragmented and frightfully banal.

In a pirated tape of a live London Symphony concert that has had a vigorous circulation in the underground market, Jascha Horenstein proved conclusively that the symphony's many problems are only surface-deep. Not only was the conductor's grasp of the subtle, complex atmosphere of the three central movements amazing, but he was also able to make the usually thin-sounding, patchwork *Finale* seem as cogent and triumphant as the finale of the Mahler Fifth.

In his superb recording with the Chicago Symphony, Claudio Abbado accomplishes many of the same things. The first four movements—especially the *Scherzo* and second *Nachtmusik*—are invested with tremendous individuality and character, and the *Finale* is perhaps the absolute high point to date in Abbado's admirable Mahler cycle. All of the themes emerge as distinct and highly charged entities carefully woven into a passionate and fabulously exciting whole. In fact, on repeated hearings of this elegantly thought-out and brilliantly executed performance, the Seventh begins to join the Sixth, Eighth, and Ninth, as one of the most powerful and original symphonies that Mahler ever wrote.

Symphony No. 8 in E-flat Major, "Symphony of a Thousand"

Harper, Popp, Auger, Minton, Watts, Kollo, Shirley-Quirk, Talvela, Vienna State Opera Chorus, Vienna Singverein, Vienna Boys Choir, Chicago Symphony, Solti. London *414493-2* [CD], 414493-4 [T].

Sir Georg Solti has said in print that he considers the Eighth to be the greatest of Mahler's symphonies, and from this stupendous Chicago Symphony recording, taped in Vienna, even the most rabid admirers of the Sixth and Ninth would be tempted to agree with him. Produced on a singularly tight recording schedule (the tension, at times, is almost palpable), Solti unleashes the music's greatness in a way that even Leonard Bernstein, in his famous London Symphony recording, is not quite able to match.

The performance of the opening movement, a setting of the medieval hymn *Veni Creator Spiritus*, is almost withering in its joyous excitement, and the lengthy setting of the closing scene from Part I of Goethe's *Faust* is wonderfully operatic in the best possible sense of the word. Solti loses no opportunity to exploit either the high drama or endless color of the score, from the hushed and sinister opening bars of the second movement to the vast and vastly moving chorus with which the symphony concludes. The massed choruses sing with tremendous accuracy and enthusiasm, and the performance boasts the strongest collection of soloists of any Mahler Eighth on the market today. Yet it is the superhuman playing of the Chicago Symphony that tips the scales—perhaps forever—in Solti's favor. Rumor has it that members of the Vienna Philharmonic who attended the recording sessions were deeply shaken by what they heard. Many left the hall speechless, while others were observed mumbling incoherently to themselves.

Astonishingly, no LP version of the Eighth Symphony was available at the time this book went to press.

Symphony No. 9

Amsterdam Concertgebouw Orchestra, Bernstein.
Deutsche Grammophon 419208-1 [LP], *419208-2*
[CD], 419208-4 [T].

Amsterdam Concertgebouw Orchestra, Haitink.
Philips 6700021 [LP], *416466-2* [CD].

Even before that historic series of concerts in May of 1920, when Willem Mengelberg presided over the first important festival of his friend's music, the Amsterdam Concertgebouw Orchestra has enjoyed the longest unbroken Mahler tradition of any of the world's major orchestras. The oser himself was a frequent guest conductor in Amsterdam, and in addition to Mengelberg's famous interpretations, those of his successors, Eduard van Beinum and Bernard Haitink, have gone a long way to cementing the Concertgebouw Orchestra's reputation as the finest Mahler orchestra in the world. Fortunately, in recent years, the greatest living Mahler conductor has begun to appear with them on a regular basis, and this live performance of the Ninth Symphony must now be counted with the three or four greatest of Mahler recordings.

In the two decades since his New York Philharmonic recordings became the principal impetus for the modern Mahler revival, Leonard Bernstein's approach to the composer's music has both deepened and grown more extreme. The surface drama has become increasingly turbulent—his detractors have called it "self-indulgent" and "over-wrought"—while its deeper implications have been plumbed with an understanding is ever more lucid and profound.

This live Concertgebouw performance of the composer's most shattering work is a triumph of extremes. Where other conductors have been intense in this music, Bernstein is almost savagely so; where others have heard the final movement as Mahler's poignant farewell to life, Bernstein transforms it into the stuff of universal tragedy, a farewell to *all* life, possibility, and hope. In essence, the conductor's most recent version of this great work is as much Bernstein's Ninth as it is Gustav Mahler's. For those who find the vision either too personal or too searingly painful to bear, Bernard Haitink's beautifully controlled recording with the same orchestra is the best alternative.

Martinu, Bohuslav
(1890–1959)

Nonet; *La Revue de Cuisine*; Trio in F Major for
Flute, Cello and Piano

> **The Dartington Ensemble. Hyperion A66084 [LP].**
>
> **Symphony No. 3; Symphony No. 4**
>
> **Bamberg Symphony, Järvi. Bis *CD-363* [CD].**

With the work of his Polish near contemporary Karol
Szymanowski, the music of Czech composer Bohuslav Martinu remains one of the last largely undiscovered treasure
troves of twentieth century music. Like Szymanowski, Martinu was a restless eclectic whose music nevertheless spoke
with a unique and thoroughly original voice. In all of the
more than four hundred works he eventually produced, one
can hear the same quality that impressed Igor Stravinsky in
Sergei Prokofiev's music—an elusive commodity Stravinsky
called "The instant imprint of personality." If the great Martinu Revival is not actually upon us yet, there has been some
encouraging recent evidence—including the two superb recordings listed above—that it may be about to begin.

In addition to bringing us some of the finest performances yet of Martinu's chamber music, the invaluable Hyper-
ion recording by England's Dartington Ensemble also provides a representative cross section of the three major phases

of Martinu's creative life. *La Revue de Cuisine* is a sassy, jazzy ballet produced during the composer's nineteen-year stay in Paris, while the Trio in F, composed during Martinu's American exile in 1944, is one of the most Czech and ebullient of all his works. But the gem of the collection is the bright and deceptively simple-sounding Nonet, conceived five months before the composer's death in 1959. In its serenity, melodic inventiveness, and structural elegance, it is easily one of the most nearly perfect and instantly enjoyable chamber works written since the end of the Second World War.

In the second installment of what will eventually become a complete cycle of all six Martinu symphonies, Neemi Järvi leads the Bamberg Symphony in some intensely committed and completely idiomatic performances of the Third and Fourth. (Volume One, which includes the First and Second Symphonies—Bis *CD-362*—is equally splendid.) Since Martinu did not produce a symphony until he was already fifty-two, both of these works are those of a mature, confident master. The Third is a brooding, frequently violent, often desperate commentary on the events of World War II; while the Fourth, written in the Spring of 1945, mixes joy, hope, and idyllic tenderness with a *Largo* whose depth and complexity rivals that of the similar movement from Dvořák's "New World" Symphony.

In short, these two recordings are an indispensable introduction to a major talent, and quite possibly a sleeping twentieth century giant.

Mascagni, Pietro
(1863–1945)

Cavalleria Rusticana

**Milanov, Bjorling, Smith, Merrill, Robert Shaw
Chorale, RCA Victor Symphony, Cellini. RCA
Victor *6510-2-RG* [CD].**

**Scotto, Domingo, Elvira, Ambrosian Opera Chorus,
National Philharmonic Orchestra, Levine. RCA
Victor CRL1-3091 [LP], CRK1-3091 [T].**

Long before he died in abject poverty and disgrace—like
Giacomo Puccini, he had been one of Mussolini's most ardent
supporters—Pietro Mascagni was one of the most tragic figures in operatic history. At the age of twenty-six *Cavalleria
Rusticana* made him world famous, and for the next fifty-six
years he was condemned to live out his life haunted by an
overwhelming early success that he was never able to repeat. "I
was crowned before I was King," was the composer's own
rueful assessment of his career, and history has been forced to
agree.

While this lurid tale of betrayal and revenge has very little
to do with "Rustic Chivalry," the literal translation of its title,
Cavalleria Rusticana has remained the most justly popular
one-act opera ever written. Like Leoncavallo's *I Pagliacci*,
with which it is usually paired, Mascagni's masterpiece is the
central work of the Italian *verismo* school. Like *"Pag"*, *"Cav"*

explodes with vivid drama and raw emotions, though it also boasts a musical subtlety and sensitivity to character that only the best of Puccini's mature operas can begin to match.

The recording that captures more of the opera's finesse and earthiness than any other is a classic RCA Victor recording from the mid-1950s that has recently been released on compact disc. Zinka Milanov was one of the century's great Santuzzas. Passionate, vulnerable, immensely feminine, she was also equipped with a voice which was as physically impressive as those of Leontyne Price and Rosa Ponselle. This recording catches her at something past her prime, but with her temperament and most of her instrument still intact the interpretation still makes for an overwhelming experience. With the insouciant and spectacularly well-sung Turridu of Jussi Bjorling, and the sensitive yet richly powerful and garlic-laden conducting of Renato Cellini, this remains, for me, the only recording of the opera to own.

Among modern recordings, the Levine version easily sweeps the field. Placido Domingo's interpretation is to our time what Bjorling's and Caruso's were to theirs. While a bit shrill and wobbly as always, Renato Scotto gives one of her most natural and affecting recorded performances, and the playing, conducting, and recorded sound are all first-rate.

Massenet, Jules (1842–1912)

Werther

Von Stade, Carreras, Allen, Lloyd, Chorus and
Orchestra of the Royal Opera House, Covent
Garden, Davis. Philips *416654-2* [CD].

At the time of his death in 1912, the suave and urbane Jules Massenet was one of the wealthiest composers who ever lived. His impeccably crafted, gently sentimental operas are among the finest and most popular ever written by a French composer. Audiences love them for their directness, dramatic realism, and inexhaustible flow of lovely melody. Singers love them because they are so carefully and gracefully written that even the most demanding Massenet role will invariably make even a fair or barely adequate singer sound exceptionally good.

While the best known of his amiable, brilliantly made masterworks is currently without a suitable recording—the best of the current crop of *Manons* features a tired-sounding, vocally eccentric Beverly Sills in the title role—*Werther*, his quiet, stunningly effective adaptation of Goethe's famous novel, can be heard in one of the most luminous operatic recordings of the last fifteen years. While Jose Carreras is vocally impressive as Goethe's doomed and tormented hero, the characterization lacks the substance of Nicolai Gedda's on

Georges Pretre's now-deleted Angel set. (And as long as Angel has been so enlightened in its policy of transferring its classic recordings from the 1950s and 1960s to compact disc, we should expect that definitive *Manon* with Victoria de los Angeles and conducted by Pierre Monteux to hit the stores any time.) Yet in spite of a hero who isn't all he could be, the Charlotte of Frederica von Stade is the most sensitive and multifaceted interpretation that one of the world's finest mezzo-sopranos ever delivered. Add to that an especially strong supporting cast and some of Sir Colin Davis' most inspired and imaginative conducting, and the result is not only the finest *Werther* ever recorded, but also the best Massenet recording available today.

Alas, both the LP and tape versions of this superb recording are apparently extinct.

Mendelssohn, Felix
(1809–1847)

Violin Concerto in E minor, Op. 64

Menuhin, violin; Berlin Philharmonic, Furtwängler. Angel *CDC-47119* [CD].

Lin, violin; Philharmonia Orchestra, Thomas. CBS IM-39007 [LP], *MK-39007* [CD], IMT-39007 [T].

This fresh, buoyant, eternally sweet-spirited work is probably the best-loved violin concerto ever written. And in spite of the apparent effortlessness of its invention, the E minor Concerto had an unusually long and painful gestation: from first sketch to finished score, it occupied the usually deft and facile composer's attention for the better part of six years.

While every important violinist of the century has recorded the work, and many of them more than once, there is still something very special in Sir Yehudi Menuhin's 1954 recording with Wilhelm Furtwängler and the Berlin Philharmonic. Unlike their monumental interpretation of the Beethoven Concerto that fills out this unusually generous compact disc, the performance of Mendelssohn is a marvel of quiet intimacy and elfin grace. Menuhin's playing—which in recent years has been seriously compromised by a neurological disorder—was never more poignantly innocent than it is here, and the conductor, who had only a few months left to live, turns in one of the freshest and most impetuous of all his recorded performances.

Among more recent versions, the sensational debut recording by the Chinese-American violinist Cho-Liang Lin is not only the most exciting recording the Concerto has received in years, but also our first glimpse at what should undoubtedly develop into one of the great careers of the next generation. Like his near contemporary, the cellist Yo-Yo Ma, Lin is already a dazzlingly equipped musician. His technique is formidably seamless, and his musical personality is an engaging combination of outgoing bravado and introspective warmth. With the lush, yet witty support supplied by the Philharmonia Orchestra and Michael Tilson Thomas, this is considerably more than a very impressive first recording by an important new artist. It is, with Menuhin's thirty-five year-old wonder, *the* recording of the Mendelssohn Concerto to own.

A Midsummer Night's Dream (Incidental Music), Op. 21 and 61

Watson, Wallis, London Symphony Chorus and Orchestra, Previn. Angel *CDC-47163* [CD].

Mathis, Boese, Bavarian Radio Chorus and Orchestra, Kubelik. Deutsche Grammophon 415840-1 [LP], 415840-4 [T].

The famous overture that Felix Mendelssohn composed for Shakespeare's Festive Comedy, *A Midsummer Night's Dream*, has a fair claim to being the greatest single musical work ever written by a teenager. Only Mozart and Schubert produced music of similar quality at a comparable age. The remainder of the incidental music that Mendelssohn would write over the next twenty years was also of a very high caliber, including the finest example of a form he would make forever his own, the quicksilver *Scherzo*, and one of the most famous five minutes in all of music, the stirring, and for many *blood-*

curdling Wedding March, to whose famous strains countless freedom-loving people have trooped off to join the ranks of the Living Dead.

On records, André Previn has established a hard-earned reputation as one of the finest interpreters of the music of the major modern English composers and of other mainline twentieth century figures from Rachmaninoff and Prokofiev to Debussy and Ravel. That he is equally comfortable in the mainstream of the Austro-German tradition is amply documented by a recording like this one in which he proves, quite conclusively I think, that he is the finest Mendelssohn conductor in the world today.

All of the familiar moments—the *Overture, Scherzo, Intermezzo, Nocturne,* and *Wedding March*—are invested with an exhilarating freshness and immensely individual character, while the less familiar set pieces and linking passages are given a weight and significance that no other recording can begin to match. The spooky menace and rhythmic point of *You Spotted Snakes* is alone worth the price of the recording.

Since the original LP from which the compact disc was made has now been withdrawn, Rafael Kubelik's frequently eccentric, but thoroughly ingratiating Deutsche Grammophon interpretation is clearly the first choice among all available LPs and cassettes.

Octet in E-flat for Strings, Op. 20

Academy of St. Martin-in-the-Fields Chamber
Ensemble. Philips *420400-2* [CD].

Cleveland Quartet, Tokyo Quartet. RCA Victor
ARL1-2532 [LP].

When I was sixteen I read something from the second volume of George Bernard Shaw's *Dramatic Opinions and Essays* that struck a painfully responsive chord:

> With the single exception of Homer, there is no eminent writer, not even Sir Walter Scott, whom I can despise so entirely as I despise Shakespeare when I measure my mind against his. It would positively be a relief to me to dig him up and throw stones at him.

At a time when I was wasting my life fighting acne and the oboe, yelling at girls, and trying to beat out three other guys for one of the two defensive end spots on my high school football team, Felix Mendelssohn was composing his miraculously inspired E-flat Major Octet. After weeks of excruciating soul-searching, leavened by the then major triumphs of making the team and thereby attracting the attentions of an exceedingly cute cheerleader, I resolved to stop hating Mendelssohn by simply facing the irrefutable facts. I was a perfectly normal Midwest high school kid; he was a genius.

Nowhere is Mendelssohn's youthful brilliance revealed more felicitously than in the finest single work ever composed for this particular combination of instruments. The level of melodic inspiration and richness of ornamental detail is so phenomenal that the Octet is obviously the work of a mature master, not a boy of sixteen. Both of these superlative recordings capture almost all of the Octet's melting warmth and blindingly brilliant inspiration. In fact, a choice between them will depend largely on your preference for the LP or the compact disc format. On tape, your best bet is the stylish version by the Melos Ensemble from Arabesque (9017).

Symphony No. 3 in A minor, Op. 56, "Scottish"

London Symphony, Maag. London 421125-4 [T].

Chicago Symphony, Solti. London 414665-1 [LP],
414665-2 **[CD], 414665-4 [T].**

It is no accident that in Great Britten, Felix Mendelssohn is revered as one of the most important of all composers. In addition to writing the incidental music for Shakespeare's *A Midsummer Night's Dream*, he supplied the Oratorio-mad English with *Elijah*, one of the greatest nineteenth century examples of their favorite form of musical entertainment. And with the *Hebrides Overture* and "Scottish" Symphony—the latter dedicated to Queen Victoria—he wrote two of the best and most popular of all musical travelogues based on British themes.

Since it was first released more than thirty years ago, no recording of the "Scottish" Symphony has come within hailing distance of that astonishingly vivid and spontaneous performance by the London Symphony led by the Swiss conductor, Peter Maag. Impulsive yet highly polished, beautifully detailed yet sweepingly cinematic, the interpretation remains one of the great glories of the stereo era. Unfortunately, only a cassette version is currently available. Until it makes its triumphant appearance on compact disc, Sir Georg Solti's slightly driven yet compellingly dramatic Chicago Symphony recording is the best alternative. With thrilling playing and dazzling recorded sound, this would actually be the first choice among all "Scottish" Symphony recordings, were it not for the once-in-a-lifetime combination of freshness and poetry that Peter Maag found in the score so long ago.

Symphony No. 4 in A Major, Op. 90, "Italian"

Cleveland Orchestra, Szell. CBS MY-37760 [LP],
** *MYK-37760* [CD], MT-37760 [T].**

More than any other work, it is the colorful, impeccably crafted "Italian" Symphony which best fixes Mendelssohn's place in the development of Western music. Essentially a Classicist who was touched by the first winds of the Romantic movement, Mendelssohn reconciled eighteenth century structural decorum with nineteenth century emotionalism more comfortably than any other composer of his time. The "Italian" Symphony is one of the great transitional works of the early Romantic era, a piece whose formal organization is as tightly knit as the symphonies of Haydn and Mozart, but whose expressiveness clearly points the way to Berlioz, Chopin, and Schumann.

The performance that most successfully projects both sides of the "Italian" Symphony's essential character is an immaculate and exciting CBS recording by the Cleveland Orchestra and George Szell. Along with the highly buffed playing of the finest Mozart orchestra of modern times, Szell finds countless ways to remind us that this is also an intensely Romantic work. The Pilgrim's March, even at a rather brisk tempo, has a wonderfully melancholy grandeur, and in the concluding *tarantella*, taken at a break-neck clip, there are many dark and disquieting moments lurking beneath the swirling, giddy surface. With equally lucid and revealing performances of the best known moments from the *Midsummer Night's Dream* music, this is one of the classic Mendelssohn recordings of the stereo age.

Milhaud, Darius
(1892–1974)

Création du Monde

National Orchestra of France, Bernstein. Angel
CDC-47845 [CD].

Boston Symphony, Munch. RCA Victrola ALK1-5391
[T].

Contemporary Chamber Ensemble, Weisberg.
Nonesuch 71281 [LP].

One of the most prolific and entertaining composers that history has known, Darius Milhaud was also one of the largest. In fact, to find a composer of comparable girth, one has to go back to the late-eighteenth century Bohemian composer and keyboard virtuoso, Jan Ladislav Dussek, who became so obese toward the end of his career that his hands could no longer reach the keyboard of his piano. (Fortunately for posterity, Milhaud never learned to play the instrument and thus was free to compose all of his music while seated at a desk.)

La Création du Monde (The Creation of the World), the ballet written after the composer's encounter with American jazz in 1923, is probably Milhaud's finest and most characteristic work. It is given racy, vibrant performances in all of the recordings listed above, and a choice among them will depend largely on your preference of format. The Bernstein compact disc also includes spirited interpretations of Milhaud's *Saudades do Brasil* and *Le Boeuf sur le Toit*—the equally jazzy and surrealistic ballet whose scenario, by Jean Cocteau, calls for (among other things) a Paris gendarme to be decapitated by an overhead fan. The Munch tape includes the only available performance of the enchanting *Suite Provençale*, Milhaud's lively and loving evocation of the folk music of his native Provence.

Monteverdi, Claudio
(1567a–1643)

Orfeo

Rogers, Kwella, Kirkby, Smith, Varcoe, Chiaroscuro, London Baroque Ensemble, London Cornett and Sackbutt Ensemble, Rogers and Medlam. Angel *CDCB-47141* [CD].

While Jacopo Peri's *Dafne* predates it by about a decade, Monteverdi's *Orfeo* is now generally regarded as the first genuine opera, as the word is commonly understood today. While *Orfeo* is an extended vocal work which *does* attempt to tell a continuous, coherent story, it is not "operatic" in the same sense that *Carmen* and *Aida* are. The action, as in most operas before those of Mozart, tends to be static to the point of stagnation, and the characters are often less than two dimensional. As a matter of fact, to the untrained ear, *Orfeo* can seem little more than a sequence of one and two-part madrigals (if that's not a contradiction in terms), thrown together with exquisite imagination and taste.

This attractive performance from Angel makes the strongest case for *Orfeo* that has been made in the recording studio. The movement of the music is gracefully fluid, and the singing of all the principals is lovely and memorable. Especially brilliant is the contribution of Nigel Rogers, whose command of florid ornamentation reminds us of something that Fritz Kreisler once said of John McCormack: "The man must have a Stradivarius in his throat." If only these same forces would now turn their attention to Monteverdi's wonderfully lurid *L'Incoronazione di Poppea*, which is currently represented only by Nikalous Harnoncourt's interminably dull and pedantic Teldec recording.

On a consistently high, though generally less exalted level, the fine Erato recording (NUM 75212, MCE-75212 [T]) led by Michel Corboz will service the needs of those who have not yet made the conversion to compact discs.

Mozart, Wolfgang Amadeus (1756–1791)

Once, when filling out an application for a summer job, on that line next to "other" in which the employer asks the prospective employee to list his or her religion, I wrote the word "Mozart." The personnel officer was *not* amused, but then again, I hadn't intended it as a joke. For there was a time when I was absolutely convinced that Mozart was at least as divinely inspired as Moses, Christ, the Buddha, Lao-tse, or Mohammed, and I suppose I still am. For in no other works of the human imagination can the divine spirit be heard more distinctly than in the *literally* miraculous music that this often vulgar, unpleasant, and difficult man produced during his pathetically brief thirty-five years. Were this book to do him any justice, the section devoted to Mozart's music would take up more than half of this total book. What follows, therefore, is a painfully compressed selection.

> **Concerto in A Major for Clarinet and Orchestra, K. 622 [LP]; Sinfonia Concertante in E-flat Major for Violin, Viola and Orchestra, K. 364 [LP].**
>
> **Marcellus, clarinet; Druian, violin; Skernick, viola; Cleveland Orchestra, Szell. CBS MY-37810 [LP], *MYK-37810* [CD], MT-37810 [T].**

This is one of the most nearly perfect Mozart recordings ever made. Robert Marcellus, the Cleveland Orchestra's principal clarinettist, gives a flawless, dramatic performance of the late and strangely uneven Clarinet Concerto with some customarily precise and enthusiastic support provided by his colleagues under George Szell, and the gleaming version of the great Sinfonia Concertante is probably Szell's finest Mozart recording. Instead of big name soloists, the conductor wisely chose to place the Cleveland's immensely accomplished concertmaster and principal violist in the spotlight. The result is an interpretation of such total generosity and uncanny unanimity of purpose that even after thirty years, it must still be heard to be believed. For much of the time, the soloists seem like a single player with two sets of arms. Each of the beautifully wrought phrases is shaped with precisely the same dynamic shading and inflection, and even the tiniest details are never left to chance. For instance, the trill at the end of the second movement *cadenza* is a miracle of timing and expressiveness. Szell's accompaniment is as energetic as it is patrician, and at the time the recording was made, the orchestra, as a Mozart ensemble, had no rival in the world.

Concertos (4) for Horn and Orchestra

Brain, horn; Philharmonia Orchestra, Karajan. Angel
CDH-61013 [CD].

Tuckwell, horn; London Symphony, Maag. London
421199-1 [LP], 421199-4 [T].

Written for a man named Ignaz Leutgub (or Leutgeb), one of the most delightfully vulgar of his Salzburg cronies and the favorite butt of many of the composer's practical jokes, the four Horn Concertos are among the most enchanting of all of Mozart's works. From the evidence of the difficult solo parts, Leutgub must have been a virtuoso of considerable accomplishment. For as taxing as they are even for the modern performer, the concertos were originally written for the *waldhorn*, an instrument without valves.

In their recent compact disc reissue, the classic recordings from the mid-1950s made by the legendary Dennis Brain
are a moving, inspiring reminder of a man who was not only
the century's greatest horn player, but also one of its finest
musicians. The secret of Brain's art lay in the fact that his
approach to the instrument was that of a great vocalist. His
phrasing, command of dynamics, and dramatic coloration
rivalled those of the finest Mozart singers of his generation. In
fact, the slow movements of the Concertos become, in effect,
hauntingly beautiful arias without words.

The modern recording that comes closest to duplicating
Brain's achievement is the second of three recordings made
thus far by Barry Tuckwell. With Peter Maag's incisive, sensitive support, Tuckwell gives the liveliest and most technically
accomplished performances heard on records since Dennis
Brain's death. If they lack the final measure of depth and
tenderness that Brain brought to his famous recordings, they
are still a magnificent accomplishment in their own right and
are vigorously recommended.

Concertos (25) for Piano and Orchestra

Perahia, piano and conductor; English Chamber
    Orchestra. CBS M13-42055 [LP], *MK-42055* [CD],
    M3T-39044 [LP], M3T-42115 [LP], M3T-39246
    [LP], M4T-39689 [T].

Brendel, piano; Academy of St. Martin-in-the-Fields,
    Marriner. Philips 412856-1 [LP], *412856-2 PH10*
    [CD], 412856-4 PH9 [T].

With the possible exceptions of his operas and last half
dozen symphonies, it is in the series of piano concertos he
wrote throughout his career that the full scope of Mozart's
achievement can best be understood. From the earliest of these
pieces, some of which were merely arrangements of the music
of his teacher, Johann Christian Bach, through the towering

masterworks of his final years, the concertos also offer the most dramatic evidence of Mozart's evolution from the most celebrated child prodigy in the history of music to the greatest composer who has ever lived.

Each of these triumphant sets of the complete piano concertos is a milestone in the recent history of recording, and since Murray Perahia and Alfred Brendel are among the most compelling Mozart performers of the last three decades a choice between them will have to be made on personal, rather than musical grounds. For those who respond to the "intellectual" approach to Mozart, Brendel's thoughtful, always self-possessed and disciplined playing serves almost all of the concertos exceptionally well. Like his teacher, Edwin Fischer, Brendel is always acutely aware of the shape and architecture of the music. Everything is calculated—in the best possible sense of the word —to make the individual details subordinated to the needs of the greater whole. Which is not to say that Brendel's playing is in any way academic or lacking in emotion. Whereas other pianists—including Murray Perahia—can never resist the temptation of letting an especially grateful episode pass them by without embellishing it with the stamp of their own personality, Brendel always does. The results are many of the most satisfying and natural-sounding Mozart recordings available today.

Sir Neville Marriner's accompaniments are invariably invigorating, refined, and stylish, and the recorded sound, primarily from the 1970s, is both as brilliantly detailed and as warmly unobtrusive as the performances themselves.

Like Daniel Barenboim and the late Geza Anda before him, Murray Perahia serves as his own conductor in his consistently fascinating CBS set. As it turns out, the decision was a sound one, not only because the arrangement helps to underscore Perahia's essentially chamberlike approach to the concertos, but also because his ideas are so firm and intensely personal that the presence of another musical "personality" would have simply gotten in the way.

If in the most general and over-simplified terms, the Brendel recordings represent the modern Classical vision of

Mozart, then Perahia's are a bold and generally successful attempt to re-think the Romantic approach taken by the great pianists of a half century ago. In virtually all of the recordings, Perahia always finds something fresh and personal to say, especially in the slow movements that are drawn out almost to the point of languorousness. The phrasing is consistently imaginative and spontaneous, and the physical sound of both the soloist and the orchestra, while decidedly hedonistic, also has a wonderful feeling of openness and inevitability. While many will find the performances a trifle precious and fussy, as many others will hear them as an endless source of discovery and delight.

A clear-cut choice between these two superb cycles is not an easy one to make. And needless to say, either of them— especially given the current highway robbery pricing of compact discs—represents a substantial investment. The wise collector should probably just bite the bullet (or perhaps persuade one of the kids to take a part-time job at McDonald's), and acquire them both.

*P*iano Concerto No. 19 in F Major, K. 459; Piano Concerto No. 20 in D minor, K. 466

Serkin, piano; Cleveland Orchestra, Szell. CBS MY-37236 [LP], *MYK-37236* [CD], MYT-37236 [T].

Why the nineteenth century tended to take a rather dim view of Mozart remains one of music's most perplexing historical mysteries. Of course, that it chose to venerate its own, far lesser figures at his expense was nothing particularly unusual or new. The wholesale dismissal of the accomplishments of preceding ages was already a time-honored institution by the late fifteenth century: "The Dark Ages"—and for that matter "Renaissance"—were both terms that Renaissance propagandists coined.

Even so, how the Romantic era could have dismissed Mozart as a rococo lightweight with a powdered wig is all but impossible to fathom, especially in light of works like the D minor Piano Concerto, which with *Don Giovanni*, the 40th Symphony, and the G minor String Quintet is one of the darkest outpourings of tragedy in all of music.

Having known each other since their student days, George Szell and Rudolf Serkin—an especially formidable combination in the music of Mozart, Beethoven, and Brahms—always managed to communicate with one another as if by some mysterious musical telepathy. Their performance of the D minor Concerto is one of the most profound and deeply serious ever recorded. Serkin's playing seethes with a brooding, impassioned intensity, and Szell's contribution, as usual, is a model of cooperative understanding that still maintains a distinct and potent personality of its own. The interpretation of the F Major Concerto is just as impressive, lending to what is often tossed off as a far lighter work an unexpected and startlingly novel significance and weight.

*P*iano Concerto No. 21 in C Major, K. 467; Concerto No. 27 in B-flat Major, K. 595

Barenboim, piano and conductor; English Chamber Orchestra. Angel AE-34485 [LP], *CDC-47269* [CD], 4AE-34485 [T].

Since its memorable appearance in Bo Widerberg's lovely 1967 film *Elvira Madigan*, the C Major Piano Concerto, or at very least its ravishing second movement, has become one of the most popular of all Mozart's works. Daniel Barenboim's performance was always one of the best things in his now deleted cycle of the complete concertos for Angel. The fiery, poetic interpretation is a blissfully Romantic one and contains such an achingly beautiful run-through of the slow movement that it is almost guaranteed to break your heart.

The performance of the B-flat Major Concerto is equally memorable and just as controversial. It is a huge and hugely dramatic reading, in which Barenboim seems intent on making the case that Mozart has a closer stylistic affinity with Schumann than with Haydn. While obviously not for purists, Barenboim's fearlessly red-blooded approach serves both works extremely well.

*P*iano Concerto No. 23 in A Major, K. 488; Piano Concerto No. 19 in F Major, K. 459

Pollini, piano; Vienna Philharmonic, Böhm. Deutsche Grammophon 2530716 [LP], *413793-2* [CD].

With the brilliant Ivan Moravec, whose recordings are becoming increasingly impossible to find, the mercurial Italian pianist Maurizio Pollini is one of the most accomplished and individual Mozart interpreters before the public today. Unfortunately, only two Pollini Mozart recordings are currently available; fortunately, each one is a gem. Only Ivan Moravec, on a now deleted Quintessence recording, has given a more probing or poetic interpretation of the popular A Major Concerto. The outer movements are unhurried, expansive, and magnificently shaped, while the playing in the passionately moving slow movement—one of the greatest moments in all of Mozart—is a model of restrained intensity and poise. While not always the most satisfying of Mozart conductors, Karl Böhm provides Pollini with excellent support in both concertos, and the often cranky Vienna Philharmonic is on its best behavior throughout.

*P*iano Concerto No. 24 in C minor, K. 491; Piano Concerto No. 21 in C Major, K. 467

Casadesus, piano; Cleveland Orchestra, Szell. CBS MY-38523 [LP], *MYK-38523* [CD], *MT-38523* [T].

The ideal companion piece to the stormy C minor Concerto is the equally troubled D minor Concerto, K. 466. In that coupling, the most distinguished of all available recordings is one that the supremely gifted Clara Haskil made in 1960, a few months before her death. Recently issued on a compact disc from Philips (*412254-2*), the interpretations are a touching reminder of one of the most patrician, yet curiously unassuming musicians of her generation.

On the other hand, as a *performance* of the D minor Concerto, none has seriously challenged that classic recording by Robert Casadesus and George Szell. On the face of it, the Casadesus-Szell partnership—and they recorded many of the Mozart concertos together—must have seemed to many a rather peculiar one. On the one hand, there was Szell the fanatical perfectionist; on the other, the frequently inspired Frenchman whose approach to technical niceties could be shockingly cavalier. Yet somehow, together, their differences always seemed to cancel each other out.

Their version of the D minor Concerto is as poised and turbulent as any Mozart concerto recording ever made. While the soloist's contribution is not the last word in mechanical perfection, the playing communicates a sense of tragic grandeur that no other performance does. Szell, as he did so often, rises not only *to*, but frequently *above* the occasion. The conducting is so quick to pick up the music's dark and shifting moods, so tightly coiled in its pent-up intensity, that we can only wonder what kind of unspeakably shattering experience a Szell recording of *Don Giovanni* might have been.

Piano Concerto No. 25 in C Major, K. 503; Piano Concerto No. 26 in D Major, K. 537, "Coronation"

Ashkenazy, piano and conductor; Philharmonia Orchestra. London 411810 [LP], *411810-2* [CD], 411810-4 [T].

If conclusive proof was ever needed for the case that an artist's work need not necessarily reflect the circumstances of the artist's life, it is to be found in the final two piano concertos that Mozart composed during the last year of his life. By any standard, 1791 was a nightmare for the composer: his spendthrift wife was seriously ill, and the always fickle Viennese public had clearly grown tired of his music. He was living in abject penury, and his health—which had been frail to begin with—was slowly succumbing to at least a dozen potentially fatal diseases. Depressed, discouraged, and racked by what amounted to continuous pain, he nevertheless produced two of the greatest and most buoyantly extroverted of all his piano concertos during this period: the magisterial "Coronation" Concerto, and the irrepressibly optimistic B-flat Major Concerto, K. 595.

As both soloist and conductor, Vladimir Ashkenazy is close to the top of his form in his recordings of both works. The performance of the "Coronation" Concerto, while capitalizing fully on the work's overtly ceremonial elements, makes it seem far more personal and significant than it usually does. On the other hand, Ashkenazy's interpretation of the B-flat Major is an irresistible explosion of gaiety and sunshine, made all the more brilliant by the lustrous playing of the Philharmonia Orchestra and the equally gleaming recorded sound.

Così fan tutte

Schwarzkopf, Ludwig, Steffek, Kraus, Taddei, Berry, Philharmonia Chorus and Orchestra, Böhm. Angel S-3631 [LP].

Caballé, Cortrubas, Baker, Gedda, Ganzarolli, Van Allen, Chorus and Orchestra of the Royal Opera House, Covent Garden, Davis. Philips 6707025 [LP], *416633-2* [CD], 416633-4 [T].

While it has never attained the popularity of *Don Giovanni*, *The Marriage of Figaro*, and *The Magic Flute*, the effervescent *Così fan tutte* certainly belongs in the company of the greatest operas that Mozart—which is to say, anyone— ever wrote. Its lightweight but enchanting plot about the ever- present danger of female infidelity (the best approximation of the title is "So do they all" or "They're all like that") is not as chauvinistic as it might seem, and Lorenzo da Ponte's witty and ingenious libretto drew from Mozart some of the most inspired music he would ever write for the stage.

Since as characters, the two romantic couples are as purposefully interchangeable as the four ditzy lovers in Shake- speare's *A Midsummer Night's Dream*, and since the old misogynist Don Alfonso and the scheming maid Despina merely exist to move the delightfully complicated plot along, *Così fan tutte* is of necessity an ensemble opera, and probably the finest ever composed. While it has its share of memorable arias, its greatest moments are the duets, trios, and quartets in which operatic polyphony reached heights of inventiveness it would never again approach.

Among all the recordings the opera has ever received, none can equal the wit, unanimity, and astonishingly gener- ous give-and-take that can still be heard in the historic Angel recording from the early 1960s. While vocally and dramat- ically all of the principals are dazzling, Elizabeth Schwarz- kopf and Christa Ludwig, as the sisters Fiordiligi and Dor- abella, give two of the most delectable performances ever put on record, and the elfin, yet ruefully world-weary Don Alfonso of Walter Berry is one of the great comic portrayals of modern times.

On a slightly less exalted but still immensely entertaining level, the more recent Philips recording offers some particularly captivating singing from Monserrat Caballé and Dame Janet Baker, spirited conducting from Sir Colin Davis, together with a wider choice of formats, and more modern recorded sound.

Don Giovanni

Sutherland, Schwarzkopf, Sciutti, Alva, Wächter, Cappuccilli, Frick, Philharmonia Chorus and Orchestra, Giulini. Angel *CDCC-47260* [CD].

Allen, Vaness, Ewing, Gale, Van Allen, Lewis, Glyndebourne Festival Chorus, London Philharmonic, Haitink. Angel DSX-3953 [LP], *CDCC-47036* [CD], 4D3X-3953 [T].

Since the Giulini *Don Giovanni* was first released in 1963, there have no doubt been a few people who've waited for a finer recording of the greatest opera ever written. Good luck to them and to those who await the Great Pumpkin, the Tooth Fairy, honest politicians, and anything worth hearing from Philip Glass.

While in the title role, Eberhard Wächter may not have had the animal magnetism and dramatic savvy of a Cesare Siepi or Ezio Pinza, his performance was nevertheless exceptionally musical and intelligent and very beautifully sung. And Wächter was the *weakest* link in the chain. All the other roles are represented by what still remain their finest recorded performances: from the suave, sweet-spirited Don Ottavio of Luigi Alva—who for once, makes the character seem like something other than the mealy-mouthed chump he probably is—to the horrifying Commandatore of Gottlob Frick. Yet it is that incomparable trio of ladies, Elisabeth Schwarzkopf, Joan Sutherland, and Graziella Sciutti, together with phenomenally inspired direction from the man in the pit, which levitates this *Don Giovanni* onto a plane shared by only a handful of operatic recordings.

Although the original sound has been greatly improved in Angel's compact disc transfer, for those who absolutely insist on something more modern—or who have yet to acquire a compact disc player—Bernard Haitink's richly dramatic interpretation is the obvious second choice.

The Magic Flute

Popp, Gruberová, Lindner, Jerusalem, Brendel, Bracht, Zednik, Bavarian Radio Chorus and Orchestra, Haitink. Angel *CDCC-47951* [CD], 4D3X-3918 [T].

For Bruno Walter, *The Magic Flute*, and not the *Requiem*, was Mozart's last will and testament. For in the characters of the questing hero Tamino, the noble priest Sarastro, and the vulgar, buffoonish bird-catcher Papageno, Walter saw the three essential components of Mozart's complex and often contradictory personality. Like most of the great conductor's speculations, this one carries a certain gentle authority and in fact may contain more than a grain of truth. The most divinely simple of all his great operas, *Die Zauberflöte* affords some even more tantalizing grist for the speculation mill: had he lived, would Mozart have continued the process of simplification heard here and in other later works? And if so, what effect would this new directness have had on the infant Romantic movement?

In his recording debut as an operatic conductor, Bernard Haitink leads one of the warmest and most dramatic performances the opera has ever received. The unusually strong cast includes many of the finest living Mozart singers. Lucia Popp is an adorably sensual Pamina, Siegfried Jerusalem a subtle yet vocally exciting Tamino, and Edita Gruberová, as the Queen of the Night, recalls the most brilliant and commanding German coloraturas of the past. In all, this is one of the great Mozart recordings of the last decade and will probably tower above the competition for years to come.

Surprisingly, there is no completely acceptable recording of the opera currently available on LP. Karl Böhm's Deutsche Grammophon recording (419556-1), while the strongest of all, is still a very mixed bag. On the one hand, it offers the magical Tamino of Fritz Wunderlich and an imposing Sarastro in Franz Crass; on the other, it asks you to endure Roberta Peters' rather shrill Queen of the Night and, worse, the mugging and shameless hamming of Dietrich Fischer-Dieskau as Papageno.

The Marriage of Figaro

Schwarzkopf, Moffo, Taddei, Wächter, Cossotto,
  Philharmonia Chorus and Orchestra, Giulini. Angel
  S-3608 [LP], 4X3X-3608 [T].

Te Kanawa, Popp, Von Stade, Ramey, Allen, Moll,
  London Philharmonic Chorus and Orchestra, Solti.
  London 410150-1 [LP], *410150-2* [CD], 410150-4
  [T].

The same qualities that made the Giulini *Don Giovanni* one of the classic operatic recordings of the stereo era can be heard to equally memorable advantage in his version of what is widely regarded as the greatest comic opera ever written. While the contributions of the stunning cast cannot be praised too highly—for instance, the Countess of Elisabeth Schwarzkopf is in every way as great a creation as her Marschallin in Strauss' *Der Rosenkavalier*—it is Giulini's magical conducting that seems to place a stamp of immortality on the recording.

Only Erich Kleiber, in his famous, early-stereo version for London, managed to draw as much from both the singers and from the score itself. Yet if the Kleiber performance offered an abundance of sparkling wit, vocal beauty, and effortless grace, then the Giulini offers even more. While virtually every moment of the performance offers some startling yet utterly natural insight, the ineffable purity Giulini conjures out of the Act IV *Finale* makes it one of the most ethereally beautiful five minutes ever heard on a commercial recording.

Until this eternal performance makes its way onto compact disc, Sir Georg Solti's delightful London recording fills the gap more than admirably. Dame Kiri Te Kanawa, while she sings beautifully, is still no match for Schwarzkopf in her prime. The rest of the cast is unusually strong, Solti's conducting is both relaxed and pointed, and the recorded sound is easily the most impressive the opera has yet enjoyed.

Mass in C minor, K. 427, "The Great"

Cortrubas, Te Kanawa, Krenn, Sotin, John Alldis Choir, New Philharmonia Orchestra, Leppard. Angel AM 34710 [LP], *CDC-47385* [CD], 4AM-34710 [T].

With the unfinished *Requiem*, the C minor Mass is the most important of all of Mozart's choral works, and equal to the finest of that towering series of masses his friend Franz Joseph Haydn completed at the end of his career. Like the *Requiem*, "The Great" C minor Mass is a dark and disturbing work, full of uncharacteristic doubts and unsettling tensions.

Raymond Leppard leads an extremely humane and civilized interpretation of the work in a performance which features both a choir and orchestra of chamber proportions. While the soloists are all very individual and moving, Kiri Te Kanawa gives us one of her finest recorded performances.

While her singing—as well as that of Ileana Cortrubas—is as physically beautiful as any to be heard on records today, she also invests the music with a character and sense of involvement that most of her recordings rarely reveal.

String Quartets 14-19, "Haydn Quartets"

Melos Quartet. Deutsche Grammophon 2740249 [LP], 415870-2 [CD].

Alban Berg Quartet. Teldec 6.35485 [LP].

Quartetto Italiano. Philips 6747097 [LP].

Begun in 1782 after a nine-year period during which he composed no string quartets at all, the six works that Mozart wrote under the influence of, and eventually dedicated to, his friend Franz Joseph Haydn, constitute one of the great summits in the history of chamber music. Haydn himself was overwhelmed by his young friend's touching act of homage. It was this music which led Haydn to tell Mozart's father, "I swear before God and as an honest man, that your son is the greatest composer known to me, either in person or by reputation."

Collectors who would like to buy the six quartets together in a convenient package now find themselves in one of those difficult quandaries that seem to delight recording companies. The most charming and completely memorable versions of the "Haydn" Quartets—those classic performances by Quartetto Italiano—are now only available on a nine-record set from Philips (LP only), which also brings us superb performances of the rest of Mozart's twenty-three quartets. A superlative set from Vienna's Alban Berg Quartet can be found in a five-record Teldec box, which also includes gleaming performances of the four late "Prussian" Quartets, but only two of the "Haydn" series (Nos. 14 and 19) are available on compact disc.

This leaves us with the stylish, utterly professional yet slightly less effective performances by Stuttgart's gifted Melos Quartet. While they play with an abundance of grace, finesse, and wit, the principal selling points of their cycle are: 1. It includes only the "Haydn" Quartets, and, 2. It can be found on both LP and compact disc. As the celebrated philosopher Anonymous said so eloquently, "You pays your money and takes your choice."

Quintet in A Major for Clarinet and Strings, K. 581

Shifrin, clarinet; Chamber Music Northwest. Delos *DCD-3020* [CD].

Pay, clarinet; Academy of St. Martin-in-the-Fields Chamber Ensemble. Philips 9500772 [LP], 420961-4 [T].

Unlike the flute and the tenor voice, two instruments he thoroughly despised, Mozart's initial reaction sounds from the recently invented clarinet was love at first sight. He first heard them at the court of Mannheim in the late 1770s and, during the next decade, he would compose the first great works written for this instrument: the E-flat Major Trio, K. 498, and the most popular of all his chamber works, the great A Major Clarinet Quintet.

From the recording made during the 78 era by legendary English clarinettist Reginald Kell to that poignant little performance with a group of captured Chinese musicians led by Major Charles Emerson Winchester III (David Ogden Stiers) in the concluding episode of *M.A.S.H.*, the Quintet has received countless memorable performances over the years and is currently represented by at least a half dozen superlative recordings.

While less well-known than his glamorous near-contemporary Richard Stoltzman, David Shifrin is every bit his equal, as this sterling Delos recording clearly shows. Physically, Shifrin's sound is as large and beautiful as any in the world today. Musically, he is one of the most imaginative and individual performers of his generation, mixing an attractive, instantly recognizable musical personality with an unerring sense of decorum and good taste. While cast on a somewhat grand and Romantic scale, Shifrin's interpretation is also superbly detailed and intimate. With sensitive and enthusiastic support from four of his Chamber Music Northwest colleagues, coupled with its dazzling recorded sound, this is easily the most appealing recording the Quintet has received in at least a dozen years.

Although he plays with less personality than Shifrin, the fine English clarinettist Anthony Pay gives a breathtakingly sensitive performance with members of the Academy of St. Martin-in-the-Fields for Philips. As a bonus, this lovely and unusually generous recording offers two of the best available versions of the composer's Oboe Quartet and E-flat Major Horn Quintet.

Requiem K. 626

Price, Schmidt, Araiza, Adam, Leipzig Radio Choir, Dresden State Orchestra, Schreier. Philips 411420-1 [LP], *411420-2* [CD], 411420-4 [T].

Among so many other things, the East German tenor Peter Schreier has what must certainly be one of the most wildly *inappropriate* names in recent musical history. "Schreier" literally means "screamer," "howler," "shrieker," and other unpleasant things, and for more than twenty years he has been *anything* but that. After Fritz Wunderlich, his was probably the most beautiful tenor voice to have come out of Germany since the end of the War. And now, as his singing career draws inevitably to a close, he is proving to be an equally polished and sensitive conductor.

Schreier's Philips recording of the great unfinished *Requiem* is as perceptive and powerful as any recorded performance has ever been. Tempos are judiciously judged; the brilliantly disciplined chorus sings with equal amounts of gusto and devotion, and the Dresden State Orchestra has been honed to a fine cutting edge. Yet as in his stunning recording of Bach's *St. Matthew Passion*, it is with his stellar quartet of soloists that Schreier gets the most electrifying results. Perhaps it is simply because he has a natural understanding of their needs and problems, or perhaps it is because *they* know they are singing for one of the greatest singers of his time, but each of these fine singers—particularly Margaret Price—gives one of the most impressive recorded performances of his or her career. Philips' recorded sound is as warm and dramatic as the performance itself, rising to shattering heights in the *Dies Irae*, while fading to a hushed whisper in the *Lacrimosa*.

Serenade in G Major, K. 525, "Eine kleine Nachtmusik"

Columbia Symphony, Walter. CBS MY-37774 [LP], *MK-37774* [CD], MT-37774 [T].

Recordings of this imperishable charmer come and go, but none has ever seriously challenged that miracle of freshness and amiability that Bruno Walter recorded in the final years of his career. If the strings of the Columbia Symphony are not as clean and precise as they could have been, or the remastered recorded sound still retains its tubby bottom and hissy top, what does it matter? The music unfolds with such affectionate deftness and spontaneity that you'll almost suspect the ink was still wet on the page.

In addition to this most ingratiating of all recorded versions of the Serenade, the album also features vintage Walter interpretations of *The Impresario*, *Così fan tutte*, *Marriage of Figaro*, and *Magic Flute* Overtures, together with the moving, important, yet rarely heard *Masonic Funeral Music*.

*S*ymphony No. 25 in G minor, K. 183; Symphony No. 29 in A Major, K. 201

Academy of St. Martin-in-the-Fields, Marriner.
London 411717-1 [LP], 411717-4 [T].

Because London has yet to issue a compact disc version of Sir Neville Marriner's excellent versions of two of the finest of Mozart's early symphonies, there may be reason to hope they will eventually come through with what would be the ideal compact disc coupling: the recordings that Benjamin Britten made with the English Chamber Orchestra. With Britten's lush but controversial version of the Fortieth Symphony—in observing all of the repeats, he transformed the work into something on the scale of Beethoven's "Eroica" Symphony—these are two of the indispensable Mozart recordings of the modern era, and they *must* be returned to circulation soon.

Until they are, Marriner's taut, elegantly polished performances will have to hold the fort. Alas, none of the current compact disc versions of either work can be recommended with any enthusiasm. James Levine, on Deutsche Grammophon, is brusque and generally insensitive. Christopher Hogwood's Oiseau Lyre recording is edgy and irritating. And even with the great Amsterdam Concertgebouw Orchestra at his disposal for his Philips recording, Nikolaus Harnoncourt is, as usual, a joke.

Symphony No. 35 in D Major, K. 385, "Haffner"; Symphony No. 32 in G Major, K. 318; Symphony No. 39 in E-flat Major, K. 543

English Chamber Orchestra, Tate. Angel AE-34439 [LP], *CDC-47327* [CD], 4AE-34439 [T].

Under its gifted new music director, Jeffrey Tate, the English Chamber Orchestra has undergone a dramatic resurgence in the last several years. That is saying quite a bit more than meets the eye, since even before Tate began to guide its fortunes, the ECO had a reasonable claim to being the finest chamber orchestra in the world.

What Tate has accomplished in the last few seasons is to imbue the orchestra with a distinct personality, a quality which their work, with so many different conductors over the years, made difficult to sustain. Their storied precision and virtuosity are still intact, but under Tate they play with a zesty *esprit de corps* that hasn't been heard in many years. The strings have a new unanimity and warmth, and the solo winds are playing with such clearly defined individuality that they almost remind us of the old Royal Philharmonic during the best of the Beecham years.

That Tate is also one of the finest Mozart conductors of his generation can be heard in his admirable cycle of the late symphonies. The performances of the "Haffner" and 39th Symphonies contained on this handsome Angel album are consistently insightful, without ever seeming fussy or pointlessly unorthodox. Tate's basic approach to Mozart seems to have much in common with the classic one favored by Otto Klemperer: a combination of broad tempos and crisp rhythms that create an aura of lively spaciousness in which the details emerge in sharp relief while the music is given ample room to breathe. In short, a wonderful recording by a major new talent.

Symphony No. 36 in C Major, "Linz"; Symphony No. 38 in D Major, "Prague"

Vienna Philharmonic, Bernstein. Deutsche Grammophon 415962-1 [LP], *415962-2* [CD], 415962-4 [T].

Bernstein's vision of these two popular symphonies by Mozart has much in common with his recent recordings of Haydn's music. Shunning both the chamber dimensions and drier sound favored by younger conductors in recent years, Bernstein's Mozart remains a bracing anachronism. The interpretations are ripe and richly Romantic, characterized by luscious textures, extreme but always persuasive tempos, powerfully dramatic gestures, and forward thrust. The opening of the "Prague" Symphony has never sounded more vividly operatic—after all, it *was* written at the same time as *Don Giovanni*—nor has the "Linz" ever sounded quite so exhilarating or rhapsodic. In recent years, the Vienna Philharmonic has rarely played better for anyone. In fact, only the sense of electric excitement hints that these recordings were made during actual concert performances.

Symphony No. 40 in G minor, K. 550; Symphony No. 41 in C Major, K.551, "Jupiter"

Philharmonia Orchestra, Klemperer. Angel AE-34405 [LP], *CDC-47852* [CD], 4AE-34405 [T].

With their transcendentally serene and good-natured companion piece in E-flat, the G minor and "Jupiter" Symphonies form a trilogy that marks the absolute high-water mark of eighteenth century symphonic thought. In these great and mysterious works—why or for what occasion Mozart wrote them has never been known—the Classical symphony reached its final stage of perfection. After Mozart, there was literally no place left for the form to go other than through the

bold and convulsive experiments of Beethoven, which sig-
nalled the beginning of the Symphony's inevitable death.

Otto Klemperer's monumental performances from the
early 1960s stake a fair claim to being the greatest recordings
each of the last two symphonies have ever received. It is not
simply the breadth of the interpretations which make them so
extraordinary, for other conductors have adopted tempos in
the outer movements which are nearly as slow. It is the conductor's Olympian insight, whether in probing the depths of
despair in the Fortieth or the heights of the "Jupiter's" exulta-
tion, that gives the performances a sense of scale and scope
and makes them unique. While there have been more turbulent recordings of the G minor Symphony and more exciting readings of the "Jupiter," there are none that capture
more of the tragedy and triumph of Mozart's farewell to the
symphony than these.

Mussorgsky, Modest
(1839–1881)

Boris Godounov

Vedernikov, Arkhipova, Koroleva, Sokolov,
Shkolnikova, USSR Radio and Television Orchestra
and Chorus, Fedoseyev. Philips 412281-1 [LP],
412281-2 [CD], 412281-4 [T].

In any of its several versions—the two by the composer
himself, and the famous revision by a well-intentioned
friend— Mussorgsky's *Boris Godounov* is not only the most
powerful and original Russian opera ever written, but also
one of the most relentlessly gripping theatrical experiences of
the operatic stage. Since the days that Feodor Chaliapin's
famous, overwhelming interpretation made it a major box-
office attraction in the West, most listeners have come to know
Boris through Rimsky-Korsakov's brilliant arrangement.
While that wizard of the late-Romantic orchestra deserves the
lion's share of credit for the opera's subsequent popularity, in
the composer's 1872 revision, the opera emerges as a cruder,
rougher, and more starkly original piece.

For years we have needed an absolutely convincing recorded performance of Mussorgsky's final revision, and this
admirable Philips recording is probably as close as we are
likely to get in the foreseeable future. The greatest strengths in
the performance are precisely what they need to be: the

intensely dramatic conducting of Vladimir Fedoseyev and the broodingly powerful Boris of Alexander Vedernikov. Other basses—Chaliapin, Alexander Kipnis, Boris Christoff, George London— have brought finer voices and more refined musicality to the part, but in the big scenes, Vedernikov more than delivers the goods. The "Clock Scene" is especially unhinging in the way Vedernikov slowly begins losing his grip, and in Boris' Farewell and Death, he is perhaps more convincing (and genuinely moving) than any performer since George London. The supporting cast is generally excellent, though the Pretender is more wobbly and inadequate than usual. In the massed choral scenes—and in *Boris*, as in Puccini's *Turandot*, the chorus is at least as important as any of the opera's other major characters—the USSR Radio and Television Chorus sings magnificently, with that characteristic Russian combination of wild exuberance and ink-black despair.

Pictures at an Exhibition

New York Philharmonic, Bernstein. CBS MY-36726 [LP], *MYK-36726* [CD], MYT-36726 [T].

Richter, piano. CBS Odyssey Y-32223 [LP], YT-32223 [T].

Either in its original piano version, or in the familiar orchestration that Serge Koussevitzky commissioned from Maurice Ravel in 1925, *Pictures at an Exhibition* is among the most inventive and original works ever written by a Russian composer. Beginning with the pioneering recordings by Koussevitzky and Arturo Toscanini, the Ravel edition of the *Pictures* has probably received more great recordings than any other twentieth century orchestral score.

One of Leonard Bernstein's earliest recordings after assuming the directorship of the New York Philharmonic in 1958 also remains one of his best. It was also the most impressive stereo recording that CBS (then Columbia) had made up to that time. Bright and richly detailed, with a particularly solid and resonant bottom end, the physical sound remains astonishingly impressive in its compact disc transfer, and Bernstein's performance, after nearly thirty years, still remains the one to beat. In no recording do all of the individual pictures emerge with such character and clarity, from the heavy ponderousness of the Ox-cart section to the delicate humor of the "Ballet of the Chicks in Their Eggs." Yet it is with the final two portraits that Bernstein leaves the competition at the museum door. The "Hut on Fowls' Legs" is a wonder of demonic fury and intensity, and the performance concludes with the most thrilling and majestic "Great Gate of Kiev" ever put on records.

Among recordings of the original piano suite, none—not even Vladimir Horowitz' famous Carnegie Hall recording, or the gleaming new version by the recent Tchaikovsky Competition winner, Barry Douglas—can be mentioned in the same breath with Sviatoslav Richter's historic 1960 recording. In spite of the relatively drab and distracting recorded sound (it was taped at a recital in Sofia, Bulgaria, on a night when the entire city, apparently, was dying of terminal smoker's hack), there has never been a version of the *Pictures* to match it. It is not only the most electrifying performance that Mussorgsky's suite is ever likely to receive, but also one of the dozen greatest recordings that any modern pianist has made of *anything*.

Nielsen, Carl (1865–1931)

Symphony No. 3, Op. 27, "Sinfonia Espansiva"

Royal Danish Orchestra, Bernstein. CBS MP-39071 [LP], MT-39071 [T].

Gothenburg Symphony, Chung. Bis *CD-321* [CD].

For a time during the mid-1960s, it seemed to many that the late-Romantic Danish composer Carl Nielsen was belatedly going to join his Finnish contemporary Jean Sibelius as one of the last and most popular practitioners of modern symphonic form. While the Nielsen revival has obviously begun to lose momentum in recent years—there were once *two* complete recorded cycles of all six symphonies, today there are none—Nielsen's remains a charming, provocative, and utterly original voice, especially in this first of the three major symphonies upon which most of his future reputation will be based.

It's difficult to imagine a more inspired performance of the "Sinfonia Espansiva" than the one contained on this CBS recording that did so much to advance the Nielsen revival. Bernstein's enthusiasm for the work is as obvious as it is infectious. The Royal Danish Orchestra catches fire in what is probably the finest performance it has given in its collective memory, from their thunderous exuberance in the swaggering opening movement, to the way they assault the normally flaccid *Finale* as though it were an undiscovered masterwork of Johannes Brahms. For some reason, Bernstein's equally triumphant readings of the Fourth and Fifth Symphonies have been allowed to slip out of print. Perhaps a compact disc reissue of all three symphonies would help the composer and his music get back on track again.

The gifted Korean conductor Myung-Whun Chung leads an enjoyable performance for the small Swedish label Bis. While no match for the driven ferocity of the Bernstein, or quite as fine as his own spirited performance of the Nielsen Second Symphony, this is the best compact disc version of the "Sinfonia Espansiva" that has yet appeared.

Symphony No. 4, Op. 29, "Inextinguishable"

Berlin Philharmonic, Karajan. Deutsche Grammophon 2532029 [LP], *413313-2* [CD], 3302029 [T].

While certainly not an ideal recording of this great symphony—for that, the now-deleted versions by Bernstein and the New York Philharmonic, or Jean Martinon and the Chicago Symphony, both came breathlessly close—this surprisingly fine effort from Herbert von Karajan is the best on the market today. (Admittedly, there isn't much competition. Everyone had high hopes for the brilliant Esa-Pekka Salonen's recent CBS recording, which proved to be so senselessly willful that many, myself included, initially suspected that the CBS editors were indulging in a very expensive practical joke.)

Karajan, here, shows flashes of the Karajan he used to be in the 1950s and 1960s. Gone are most signs of the smooth-shod cynicism that has infected almost all of his recordings in recent years. In place of the arrogant sterility, he gives us what appears to be genuine emotion; instead of homogenized (albeit sophisticated) orchestral mush, actual *entrances* and more than a few rough edges. The Berlin Philharmonic, as always, plays with a breathtaking grandeur and precision. That this great ensemble has been wasted so remorselessly over the past two decades is one of the major musical tragedies of modern times.

Offenbach, Jacques
(1819–1880)

Gâité Parisienne (Ballet, arranged by Manuel Rosenthal)

Pittsburgh Symphony, Previn. Philips 411039-1 [LP],
411039-2 **[CD], 7337367 [T].**

Like *Les Sylphides* and *La boutique fantasque*, those ersatz ballets arranged from the piano music of Chopin and Rossini, *Gâité Parisienne*, Manuel Rosenthal's inspired adaptation of melodies from the Offenbach operettas still tends to raise eyebrows (and many noses) among the Serious Music Lover set. While as a smug and jaded musical curmudgeon I yield to no one in my arrogance or pickiness, I've never understood how it's *not* possible to like dazzling confection, especially in a performance as lively and charming as this.

The ballet has received numerous fine recordings, including one by Manuel Rosenthal himself, but none can approach the urbane wit and Gallic grace of this superb Philips recording by André Previn. All of the great set pieces— the *Barcarole* from *The Tales of Hoffman*, the "Can-Can" from *Orpheus in the Underworld*— are given the most lively and affectionate performances imaginable. In fact, the recording is a triumph of bracing rhythms, inventive phrasing, and tasteful sentimentality from beginning to end.

The Tales of Hoffman

Sutherland, Domingo, Tourangeau, Bacquier, Cuenod,
Chorus and Orchestra of Radio Suisse Romande,
Bonynge. London *417363-2* [CD].

Throughout his long and lucrative lifetime as the father
of the operetta—his astonishing output of tuneful, racy, frequently *naughty* musical satires earned him the sobriquet,
"The Mozart of the Boulevards"—Jacques Offenbach dreamed
of writing single, serious opera that would be the crowning
achievement of his career. With *The Tales of Hoffman*,
finished a few months before the composer's death (Offenbach
died while it was in rehearsal for the first production), the
diminutive German-born cellist turned light-hearted French
composer did precisely that. While overshadowed in popularity by Gounod's once-ubiquitous *Faust*, Offenbach's immortal adaptation of stories by E. T. A. Hoffman is the only
French opera that, in the quality and consistence of its inspiration, can be mentioned in the same breath with *Carmen* and
Debussy's *Pelléas et Mélisande*.

The stunning London recording from the early 1970s is
still the single most satisfying recorded performance that
Hoffman has ever received. Joan Sutherland, who undertakes
all four of the opera's heroines, has never been more impressive. While Antonia and Giulietta are a trifle lacking in
character, both are splendidly sung. As the doll Olympia,
however, she turns in a virtuoso *tour de force* of such staggering dimensions that even those of us who do not count ourselves among the most rabid Sutherland fans come away in a
state of slack-jawed amazement. As the opera's several villains,
Gabriel Bacquier is as suavely malevolent as any singer who
has ever undertaken the roles, but the gem of the production is
Placido Domingo's Hoffman. For nearly two memorable decades now, Domingo's achievements have rivalled those of the
greatest tenors of the century's Golden Age. Vocally and dramatically, this Hoffman is one of his most impressive creations, a performance which—if it isn't already—will one day
become the stuff of legend.

Amazingly enough, there are no LP versions of the opera listed in the current Schwann catalogue. Among available tapes, the old Schwarzkopf, Gedda, Cluytens recording for Angel (4X3X-3667) remains the most rewarding of all.

Orff, Carl (1895–1982)

Carmina Burana

**Armstrong, English, Allen, St. Clement Danes Boys'
Choir, London Symphony Chorus and Orchestra,
Previn. Angel AM-34770 [LP], *CDC-47411* [CD],
AAM-34770 [T].**

Like acne and an insatiable lust for Milk Duds, Carl
Orff's *Carmina Burana* is a juvenile affliction that most people eventually outgrow. As that torrent of unspeakably dull
and repetitious music clearly proved, Carl Orff was not only a
one work, but also a one *idea* composer. That none of his
subsequent pieces ever achieved a fraction of *Carmina Burana*'s popularity is hardly surprising. This astonishingly simple, musically primitive setting of some bawdy medieval lyrics
can be a dazzlingly effective experience the first couple of
times you hear it. It is only after repeated encounters that the
vulgarity and yawning vapidity of *Carmina Burana* really
begin to get on a person's nerves.

For those who have an incomprehensible affection for
this trash—and I must admit that *I* always have—André Previn's Angel recording is one of the finest ever made. To his
credit, Previn does nothing to cheapen the work further than
its composer already has, but instead constantly seeks out its

humor, limited subtlety, and frequently engaging wit. Which is not to say that the performance attempts to house-break *Carmina Burana*. For at the end, we are thoroughly convinced that this is music that a gland would write, if only it could.

Pachelbel, Johann
(1653–1706)

Kanon in D

Stuttgart Chamber Orchestra, Munchinger. London
411973-1 [LP], *411973-2* [CD], 411973-4 [T].

What violent emotions Pachelbel's sweet little Kanon continues to provoke! While it is now one of the most frequently recorded of all classical works, there are those of us who still can't quite understand what all the shouting is about. At best, Pachelbel was a third-rate baroque nonentity who occasionally rose to the level of the second-rate in some of his organ music. And while the Kanon was composed more than a century before Napoleon showed the world what *really* heavy ordnance could do, it still unquestionably qualifies as *large bore*.

If you really *must*, Karl Munchinger leads the Stuttgart Chamber Orchestra in a tender, yet admirably disciplined performance on London. The compact disc version is especially useful, in that you can program the Kanon to repeat again and again and thus save yourself untold thousands of dollars by putting off that frontal lobotomy you had planned.

Paganini, Niccolo
(1782–1840)

Caprices (24) for Unaccompanied Violin, Op. 1

Perlman, violin. Angel S-36860 [LP], *CDC-47171* [CD], 4XS-36860 [T].

Unlike his rather lumpy and charmless violin concertos, the Paganini Caprices are among the most intriguing works ever written for the violin by the man who was, by all accounts, its greatest master. Stories of Paganini's virtuosity are legion. For a week after a concert during which he played the whole of Beethoven's "Kreutzer" Sonata on a single string, he was the talk of Paris; when his chauffeur asked for a considerable raise since his master was becoming so famous, Paganini readily agreed, provided he be driven everywhere on a single wheel.

Musically and technically, the recordings made by Itzhak Perlman in the early 1970s have yet to be bettered. The playing is as sensitive as it is audacious, and for once even the most difficult of the individual pieces emerge with a color and freshness that suggest miniature tone poems instead of mere excuses for wanton virtuoso display.

Ponchielli, Amilcare
(1834–1886)

La Gioconda

Callas, Cossotto, Companeez, Ferraro, Cappuccilli,
Vinco, La Scala Chorus and Orchestra, Votto. Angel
CDCC-49518 [CD].

Caballé, Baltsa, Pavarotti, Milnes, Hodgson, London
Opera Chorus, National Philharmonic, Bartoletti.
London LDR-73005 [LP], *414349-2* [CD],
LDR5-73005 [T].

The next time you're at a party with people who really
think they know a lot about opera, challenge any one of them
to relate, in its simplest terms, the plot of *La Gioconda*. In
retrospect, it's almost impossible to fathom how the future
librettist of Verdi's *Otello* and *Falstaff* and the composer of
Mefistofele, Arrigo Boito, could have come up with such a
hopelessly confusing pile of gibberish, or how Amilcare
Ponchielli, a composer of limited abilities, could have fash-
ioned from it one of the most powerful and enduring works of
the Italian operatic stage. *La Gioconda* would have a decisive
influence on almost every Italian opera that followed it, including the later operas of Verdi and those of Ponchielli's most
celebrated pupil, Giacomo Puccini.

For more than three decades, the only *Gioconda* has
been that of Maria Callas. It is one of the most gripping of all

her recorded characterizations and one which inspires everyone around her—from the other principal singers to every
member of the chorus and orchestra—to give of his or her
absolute best. The recorded sound, from 1960, is surprisingly
lively and realistic in Angel's compact disc transfer.

The only real modern competition for this classic recording comes from the splendid London set which counts,
among its principal strengths, recorded sound of astonishing
clarity and presence, and one of the finest performances that
Luciano Pavarotti has given in years. The rest of the cast, other
than Caballé's rather stiff and unimaginative heroine, is generally excellent, and Bruno Bartoletti, like Antonino Votto on
the Angel set, conducts like a man possessed.

Poulenc, Francis
(1899–1963)

Concert champetre for Harpsichord; Concerto in G minor for Organ, Strings, and Timpani

Koopman, harpsichord; Alain, organ; Rotterdam Philharmonic, Conlon. Erato NUM-75210 [LP], *ECD-88141* [CD], MCE-75210 [T].

If ever a composer wrote music that bore an uncanny resemblance to the way he actually looked, that composer was undoubtedly the tall, gangly, always slightly off-kilter Francis Poulenc. There is a pervasive and goofy oddness in all the work that this deft, graceful, and fabulously original composer produced. Had he been just a little less peculiar he may have been as important a composer as Debussy; as it stands, he is responsible for some of the major French art songs of the twentieth century and is, perhaps, France's major modern composer of sacred music.

Two of Poulenc's most entertaining and individual works are given superb performances on this brilliant Erato recording. The magisterial Organ Concerto has never sounded more grand or imposing, and if the *Concert champetre*, written originally for Wanda Landowska, has had wittier performances on record, few can match the elegance and panache of this one. Unfortunately, the orchestra, led with great zest and individuality by James Conlon, badly overbalances Ton Koopman's extremely sophisticated performance of the solo part. This is obviously less a fault of the conductor than of Erato's usually meticulous engineers.

Gloria in G Major

Carteri, soprano; French National Radio Chorus and Orchestra, Pretre. Angel *CDC-47723* [CD], 4AE-34492 [T].

Composed only two years before his death, Poulenc's *Gloria* is one of the composer's most consistently inspired, touching, and exhilarating works. Not since Haydn had another composer set the *Laudaumus Te* quite as joyously, and the work's closing bars easily rank with the most divinely inspired moments composed in this century.

George Pretre's Angel recording was not only the first to be made of this great modern sacred work, but also to be done with the composer himself in attendance. Only Leonard Bernstein—in a CBS recording now available only as a CBS cassette—found the same immensely appealing combination of fun and devotion in the *Gloria*, although for the most part the Pretre interpretation is far more charming, and hence, far more French.

On LP, the *Gloria* is best served by Robert Shaw's recording for Telarc (DG-10077); a competent performance, but in light of his earlier, incandescent interpretation for RCA Victor, a somewhat disappointing one.

Praetorius, Michael
(1571–1621)

Terpsichore Dances

London Early Music Consort, Munrow. Angel
   AM-34728 [LP], *CDM-69024* [CD], 4AM-34728
   [T].

When the extravagantly gifted David Munrow died by his own hand a dozen years ago, the cause of early music lost one of its most devoted and appealing advocates. While he was as committed to the "authentic" performance of renaissance and medieval music as any musician of his generation, Munrow was also a great entertainer and a compelling performer, as this stupendous 1973 recording of music by Praetorius clearly shows.

Rarely have the famous *Terpsichore Dances* sounded more lively, lovely, or utterly infectious, and the lesser-known, but stunningly beautiful motets from *The Muses of Zion* here emerge as one of the most important vocal collections of the period.

If, like a highly respected critic and my some-time tennis partner is, you are usually tempted to dismiss renaissance dance fare as "Village Idiot Music," this wonderful monument to David Munrow's towering talent will make a believer out of almost anyone.

Prokofiev, Sergei
(1891–1953)

Piano Concerto No. 3 in C Major, Op. 26

Graffman, piano; Cleveland Orchestra, Szell. CBS MY-37806 [LP], MT-37806 [T].

Argerich, piano; Berlin Philharmonic, Abbado. Deutsche Grammophon 415062-2 [CD].

The most popular of Sergei Prokofiev's five piano concertos has received numerous first-rate recordings since the composer himself left his historic account of this profound, ebullient piece in the 1930s. Incidentally, that exhilarating performance with the London Symphony conducted by Piero Coppola (grandfather of the film director) can still be found on an audio cassette from the In Sync label (C-4148). The greatest modern performance of the Third Concerto can be found on a CBS recording that also includes equally gripping run-throughs of the audacious First Concerto and the Third Piano Sonata. This generously packed reissue includes some of the finest playing that Gary Graffman ever left in a recording studio, and is further cause for lament that his brilliant career was cut short by a neurological disorder. In both concertos, George Szell's accompaniment is spellbinding, and the late 1960s recorded sound is still more than adequate.

Among available compact discs, none is finer than the version made by the young Martha Argerich in 1968. While the performance is less brilliant and commanding than Graffman's, it has a perceptive and languorous beauty of its own, and coupled with one of the better Tchaikovsky Concertos to have emerged on compact disc, it represents a considerable bargain.

Concertos (2) for Violin and Orchestra

Mintz, violin; Chicago Symphony, Abbado. Deutsche Grammophon 410 524-1, *410524-2*, 410534-4 [T].

No two works will better explain Sergei Prokofiev's position as one of the most popular of all twentieth century composers than will these two magnificent violin concertos, written just before and immediately after his long, self-imposed exile from the recently created Soviet Union. While the youthful D Major Concerto is one of the freshest and most original works Prokofiev had written up to that time, the G minor Concerto is among the greatest modern works written for the instrument. Lyrical, dramatic, sardonic, and overflowing with an utterly distinctive melodic personality that makes all of Prokofiev's music so unique, the Second Concerto ranks with the finest of all the composer's mature works, which is to say with the finest music written since the turn of the century.

The Israeli violinist Schlomo Mintz is an ideal advocate of both of these wonderful works. His technique and temperament easily overcome all of the formidable challenges the music presents. The accompaniments provided by Claudio Abbado are as poised and passionate as one could hope for, and Deutsche Grammophon's recorded sound is something close to ideal.

Lt. Kijé Suite; The Love For Three Oranges Suite

**Dallas Symphony, Mata. RCA Victor ARC1-5168,
RCD1-5168, ARE1-5168 [T].**

This is a thoroughly satisfying coupling of two of Prokofiev's most justly popular scores. For most of the time the
Dallas Symphony sounds like one of America's major orchestras: they play with great color and finesse throughout the
Lt. Kijé music, and with a measure of wit and ferocity in the
Love for Three Oranges Suite that makes one wonder why
this charming and endlessly inventive opera isn't heard at
least as frequently as Verdi's *Aida* or Puccini's *La Bohème*.

For those who are interested in *Lt. Kijé* alone, the magic
of two performances from the 1960s has never been surpassed. George Szell's CBS recording (MY-38527, *MYK-
38527*, MT-38527) is teamed with that finest of all recorded
performances of Kodály's *Háry János Suite*, and Fritz Reiner's
dazzling RCA Victor recording (*5605-2-RC*, compact disc
only) accompanies that conductor's incomparable—though
alas, English language—version of Prokofiev's stirring cantata
from Sergei Eisenstein's 1938 film, *Alexander Nevsky*.

Peter and the Wolf

**Perlman, narrator; Israel Philharmonic, Mehta. Angel
DS-38190 [LP], *CDC-47067* [CD], 4DS-38190 [T].**

You have to be a pretty irretrievably crusty curmudgeon
not to respond to the warmth and wonder of Prokofiev's best-
known work. Like *Hänsel und Gretel*, *Peter and the Wolf*
transcends the traditional limits of a conventional "children's
work;" its simplicity can be grasped and loved by the tend-
erest of musical ears, while its immense wit and sophistication
can appeal to the most refined of musical tastes.

For years, the most delectable of all recordings of the

work featured a wonderfully sly narration (complete with some marvelously personal sound effects) by the late Michael Flanders, a performance which can still be found on a Seraphim cassette (4XG-60172). Since the recording will probably never appear on compact disc—and in fact, may disappear altogether at any moment—the best alternative for the foreseeable future is Zubin Mehta's fine Angel recording. While superbly played by members of the Israel Philharmonic, by far the best thing in the recording is the endearing narration by Itzhak Perlman, who somehow manages to transform Prokofiev's Grandfather into a Jewish Mother without doing significant disservice to either the spirit or the letter of the score. A sparkling performance of Saint-Saëns' *Carnival of the Animals* rounds out this extremely desirable release.

Symphony No. 1 in C Major, "Classical"; Symphony No. 7 in C-sharp minor, Op. 131; *Lt. Kijé Suite*

London Symphony, Previn. Angel AM-34711 [LP], *CDC-47855* [CD], 4AM-37411 [T].

This unusually generous Angel package conveniently brings together Sergei Prokofiev's "Classical" Symphony, that slyly elegant act of homage to the music of Haydn and Mozart, and the deceptively simple-sounding C-sharp minor Symphony, with which the ailing composer all but concluded his career. For two decades this has been one of the most thoroughly enjoyable of all Prokofiev recordings. Previn's interpretation of the familiar "Classical" Symphony is full of an appealing dash and freshness, and he makes one of the strongest cases ever for the Seventh Symphony, a very great, but still unfairly neglected work. One of the best modern performances of the *Lt. Kijé Suite* rounds out a recording that no Prokofiev-lover should be able to resist.

Symphony No. 5 in B-flat Major, Op. 100

Israel Philharmonic, Bernstein. CBS IM-35877 [LP],
MK-35877 [CD], MHT-35877 [T].

Since it first began to be known in the late 1940s, the
Fifth has remained the most popular, and is probably the
most important of the composer's seven symphonies. Like
the equally celebrated Fifth Symphony of Dmitri Shostakovich, it is the one large-scale symphonic work to emerge from
the Soviet Union that seems destined to occupy a permanent
place in the standard repertoire, and rightly so. For the Prokofiev Fifth, like the Shostakovich, is a big, powerful, intensely
dramatic, and unmistakably *Russian* composition, which will
probably continue to move and inspire audiences well into the
next century, and beyond.

While the Prokofiev Fifth has had some memorable recordings in the last thirty years (a brilliant London recording
by Jean Martinon, and a superlative Chicago Symphony version with André Previn have been inexplicably withdrawn),
this latest entry from Leonard Bernstein is easily the most
overwhelming recording that this popular work has yet received. Bernstein's earlier New York Philharmonic recording—which is still available on CBS—was controversial a
quarter century ago. Suffice it to say that Bernstein's interpretation has only grown more personal and powerful over the
years: tempos are all on the extreme side, as is the emotional
content of what can often be heard as a rather cool and
sardonic work. Bernstein builds some of the most tremendous
climaxes heard these days on commercial recordings. The
Scherzo whips by with a tremendous sense of urgency, and
the *Finale* contains some of the most exhilarating moments
that this conductor—which is to say *any* conductor—has ever
left in a commercial recording.

Puccini, Giacomo
(1858–1924)

La Bohème

De Los Angeles, Bjorling, Amara, Merrill, RCA Victor
Chorus and Orchestra, Beecham. Angel Seraphim
S-6099 [LP], *CDCB-47235* [CD], 4X2G-6099 [T].

This astonishing recording—certainly one of the greatest
commercial recordings ever made—was thrown together at
the last possible moment, and in fact was very nearly never
made at all. For more than thirty years it has remained the
standard recording of Giacomo Puccini's most popular opera
and will undoubtedly continue to remain so for as long as
recordings are made.

Along with a superlative cast (De Los Angeles and Bjorling are especially wonderful as the lovers), most of the real
magic of this most magical of all Puccini recordings comes
from the pit. Several volumes could be written about the
special insights, the beautifully shaped phrases, the aching
tenderness, and surging passion that Sir Thomas Beecham
finds in Puccini's score. No one has ever made the love music
bloom as tenderly or captured more of the high spirits or

bitter tragedy of the work than did Beecham on what was an impossibly tight recording schedule. Robert Merrill, the superb Marcello, once told me that Sir Thomas caused great consternation by insisting that the duet "O Mimi, tu piu non torni" be recorded again, even though time was running out and the first try had seemed to be a virtually perfect performance. Later, when the producer, who could hear no difference in the two versions, asked the conductor why he insisted on a second take, Beecham replied with characteristic glee, "Oh, because I simply *love* to hear those boys sing it!" That this very special recording *was* a labor of love from beginning to end is as obvious now as on the day it was first released.

Madama Butterfly

Tebaldi, Bergonzi, Cossotto, Sordello, Santa Cecilia Academy Chorus and Orchestra, Serafin. London 411634-1 [LP], *411634-2* [CD], 411634-4 [T].

That this radiant, heart-stopping opera was a fiasco at its world premiere in 1904 still seems impossible to most operalovers today. We forget that the audience at Milan's La Scala was not exactly anxious to embrace a love story between an occidental and a fifteen-year-old Japanese girl, and that the composer—as he later admitted—had made a serious miscalculation in the structure of his new work. What we now know as the Second and Third Acts of the opera were once a single, uncomfortably lengthy act that would have tested the patience of even the most ardent of the composer's admirers.

As one of the best-loved operas ever written, *Madama Butterfly* has had more than its fair share of memorable recordings, but none was ever more radiant than this classic 1958 version with the sumptuous Renata Tebaldi in the title role. Tebaldi's Cio-Cio-San is a marvel of dramatic evolution: from the innocent child of the opening scene to the towering, tragic heroine of the opera's final moments. The supporting cast, especially the beautifully-sung Pinkerton of Carlo Bergonzi and the vastly resourceful Suzuki of the young Fiorenza Cossotto, could not have been improved upon. Tulio Serafin's conducting has its usual admirable amalgam of sensitivity, understanding, and dramatic bite, and the original late-1950s acoustics have held up surprisingly well.

Tosca

Callas, Di Stefano, Gobbi, La Scala Chorus and Orchestra, De Sabata. Angel AV-34047 [LP], *CDCB-47174* [CD], 4AV-34047 [T].

If there was ever such a thing as a perfect opera recording, this is it. It features among other things, Maria Callas, the greatest Tosca of the modern era; the most elegantly sung of tenor Giuseppe di Stefano's heros; and a villain—the Baron Scarpia of Titto Gobbi—that will set your hair on edge. But what puts this *Tosca* on a nearly unapproachable level is the conducting of Victor De Sabata. While not as well known as his more famous near-contemporary, Arturo Toscanini, I think De Sabata was always the finer conductor. Like Toscanini, his dramatic sensibilities were very highly developed, yet unlike the Maestro, De Sabata had an immensely complex musical mind that not only probed the music with greater depth, but also allowed it sufficient space to breathe. His conducting throughout this inspired recording is nothing less than miraculous: from the soaringly beautiful support he lends to the love music, to that chillingly violent moment in the Second Act when the evil Baron finally "gets the point."

In short, this is a classic recording which no opera lover can afford to be without.

Turandot

Sutherland, Pavarotti, Caballé, Pears, Ghiaurov, John
Alldis Choir, London Philharmonic, Mehta. London
414274-1 [LP], *414274-2* [CD], 414274-4 [T].

The emergence of *Turandot* as an opera whose popularity has begun to challenge those of Puccini's other major works is a relatively recent phenomenon. For years, all that anyone ever knew about *Turandot* was the beautiful Third Act aria, "Nessun Dorma," and the fact that the opera remained unfinished at the time of the composer's death. For all of its obvious flaws and inconsistencies (the unfinished love duet would have undoubtedly been the crowning achievement of Puccini's career, and the problems with the hero's character would have unquestionably been ironed out had the composer been given time to revise the score), *Turandot* is a great opera—as daring, original, and phenomenally beautiful a work as Puccini would ever write.

When it was first released in the early 1970s, this now legendary London recording shocked the operatic world. What was Joan Sutherland, the reigning *bel canto* diva of her time, doing recording a role that she never had, and obviously never would, sing on stage? Whatever the reasons, the gamble paid off handsomely. As Puccini's icy princess, Sutherland gave one of her finest recorded performances. The interpretation is full of fury, dramatic intensity, and—in the final scene—a startling warmth and femininity that have never been this singer's strongest suits. Similarly, Luciano Pavarotti—who recorded the role of Calaf before he ever sang it on stage—is brilliant as the Unknown Prince. Unlike the Pavarotti of recent years, who seems to shout and croon his way through almost every performance, this is not only an interpretation by a great tenor in his prime, but also a sad reminder of what a vulgar sot this once-electrifying artist has allowed himself to become.

While I have never been Zubin Mehta's greatest fan, here he delivers one of the finest performances of his career. No detail in Puccini's astonishing orchestration is overlooked, while the conducting is as tenderly lyrical as it is compellingly dramatic. For those who have yet to make the acquaintance of what may well have become the composer's masterpiece, this is the *Turandot* for you.

Purcell, Henry (c. 1659–1695)

Dido and Aeneas

Norman, McLaughlin, Kern, Allen, Power, English
Chamber Orchestra and Chorus, Leppard. Philips
416299-1 [LP], *416299-2* [CD], 416299-4 [T].

More than any other recording of the last generation, it
is this new version of *Dido and Aeneas* that best demonstrates
why this incredible work by the thirty-year-old Henry Purcell
is the oldest of all operas which can still hold a place in the
standard repertoire today. Under Raymond Leppard's inspired direction, the work leaps to life in a way that it rarely
has on commercial recordings. Jessye Norman's Dido rivals
those of Kirsten Flagstad and Janet Baker in its depth and
intensity, and Thomas Allen is the most manly and heroic
Aeneas I can remember hearing. For those who usually find
this greatest of English operas too thin in its characterization,
or too slight in its development, this magnificent and luxuriant new version will probably change their minds.

Rachmaninoff, Sergei
(1873–1943)

Piano Concerto No. 2 in C minor, Op. 18

Richter, piano; Warsaw Philharmonic, Wislocki.
Deutsche Grammophon *415119-2* [CD].

Graffman, piano; New York Philharmonic, Bernstein.
CBS MY-36722 [LP], *MYK-36722* [CD],
MYT-36722 [T].

Although the composer himself—who was certainly one of the great pianists in history—left a series of famous, authoritative recordings of all his major works for piano and orchestra, no recording of his most popular concerto has ever generated more sheer wonder or excitement than Sviatoslav Richter's famous version from the mid-1960s. Interpretively, the performance is something of a madhouse: Tempos are invariably extreme—from the slowest of *adagios* to a breakneck clip in the final movement that will leave most listeners panting on the floor. Yet as extreme as the interpretation certainly is, it is also utterly convincing, thanks to the technique and temperament of the foremost pianist of our time.

For those who prefer an LP or cassette version of this high-cholesterol classic, Gary Graffman's version with Leonard Bernstein remains as polished as it is poetic, with one of the finest—in fact, my favorite—modern version of the *Rhapsody on a Theme of Paganini* as the extremely attractive filler.

Piano Concerto No. 3 in D minor, Op. 30

Horowitz, piano; New York Philharmonic, Ormandy.
RCA Victor CRL-1-2633 [LP]; *RCD1-2633* [CD],
CRK-1-2633 [T].

Some very reliable rumors insist that Rachmaninoff stopped playing his D minor Concerto in public shortly after he heard it performed for the first time by the young Vladimir Horowitz. And for the better part of fifty years, the Rachmaninoff D minor was a cornerstone in what was surely the tiniest concerto repertoire that any major pianist has ever possessed. While I have always felt about Horowitz much the same way I feel about his father-in-law, Arturo Toscanini, and his near contemporary, Jascha Heifetz; give the man his due: in this particular music, no pianist of the century has ever come close to him. Of course, for something close to the ultimate in hair-raising piano fireworks, the 1951 studio re-cording that Horowitz made with Fritz Reiner and the RCA Victor Orchestra (RCA AGM1-5262, AGK1-5262 [T]) sur-passes this 1978 live performance. But as a souvenir of the century's most phenomenal technician, this recording be-longs in almost every collection.

Isle of the Dead; Symphonic Dances

Amsterdam Concertgebouw Orchestra, Ashkenazy.
London 410124-1 [LP], *410124-2* [CD], 410124-4
[T].

While he is best known for his once-ubiquitous piano music, during his lifetime Sergei Rachmaninoff was equally celebrated as a composer of orchestral music and songs. The dark and richly atmospheric *The Isle of the Dead*, one of the most accomplished of all his compositions, and the four *Symphonic Dances*, his last major work, have never been served more brilliantly than in this recent London recording by Concertgebouw Orchestra, led by Vladimir Ashkenazy.

While the *Symphonic Dances* were actually composed for, and dedicated to Eugene Ormandy and the Philadelphia Orchestra—the last of their several recordings can still be found on CBS Odyssey Y-31246 or YT-31246 [T]— Ashkenazy's version is in every way more colorful, rhythmically vibrant, and intense. For those who are still persuaded that the heart of Rachmaninoff's output was the Prelude in C-sharp minor and the syrupy *Vocalise*, these wonderful performances of a pair of masterworks should come as an extremely pleasant surprise.

*P*reludes (23) for Piano

Ashkenazy, piano. London *414417-2* [CD], 421258-4 [T].

Incredibly enough, given their wealth of invention, emotional and musical variety, and fabulous melodic richness—like a Chopin melody, a Rachmaninoff tune can be maddeningly impossible to forget—there has only been one completely successful recording of all twenty-three of these miniature miracles, the London version by Vladimir Ashkenazy. The pianist is uncannily successful in drawing out the special character of each of the individual pieces, and in general the playing has a wonderful audacity mixed with a lyrical tenderness and engaging wit. While the Ashkenazy compact disc and tapes should be snapped up by anyone who is seriously interested in brilliant piano playing or the music itself, there is currently no complete version of the Preludes on LP that can be recommended with any enthusiasm.

Symphony No. 2 in E minor, Op. 27

London Symphony, Previn. Angel AM-34740 [LP],
CDC-47159 [CD], 4AM-34740 [T].

There are two ways of viewing Rachmaninoff's E minor Symphony: as a late-Romantic dinosaur completely out of step with its time, or as one of the lushest and loveliest symphonies ever written. Both views are equally correct. Compared to what was going on in music at the time it was written, Rachmaninoff's finest orchestral work was a complete anachronism, a throwback to an era when unabashed sentiment was not the cause for blushing embarrassment it would eventually become. Yet for all its old-fashioned sentimentality, the Symphony is also an utterly *genuine* expression of the essence of the Romantic spirit. For instance, if there is a Romantic symphony with a lovelier slow movement than the famous *Adagio* of this one, it has yet to be discovered.

André Previn has now recorded the Symphony three times, and to date, his second recording—made in 1973 with the London Symphony—is probably the best. It is an interpretation with great thrust and passion, but one in which the music's other qualities—its delicacy, exuberance, and darkness—are also given their full due. The London Symphony, as usual, plays the piece as though it were written for them, and the early-1970s recorded sound has held up extremely well.

Ravel, Maurice (1875–1937)

Alborada del Gracioso; Bolero; Rhapsodie espagnol; La Valse

> Montreal Symphony, Dutoit. London 410010-1 [LP],
> *410010-2* [CD], 410010-4 [T].

For anyone interested in four of Ravel's most popular show pieces in state-of-the-art performances and recorded sound, it would be difficult to improve upon one of Charles Dutoit's most impressive recordings to date. The playing of the Montreal Symphony is quite sensational: *La Valse* and *Rhapsodie espagnol*, in particular, are barn-burners; *Bolero* has rarely sounded so sensual *and* civilized, and the brief *Alborada del Gracioso* is an unmitigated delight. Superlatives fail me on this one. Buy it, and enjoy.

Daphnis et Chloé (complete ballet)

> Montreal Symphony, Dutoit. London LDR 71092 [LP],
> *400055-2* [CD], 400055-4 [T].

Ordinarily, London's withdrawal of Pierre Monteux' classic recording of the work widely regarded as Ravel's masterpiece could be viewed as an act of insensitivity bordering on criminal negligence. It was Pierre Monteux who introduced this spellbinding work to the world in 1911, and it was his recording, from the early days of the stereo era, which no one ever seriously expected to be surpassed. While for historical reasons alone, London never should have even considered withdrawing it from its catalogue, Charles Dutoit's stupendous recording takes at least some of the sting out of London's unforgivable crassness.

In many ways, the initial installment in Dutoit's already fabulous Ravel series is still the most impressive. The dynamic range of both the performance and the recording is phenomenal, from the most delicate whispers in Ravel's diaphanous orchestration to the thunderous outbursts in the orgiastic final scene. Dutoit's command of the idiom is as complete and masterly as any of the greatest Ravel conductors of the past, and the playing of his impeccable orchestra cannot be praised too extravagantly. Clearly, this is already one of the milestones of the early digital era.

Pavane for a Dead Princess; *Mother Goose*; *Le tombeau de Couperin*; *Valses nobles et sentimentales*

Montreal Symphony, Dutoit. London 410254-1 [LP], 410254-2 [CD], 410254-4 [T].

With the two brilliant recordings listed above, these stunning interpretations of four more popular works by Ravel all but conclude Charles Dutoit's triumphant Ravel cycle. Versions of the two piano concertos with Pascal Rogé, available only as a compact disc (London *410230-2*), are the only modern performances worthy of comparison with Alicia De Larrocha's hair-raising recording from the mid-1970s, yet another example of London's incredible insensitivity to both a classic recording and to the needs of its consumers.

As in the performances of *Daphnis et Chloé, Bolero, La Valse,* and the rest, Dutoit breathes an incredible freshness and vigor into these familiar works. For once, the famous *Pavane* does not come off as the cloying wad of sentimentality it can so often become, and the other works are given performances which are as refined as they are exciting. Rarely have the closing bars of the *Mother Goose* music sounded so imposing, or the fabulously difficult music which begins *Le tombeau de Couperin* been tossed off with such apparent ease. Again, London's engineers have provided Dutoit with demonstration-quality recorded sound, and again, the Montreal Symphony sounds like nothing less than one of the greatest orchestras in the world.

String Quartet in F Major

Melos Quartet of Stuttgart. Deutsche Grammophon
419750-2 [CD].

Budapest Quartet. CBS MP-38774 [LP], MT-38774
[T].

It's a great pity that RCA Victor has seen fit to withdraw the Guarneri Quartet's ravishing account of this cornerstone of modern French chamber music, and that Deutsche Grammophon has made the Melos Quartet's equally memorable version available only as a compact disc. (There are times when I'm more convinced than ever that the motto of the recording industry as a whole should be—yea verily, always has been—"Buyer, Be Damned.") Therefore, for music lovers armed with compact disc players, the Melos Quartet recording easily sweeps the field. The playing has both edge and elegance, and the interpretation projects equal amounts of romantic abandon and iron control.

While the old Budapest String Quartet recording dates from the final years of that immortal ensemble's long and memorable history, it is a performance which exudes tremendous personality and warmth, if not the last word in mechanical perfection. On balance, this would be my first choice for those who still believe in tapes and LPs, though an ideal offering—and don't hold your breath—would be a digitally remastered reissue, in all three formats, of the Guarneri recording from RCA.

Respighi, Ottorino
(1879–1936)

Fountains of Rome; Pines of Rome; Roman Festivals

**Philadelphia Orchestra, Muti. Angel DS-38219 [LP],
CDC-47316 [CD], 4DS-38219 [T].**

How unfortunate for this tremendously gifted composer that he was also a man with virtually no musical conscience or taste. (I have always thought that it was no accident that the word "Pig" can actually be found within his name.) A wizard of the modern orchestra and Italy's only significant non-operatic composer of the pre-War era, Ottorino Respighi is best remembered for that triptych of tone poems which celebrates the sights and sounds of his beloved Rome. Respighi's command of orchestration rivalled that of any composer who has ever lived, which is largely why these three pieces of unadulterated trash rank with the most popular orchestral showpieces of the twentieth century. (And like everyone else who has ever fallen under their vulgar spell, I love all three to distraction.)

While nothing will ever make me give up my cherished RCA Victor recording of the *Fountains* and *Pines* by Fritz Reiner and the Chicago Symphony (RCA ARP1-4579, *RCD1-5407*), the performances contained on Riccardo

Muti's Angel recording are very much in that same rarified league. In addition, he also gives us a spine-tingling run-through of the grisly *Roman Festivals*, my own nomination as the greatest single piece of musical schlock produced by anyone in the last hundred years. (The only other possible contender, Richard Addinsell's *The Warsaw Concerto*, was written for a movie and only accidentally went on to a macabre life of its own.) As in so many of their recent recordings, the actual playing of the Philadelphia Orchestra really must be heard to be believed. The last vestiges of Eugene Ormandy's "Philadelphia Sound" have all but been eradicated by his dynamic successor. And while Muti may not be the most consistently profound or interesting conductor performing today, he certainly deserves enormous credit for having revitalized a great American orchestra.

Rimsky-Korsakov, Nikolai (1844–1908)

Scheherazade

Chicago Symphony, Reiner. RCA Victor ARP1-4427 [LP], *RCD1-7018* [CD], AGK1-4427 [T].

It's difficult to think of another composer who better deserves the title of History's Greatest Minor Composer. Camille Saint-Saëns actually predicted that posterity would remember him that way, but he forgot about the work of this Russian near-Giant. An orchestrator and teacher of genius (his brilliant edition saved his friend Mussorgsky's *Boris Godounov* from oblivion, and his best-known pupil, of course, was Igor Stravinsky), Rimsky-Korsakov never quite grasped the greatness that always seemed to be just outside his reach. For moments, even for entire acts of dazzling operas like *Le Coq d'Or*, *Mlada*, or *The Snow Maiden*, you can hear him on the verge of actually *doing* it, and then, inevitably, the music draws back at the very last.

By that same token, *Scheherazade*, one of history's most colorful and beautifully made orchestral scores, is also in a sense one of its most heartbreaking. It is a work that never quite adds up to much more than the sum of its fabulous parts: an elegant, vivid, brilliant, clever, colorful piece, but never a great one.

Among the many memorable recordings that *Sche-*

herazade has enjoyed over the years, none has ever made it *seem* closer to being a great piece than the performance recorded in the late 1950s by Fritz Reiner and the Chicago Symphony. In spite of formidable competition from Sir Thomas Beecham (whose legendary interpretation recorded at about the same time and recently reissued on an Angel compact disc (*CDC-47717*) still remains the last word in individuality, charm, and staggeringly inventive solo display), Reiner's combination of near-perfect execution, finesse, and unadulterated sex, makes this—by a whisker—*the* performance of *Scheherazade* to own. While the original recorded sound has been dramatically improved in all three formats, it is most spectacular in the compact disc, which, as a bonus includes that most electrifying of all recordings of Debussy's *La Mer*.

Rodrigo, Joaquin
(1902–   )

Concierto de Aranjuez for Guitar and Orchestra

**Williams, guitar; English Chamber Orchestra,
Barenboim. CBS *MK-33208* [CD].**

**Angel Romero, guitar; London Symphony, Previn.
Angel AM-34716 [LP], *CDC-47693* [CD],
4AM-34716 [T].**

With the possible exception of the dippy Pachelbel
Kanon, Joaquin Rodrigo's *Concierto de Aranjuez* has become
the great "hit" classical piece of the last dozen years, and its
popularity is richly deserved. Written with the great Andrés
Segovia in mind, Rodrigo's *Concierto* is easily the finest such
work ever written for the instrument: a work which not only
exploits virtually all of the rather limited expressive possibilities of the guitar, but also provides us with one of the
most haunting of all musical evocations of the sights and
sounds of Spain.

To date, the great John Williams has recorded the *Concierto* no fewer than four times, and it is his version with
Daniel Barenboim and the English Chamber Orchestra that is
still the most completely satisfying recording the piece has
ever received. Technically, Williams is without equal among
living guitarists, and here, as in all of his recordings, he tosses
off the *Concierto*'s formidable difficulties as though they

didn't even exist. Yet unlike his other versions, there is a freshness and spontaneity in this performance that no other recording can begin to match. Thanks, no doubt, to Daniel Barenboim's rich and flexible accompaniment, Williams is allowed to phrase and emote with a freedom he has rarely shown on records before or since. Since this interpretation is currently available only on compact disc, the Angel Romero/André Previn recording for Angel would be my first choice among available LPs and tapes. Romero's playing is nearly as brilliant and refreshing as Williams', and instead of the Villa-Lobos Guitar Concerto which comes with the Williams recording, this one offers the more conventional (and desirable) coupling of Rodrigo's equally enchanting *Fantasia para un gentilhombre*.

Rossini, Gioacchino
(1792–1868)

The Barber of Seville

Callas, Alva, Gobbi, Philharmonia Chorus and
Orchestra, Galliera.
Angel AVB-34074 [LP], *CDCB-47634* [CD],
4AVB-34074 [T].

Despite some formidable competition from the beautifully sung and brilliantly recorded Philips version led with
high and obvious zest by Sir Neville Marriner (Philips
6769100, *411058-2*, 411058-4 [T]), this imperishable Angel
recording, for all its flaws, remains the most enchanting and
infectious recorded performance of the world's most popular
opera buffa. While the supporting cast is consistently excellent—especially the late and irreplaceable Titto Gobbi and the
exceptionally suave Almaviva of Luigi Alva—the star of the
show is clearly Maria Callas, who, in one of her rare comic
roles, proves that she was every bit as successful a comedienne
as she was a tragic heroine. Listen especially to the way she
teases the phrases in "Una voce poco fa," and you'll begin to
understand why we Callas cuckoos immediately salivate at the
mere mention of the woman's name. Although there are nig-
gling cuts throughout the performance and the recorded
sound is not up to today's standards, there is a sparkling,

good-natured sense of fun in this famous interpretation that will probably never be captured in a recording studio again.

Overtures

> Academy of St. Martin-in-the-Fields, Marriner. (Complete) Philips 6768064.
>
> Orpheus Chamber Orchestra. Deutsche Grammophon 415363-1 [LP], *415363-2* [CD], 415363-4 [T].
>
> Chicago Symphony, Reiner. RCA Victor AGL1-5210 [LP], APL1-5210 [T].

For anyone seriously interested in many of the most famous and scintillating orchestral miniatures ever written, Sir Neville Marriner's four-record Philips boxed set of all the surviving Rossini overtures is an irresistible investment. The performances of these familiar pieces are among the best on the market today (they have also been wisely gathered together on a compact disc, *412893-2*), and even the least interesting of the unfamiliar works are more than worth hearing. Besides, you never know when you might receive a request for the overture to *Demetrio e Polibio*, and wouldn't it be nice to be prepared?

Among the less ambitious collections, the most impressive of the newer recordings features the brilliant Orpheus Chamber Orchestra. Performing without a conductor, they turn in interpretations which are as crisp and loaded with personality as any that are currently available.

Finally, for some of the most stylish Rossini overture recordings ever made—including the most powerfully dramatic version of *William Tell*—Fritz Reiner's classic outing for RCA Victor remains irreplaceable. All we really need now is its triumphant appearance on compact disc.

Saint-Saëns, Camille
(1835–1921)

Carnival of the Animals

New York Philharmonic, Bernstein. CBS MY-37765
[LP], *MYK-37765* [CD], MT-37765 [T].

Ironically enough, it was for a work he refused to have
performed in public during his lifetime that the vastly prolific,
and once enormously popular Camille Saint-Saëns remains
best known today. While much of his tuneful, ingratiating,
always impeccably crafted music has apparently begun to lose
its grip on the modern imagination—rather incredibly, no
complete recording of his opera *Samson and Delilah* is presently available —the ageless *Carnival of the Animals* has never
gone begging for first-class recorded performances.

I have some very vivid memories of a Leonard Bernstein
Young Person's Concert in which it was first explained to me
that the cuckoo was represented by the clarinet, the swan by
the cello and so forth. I bought the Bernstein recording soon
afterwards (one of the first records in my collection that did
not have an erotic cover) and have cherished the performance
ever since. Bernstein brings an obvious and unmistakable
enthusiasm to both his narration and to the music. The soloists and the orchestra play with passion and devotion, and
the early 1960s recorded sound is still very serviceable. In its

most recent incarnation, the performance comes with an equally memorable—and when the horns get wound up, terrifically scary—interpretation of Prokofiev's *Peter and the Wolf*.

Symphony No. 3 in C minor, Op. 78, "Organ"

Hurford, organ; Montreal Symphony, Dutoit. London
    410201-2 [CD], 410201-4 [T].

Zamkochian, organ; Boston Symphony, Munch. RCA
    ARP1-4440 [LP], *5750-2* [CD].

The last and only one of the *five* symphonies that Saint-Saëns actually composed that is ever performed these days owes much of its current popularity to the recording industry. In the mid-1950s, when the record companies were casting about for "sonic spectaculars" to show off the revolutionary wonders of stereo, the "Organ" Symphony began to enjoy a new lease on life. Along with Paul Paray's wonderful Mercury recording with the Detroit Symphony, Charles Munch's classic Boston Symphony recording dominated the catalogues for decades. The recording had fire, a healthy measure ofal Munchian madness, stupendous playing from the orchestra, and recorded sound to raise the roof—which it still does in its compact disc reissue. In fact, the Munch recording remains the first choice among all available LP versions of this popular work, but only, I am sorry to say, because Charles Dutoit's astounding London recording is now available only on compact disc and cassette.

What makes the Dutoit such a great performance is as easy to hear as it is difficult to describe. In its simplest terms, this is the one recording of the "Organ" Symphony which actually makes the piece sound like what it most assuredly is *not*: a great work. The conductor captures most of the Symphony's color and dramatic gestures, but for once the gestures seem internal and natural, as opposed to the empty, bombastic postures that they probably are. In short, along with its freshness, intelligence, and subtlety, this is the only version of the "Organ" Symphony in my experience in which we seem to be hearing music of genuine grandeur instead of something which is merely grandiose.

Scarlatti, Domenico
(1685–1757)

Keyboard Sonatas

> Kirkpatrick, harpsichord. Deutsche Grammophon
> 2533072 [LP].

> Pinnock, harpsichord. Deutsche Grammophon
> *ARC-419632-2* [CD].

> Pinnock, harpsichord. CRD 1068, 4068 [T].

> Yepes, guitar. Deutsche Grammophon 413783-1 [LP],
> 413783-4 [T].

An exact contemporary of George Frideric Handel and Johann Sebastian Bach—1685 was one of the great vintage years in the history of music—Domenico Scarlatti was to the harpsichord what Chopin would later be to the piano: the first important composer to study the special characteristics of his chosen instrument and then write music specifically designed to show off its individual character and peculiar strengths. His output of keyboard music was as prodigious as it was inspired. In 1971, a facsimile edition of the complete music for keyboard was published in eighteen densely-packed volumes.

It's a great pity that only a single recording featuring the father of modern Scarlatti scholarship, the late Ralph Kirkpatrick, is now in print. His book *Scarlatti*, published in

1953, not only instantly became the standard work written about the composer, but also helped clear up the centuries-old muddling of the order of composition of Scarlatti's numerous works. Kirkpatrick's performances are predictably enthusiastic and sympathetic, as are those of Trevor Pinnock, whose several recordings for Deutsche Grammophon and CRD are also models of modern Baroque scholarship and musical sensitivity. For those who don't give a hang about authenticity, the wonderfully delicate and entrancing arrangements by the Spanish guitarist Narciso Yepes are almost impossible to resist. (I once knew someone who absolutely hated them, but he eventually became an ax-murderer or a politician, I can't remember which. In any event, none of his friends were terribly surprised.)

Schoenberg, Arnold

(1874–1951)

Gurrelieder

**Norman, Troyanos, McCracken, Klemperer,
Tanglewood Festival Chorus, Boston Symphony
Orchestra, Ozawa. Philips 6769038 [LP], *412511-2*
[CD].**

As much as I am tempted to ride this personal hobby-horse into the ground, I will resist making any emotional (and they would be thoroughly heartfelt) appeals on behalf of the music of Arnold Schoenberg, the most significant composer of the twentieth century, and probably the *best* composer since Johannes Brahms. The Schoenberg debate will continue to rage long after all of us are gone and forgotten. (Why is it that in writing of Schoenberg, one always, almost automatically, slips into such cheerful images and turns of phrase? Perhaps because this melancholy figure remains the most thoroughly misunderstood composer in history.) In fact, the great boogie-man of the early twentieth century *avant-garde*, the man whose experiments with atonality, serialism, and the twelve-tone technique "destroyed" music as we know it, was in fact the most conservative composer since Bach: an arch-Romantic who realized—correctly—that if Western music were to go on at all, it needed an entirely new language. (The five-hundred year old system of triadic tonality which had made such music possible had simply worn out.)

Gurrelieder, Schoenberg's magnificent orchestral song-cycle/oratorio is both the perfect introduction to the composer's early style and one of the last great masterpieces of Romantic music. If you are one of those people who turn up your nose at the mere mention of Schoenberg's name, *Gurrelieder* might just be the medicine to cure you of a most unfortunate ailment.

While this Philips recording is not the ideal *Gurrelieder*, it is for the most part a very good one. It is also the only one on the market today. The strongest elements in the performance are the Tove of Jessye Norman, the speaker of Werner Klemperer, the playing of the Boston Symphony, and the excitement that a live performance always generates. The late tenor James McCracken struggles heroically with one of the most difficult parts ever written, so his is not an especially comfortable or attractive performance, and the usually reliable Tatiana Troyanos is unexpectedly wobbly as the Wood Dove. Ozawa, as usual, leads an interpretation that scores very high marks for the beauties of its physical sound and the attention to detail, but which nevertheless tends to gloss over the more profound elements in the music. Still, in spite of its flaws, this recording belongs in every collection, especially since *Gurrelieder*s from Bernstein, Carlos Kleiber or Klaus Tennstedt are *not* on the horizon and probably shouldn't be expected any time soon.

Unfortunately, the performance is not currently being offered on cassette.

Moses and Aron

Mazura, Langridge, Bonney, Haugland, Chicago Symphony Chorus and Orchestra, Solti. London 414264-1 [LP], *414264-2* [CD], 414264-4 [T].

There will always be a special place in hell for the well-known foundation (name withheld to prevent all right-thinking people from sending them several letter bombs per day) that turned down Arnold Schoenberg's modest request for sufficient funds to complete his oratorio *Jacobsleiter* and one of the great unfinished works in musical history, *Moses und Aron*. (This same foundation, by the way, regularly doles out hefty grants to feckless boobs who, to quote my grandfather, if they had to take a trip on brains wouldn't have to pack a lunch.) Be that as it may, even without the music of its Third Act (the composer did complete the moving text), *Moses und Aron* easily ranks with the most intriguing and important of all twentieth century operas. Were it given performances like this one on a regular basis, it might become, if not another *La Bohème*, then at least a work that would be performed with something approaching the frequency it deserves.

Sir Georg Solti, in one of the finest recordings he has made since the completion of London's Vienna *Ring*, places both the opera and Schoenberg where they properly belong. It has often been suggested that Schoenberg only wanted to rewrite the music of Johannes Brahms for the twentieth century. The suggestion is ludicrous, of course, but it contains at least a grain of truth. For Schoenberg, even in the most advanced of his twelve-tone works, remained an arch-Romantic to the very end. Unlike the other fine recordings of *Moses und Aron* (by Pierre Boulez and Michael Gielen, both out of print), it is the Solti version which most clearly recognizes the romantic elements in this rich and moving opera and makes them work. Rarely, for instance, has the most famous moment in the score, "The Dance Around the Gold Calf," sounded more lurid—in fact the entire scene is a triumph of prurient interest, as the composer intended —and never have the difficult principal roles been more effortlessly or beautifully sung.

The Chicago Symphony, as always, is miraculous in its poise and execution, and the recorded sound is stunning in its warmth and detail. Be warned, *Moses und Aron* is no *Aida*; still, it is a very great work that will repay in abundance any investment of time and energy the listener is willing to make.

Pierrot Lunaire, Op. 21

DeGaetani, speaker; Contemporary Chamber
Ensemble, Weisberg. Nonesuch 71251 [LP].

With Stravinsky's *The Rite of Spring*, Schoenberg's *Pierrot Lunaire* is one of the two great watersheds of modern music; a piece of such staggering originality and inventiveness that it still seems as though it might have been written yesterday, instead of in 1912. One would think that a decent compact disc recording of this path-breaking classic would have appeared by now. Alas, one has not. Nor is it possible to recommend the single available cassette tape: the strangely limp and uncommitted performance by a group of fabulously gifted musicians (including Daniel Barenboim, Lynn Harrell, and Pinkas Zukerman) led by Pierre Boulez.

So much for the bad news. The good news is that this classic recording, with Jan DeGaetani and Arthur Weisberg's Contemporary Chamber Ensemble is still alive and well on Nonesuch and *still* the closest thing we have yet had to an ideal realization of *Pierrot Lunaire*. Ms. DeGaetani, who has made her formidable reputation by singing the most impossibly difficult contemporary music as if it had been written by Stephen Foster, weaves her way through Schoenberg's eerie, mysteriously beautiful *sprech-stimme* as though she were telling us stories from Mother Goose. (Which, after all, is not that far removed from what the *Pierrot* speaker is supposed to do.) The highest praise that can be lavished on the accompaniment she receives from Weisberg and company is that it is altogether worthy of this legendary modern performance. Now, Nonesuch, when can we expect the compact disc?

Verklärte Nacht

English Chamber Orchestra, Ashkenazy. London
410111-1 [LP], *410111-2* [CD], 410111-4 [T].

Santa Fe Chamber Music Ensemble. Nonesuch 79028
[LP], D4-79028. [T]

The early *Verklärte Nacht*, written by a largely self-taught twenty-six-year-old composer is one of the most amazing works in the history of nineteenth century music. (And like Brahms, the composer he admired most of all, the percentage of masterworks to lesser pieces in Schoenberg's output is extraordinarily high.) The lush sonorities, the wealth of ornamental detail, the advanced harmonic thinking, and the expressive confidence of the work completely belie the composer's youth and relative lack of experience. Had Schoenberg never written another note of music, he would still be remembered, for this piece alone, as one of the most fascinating voices of the entire late-Romantic era.

Among recordings of the orchestral version of *Verklärte Nacht*, the London version by the strings of the English Chamber Orchestra led by Vladimir Ashkenazy is enormously rich and atmospheric. The playing has all the expansiveness and freedom that characterizes most of this conductor's recent work and a clarity and discipline that continually remind us of *Verklärte Nacht*'s inception as a string sextet.

Among recordings of the piece's original version, the Nonesuch rendition recorded at a Santa Fe Chamber Music Festival remains unapproached. In fact, the only significant drawback in this otherwise virtually perfect recording (which is coupled with a blazing account of a late Schoenberg masterpiece, the great String Trio), is that it has yet to be issued on compact disc.

Schubert, Franz (1797–1828)

Impromptus (8) for Piano

Perahia, piano. CBS IM-37291 [LP], *MK-37291* [CD].

With Mozart and Mendelssohn, Franz Schubert was one of the authentic miracles of Western art. At sixteen, he composed the first great German *lied*, "Gretchen am Spinnrade," and in the remaining fifteen years of his tragically brief life he became not only the undisputed master of German art song (he wrote more than seven hundred), but also the most important composer of symphonies, chamber music, and piano sonatas after his hero and idol, Beethoven. Though the two men lived in Vienna for years, the almost pathologically modest and self-effacing Schubert never screwed up the courage to meet the older man. He did serve as a pallbearer at Beethoven's funeral in 1827, which took place a scant twenty months before his own. No other composer, including Mozart, had a greater or more facile gift for melody, and none—even the indefatigable giants of the baroque era—was more prolific.

The two sets of Impromptus are among the most charming and characteristic of Schubert's piano works, and all have been served handsomely on records since the 78 era. On the basis of his CBS recording, Murray Perahia must be considered one of the great Schubert interpreters in the world today. The playing has a light, direct openness which is genuinely refreshing, but it also has plenty of *schwung* and sinew whenever the music demands. In fact, these popular works have probably not been in better hands since the days of Arthur Schnabel and Edwin Fischer. Since no cassette of Perahia's performances is available, the immensely individual (and often whimsical) tape by Daniel Barenboim from Deutsche Grammophon (415849-4) will fill the gap quite nicely.

Octet in F Major for Strings and Winds, D. 803

Boston Symphony Chamber Players. Nonesuch 79046 [LP], *79046-2* [CD], 79046-4 [T].

Given the fact that it contains nearly an hour's worth of some of the most sublimely charming music that Franz Schubert (or anyone else, for that matter) ever composed, it boggles the mind that there is only *one* recording of the great Octet currently listed in the Schwann Catalogue. Fortunately, that recording is a very good one. While perhaps not equal to that classic—and temporarily withdrawn—English performance by the London's Melos Ensemble for Angel, the Boston Symphony Chamber Players give a bright, sparkling interpretation of this wonderful work. If the performance could be faulted for anything, it would be for a certain lack of ease and graciousness. The recorded sound is up to Nonesuch's usual high standards, and until Angel returns the Melos version to circulation, this fine recording can more than hold the fort.

String Quartet No. 13 in A minor, D. 804; String Quartet No. 14 in D minor, D. 810, "Death and the Maiden"

Alban Berg Quartet. Angel DS-38233 [LP],
CDC-47333 [CD], 4DS-38233 [T].

String Quartet No. 15 in G Major, D. 887.

Alban Berg Quartet. Angel AM-34713 [LP],
CDC-49082 [CD], 4AM-34713 [T].

As in their recordings of the Beethoven Quartets, Vienna's Alban Berg Quartet is all but impossible to better in these performances of the last great quartets Schubert would compose. The ensemble's almost obscenely beautiful physical sound has never been captured to more thrilling effect (the hushed yet paradoxically full-bodied *pianissimos* of which they are capable continually remind me of the high notes that only Leontyne Price in her prime could pop out with such bewitching ease), but as always in their recordings, the Bergs offer us considerably more than a collection of pretty sounds. The "Death and the Maiden" Quartet—so called because one of its movements is a set of variations on Schubert's song of that name—has rarely sounded this dark and disturbing (there are, of course, ample doses of light and life as well), and the great G Major Quartet explodes with a dramatic intensity that no other recording can match. The sound that Angel's engineers have supplied is as opulent as the performances they capture. For Schubert-lovers, or simply anyone interested in three of the greatest string quartets written after those of Beethoven, these are absolute musts.

Quintet in A Major for Piano and Strings, D. 667, "Trout"

Richter, piano; Hörtnagel, double bass; Borodin Quartet. Angel *CDC-47009* [CD].

Curzon, piano; Vienna Octet. London 41019 [LP], 4-41019 [T].

Richter's recording of one of Schubert's best-loved chamber works is among the most impressive this consummate pianist of his generation has made. His authority, poetry, and complete understanding of the music are obvious from first bar to last in this exultant performance. The amazing Borodin Quartet proves they are completely at home in the music of their friend Dmitri Shostakovich. The playing has grace, point, and enormous individuality, and with the resonant contribution of Georg Hörtnagel, this should remain the "Trout" Quintet to dominate the catalogue for the next twenty years.

For those without compact disc players—and why the sudden, insensitive rush to completely ignore the needs of those who prefer to stay with their long-playing records and cassettes?—the wonderful London recording from the 1960s features the mercurial Sir Clifford Curzon at something close to the top of his electrifying form, coupled with some warm and sensitive support from the always engaging Vienna Octet.

Quintet in C Major for Strings, D. 956

Ma, cello; Cleveland String Quartet. CBS IM-39134 [LP], *MK-39134* [CD], IMT-39134 [T].

From works like the sublime and serene C Major Quintet, it would be impossible to deduce that the last eighteen months of Franz Schubert's life were an inexpressible nightmare. Dying of tertiary neurosyphilis, the composer was nonetheless able to churn out a body of work containing such unearthly beauty and purity that the only thing similar was that equally astonishing *annis mirabilis* of the English poet, John Keats.

While the great C Major Cello Quintet has had many distinguished recordings over the years—beginning with an unforgettable account by the old Hollywood Quartet dating from the mid-1950s—no recorded performance has been more sensitive or moving than this recent CBS release by cellist Yo-Yo Ma and the brilliant Cleveland String Quartet. One of the most impassioned and committed of all the Quintet's recent recordings, this is also one of the most polished and meticulous. The attentive and generous contribution made by the "fifth wheel" of the performance offers further evidence that Yo-Yo Ma is the most breathtakingly complete cellist of his generation, and with good playback equipment the amazingly lifelike recorded sound will almost persuade you that the players are in your living room.

*P*iano Sonata in C minor, D. 958; Piano Sonata in A Major, D. 959; Piano Sonata in B-flat Major, D. 960

Pollini, piano. Deutsche Grammophon 419229-1 [LP], *419229-2* [CD], 419229-4 [T].

While Schubert produced some twenty piano sonatas over the course of his career, he was never really comfortable with the form. It was only with the last three sonatas, written during the final year of his life, that Schubert, the incomparable miniaturist of the *Impromptus* and *Moments musicaux*, produced a trio of large-scale piano works whose depth and quality rival any that his admired Beethoven ever wrote. Not since Arthur Schnabel—who once said, "I play Beethoven to make my living; Schubert I play for love"—have these works had a more probing or poetic interpreter than Maurizio Pollini. If other performances of the C minor sonata have unleashed a more torrential strength, Pollini stands virtually alone in evoking the bitter tragedy of the A Major and the heroic grandeur of the Sonata in B-flat. While all of the interpretations are full of special insights (his detractors would call them "mannerisms") that have made Pollini the most deeply personal keyboard artist of his generation, the occasional eccentricities are far outweighed by the extraordinary depth and beauty of this set.

Songs

It is virtually impossible to offer any coherent recommendation of Schubert song recordings, not simply because there are so many of them, but also because so many of the best keep slipping in and out of print in a confusing variety of formats, and even labels. For example, at this writing, only one late recording by Hermann Prey—exclusive of his most recent version of the song cycle *Winterreise*—is listed as being available domestically (Denon *CO-1518*), a situation even the record companies can't be stupid enough to leave uncorrected for long, since with only two possible exceptions, the man is the greatest living interpreter of Schubert *Lieder* and has been so for more than twenty years.

By that same token, most of the wonderful Dutch soprano Elly Ameling's Philips recordings have seemingly gone into temporary hiatus, but will undoubtedly resurface on compact discs. In fact, two already have (Philips *410037-2* and *416294-2*). As with any of Hermann Prey's Schubert recordings, Ameling's should be snatched up for the gems they are. Record and tape collectors, alas, won't have much to snatch at except from the small label Etcetera (ETC-1009, KTC-1009, XTC-1009), since Philips has apparently joined the growing ranks of recording companies who have begun telling tape and record collectors what they can do with themselves, their hard-earned money, and their aging analogue equipment.

On the even more complicated subject of Dietrich Fischer-Dieskau, the problem has reached nightmarish proportions. As far as I am able to gather, Angel, which has most of the best recordings this invaluable singer ever made, has withdrawn them all: from the early collections of individual songs, when the voice was at its peaches-and-cream best, to those finest modern versions of the cycles *Die schöne Mullerin* and *Winterreise*. While there are abundant recordings available from Deutsche Grammophon, Philips, and Orfeo, these are generally less satisfactory, since the older "The Fish" got, the more arch, and finally unbearable, he became.

The moral of the story: wait to see what Philips does with its Prey and Ameling recordings, and Angel with its Fischer-Dieskaus. If we don't get some action out of the blockheads by the first of the year, write your congressman, gripe at your record store owner, or simply join me in boycotting the bastards.

Symphony No 8 in B minor, D. 759, "Unfinished"

Columbia Symphony, Walter. CBS *MK-42048* [CD], CBS Odyssey YT-30314 [T].

Vienna Philharmonic, C. Kleiber. Deutsche Grammophon 2531124 [LP], *415601-2* [CD].

The most surprising thing in Bruno Walter's famous recording of the best-loved unfinished *anything* in Western art (unless, of course, you count Chaucer's *Canterbury Tales*), is the searing intensity the old man unleashes in the powerful opening movement. There are those who insist that in the urgency of its drama and breadth of its conception, the first movement of the "Unfinished" Symphony equals anything in Beethoven, and this is one of those performances which goes a long way to making that case. Walter's ferocious, and not always perfectly controlled explosion is one of the most exciting moments of the early stereo era, and with a second movement which casts a spell of such other-worldly purity and beatific peace, this is still—by a wide margin—*the* "Unfinished" to own.

On LP, the best alternative is Carlos Kleiber's moving yet energetic performance for Deutsche Grammophon. He is neither as exciting as Walter in the first movement, nor as heartbreaking in the second, but among the ever-dwindling crop of available LPs, this one clearly sweeps the field.

Symphony No. 9 in C Major, D. 944, "The Great C Major"

Berlin Philharmonic, Furtwängler. Deutsche Grammophon *41560-2* [CD].

Boston Symphony, Davis. Philips 9500890 [LP], 7300890 [T].

Schubert's final completed symphony can be a very problematic work. Since the "Great" of the sobriquet refers as much to its massive length as to the divinity of its melodic inspiration, the C Major Symphony can—and often has—degenerated into nothing more than a collection of Sunday school tunes. Wilhelm Furtwängler's eternal recording from the early 1950s is the one version of the piece that makes it seem as structurally sound and dramatically inevitable as the Beethoven Ninth. The performance is a triumph of Furtwänglerian brinkmanship at its most magical. The unwritten yet electrifying *accelerando* that leads out of the Introduction to the first movement's principal theme, the spring in the

Scherzo's rhythm, and the headlong forward thrust of the *Finale* make this one of the most exciting orchestral recordings ever made.

Among more recent recordings by mortal men, the one led by Sir Colin Davis on Philips is very fine. The playing of the Boston Symphony is above reproach, as is the solid, and at times exhilarating interpretation, and the superlative recorded sound.

Schumann, Robert
(1810–1856)

Concerto in A minor for Piano and Orchestra, Op. 54

Richter, piano; Monte Carlo Opera Orchestra, Matacic. Angel *CDC-47194* [CD], 4AM-34702 [T].

Janis, piano; Chicago Symphony, Reiner. RCA ARP1-4688 [LP].

With Edvard Grieg's A minor Concerto, a work with which it is almost invariably paired on recordings, the Schumann Piano Concerto represents something close to the finest such work the Romantic era produced. Moody, sensual, and heroic, it was also one of Schumann's greatest achievements with music cast on a larger scale. Like his admired Chopin, Schumann is still accused of being a miniaturist who was completely incapable of sustaining extended forms; works like the Piano Concerto and the four symphonies triumphantly lay *that* nonsense to rest.

As in their version of the Grieg Concerto that accompanies this classic recording, Sviatoslav Richter and Lovro von Matacic serve up one of the most hair-raising performances any concerto has received in fifty years. Their tampering with the *letter* of the score might not be to everyone's taste, but no other recording you are likely to hear captures quite as much of the brash audacity of Schumann's spirit. Richter alternately sighs and thunders his way through the music, while Matacic conducts with such reckless abandon that you wish the two had worked together a few dozen more times.

While no available LP can match the fury and ferocity of this performance, the wonderful RCA Victor recording which mixes the fire of the youthful Byron Janis with the meticulous ice of Fritz Reiner is a very strong alternative.

Kinderscenen, Op. 15

Moravec, piano. Nonesuch 79063 [LP], 79063-4 [T].

Argerich, piano. Deutsche Grammophon *410653-2* [CD].

As a performance of Schumann's greatly beloved suite of childhood recollections, the recording of *Kinderscenen* by Ivan Moravec is probably the most beautiful ever made. Its wide-eyed innocence is matched only by its technical perfection, and it is one of several recordings making the convincing case that as a tonal colorist, Moravec is the late twentieth century equivalent of the legendary Walter Gieseking. Listen, especially, to the utterly unaffected yet gently devastating performance of the famous "Traumerei," or to the ambling miracle he makes of the celebrated opening bars of the piece, which have been pressed into service in recent films from *My Brilliant Career* to *Sophie's Choice*.

On compact disc, Martha Argerich's Deutsche Grammophon recording is a very fine one: less sensitive than Moravec's, but no less brilliantly played. As a bonus, she gives us one of the most exciting versions of *Kreisleriana* currently available.

Symphonies (4)

Amsterdam Concertgebouw Orchestra, Haitink.
Philips *416126-2* [CD], 412852-4 [T].

While there have been performances of the individual symphonies which have more flair and color—George Szell's CBS recording of the "Spring" and Fourth Symphonies is especially riveting (CBS MY-38468, *MYK-38468*, MYT-38468 [T]), and Carlo Maria Giulini's Los Angeles version of the "Rhenish" (Deutsche Grammophon *400062-2*) is unique in its poetry and adult passion—the most consistently satisfying set of Robert Schumann's four great symphonies is the one led by Bernard Haitink. The interpretations are utterly free of exaggeration: tempos are judicious, textures are beautifully controlled and balanced, and throughout all of these carefully judged, meticulously executed performances, there is a sense of inevitability and rightness which few modern recordings can equal. Compared to some of the more strong-willed recordings on the market—those by Levine, Bernstein, and Furtwängler, together with those listed above—Haitink, at first, might seem a trifle colorless and bland. However, with repeated exposure his maturity and enormous dignity, together with the fabulous playing of the orchestra, more than carries the day.

Among the currently available LP sets, the impassioned, if frequently wayward interpretations by James Levine and the Philadelphia Orchestra (RCA ARL3-3907) are clearly the ones to own.

Shostakovich, Dmitri
(1906–1975)

String Quartets (15)

Borodin String Quartet. Angel *CDC-49266-70* [CD].

If there was ever the slightest question that the fifteen string quartets of Dmitri Shostakovich rank not only with the major chamber works of the twentieth century, but also with the most significant works in the form since Beethoven, this triumphant new recorded cycle by the Borodin String Quartet should lay all remaining doubts to rest. Begun in 1935, when the composer already had four symphonies to his credit, the quartets eventually became—as they had for Beethoven before him—the vehicle for expressing the most private of all his thoughts and emotions. (Nevertheless, Shostakovich vigorously discouraged any suggestion that the symphonies were the public statements of the "official" Shostakovich, and that the quartets were the ruminations of the introverted, painfully shy man within. However, given that some of the early quartets are genuinely symphonic in their structure and expression, and some of the later symphonies are almost chamberlike in their size and proportions, the over-simplified generalization seems to fit.)

For a time, a superb series of all fifteen quartets in performances by England's Fitzwilliam Quartet was available domestically on Oiseau-Lyre. As fine as those interpretations certainly were, they have now been superceded by this incredible, and probably historic version by the Borodin Quartet. Having studied with the composer extensively (they were his favorite chamber ensemble after the celebrated Beethoven Quartet, which gave most of these quartets their world premieres), the Borodins bring an incomparable authority and understanding to the music that no other ensemble can begin to rival. They also possess one of the most individual physical sounds in the musical world today: a sound which is at once rich and sparse, pointed and flexible, from a collection of clearly defined individuals who work as a completely unified, indissoluble whole.

With the exception of the autobiographical Eighth Quartet—with its programmatic allusions to the Second World War and quotations from many of the composer's previous works—none of these extraordinary pieces has yet to enter the standard chamber repertoire, nor are they likely to do so any time soon. Still, they represent as individual and uncompromising a body of work as has been produced so far in this century: from the formal complexity of the early works to the wrenching, often lugubrious death throes of the final works in the series. The Quartet No. 15, for instance, is a series of six unrelentingly gloomy *adagios*, all cast in the key of E-flat minor. In short, while this is certainly not a series of recordings that will appeal to admirers of the *1812 Overture* and *Victory at Sea*, it represents one of the most daring and significant recording projects of the last decade. At present there seem to be no plans to release these amazing performances on LP or cassette, which means we will have to content ourselves with one of the first authentic milestones in the brief history of the compact disc.

Symphony No. 1, Op. 10

New York Philharmonic, Bernstein. CBS MK-38750 [LP], MT-38750 [T].

London Philharmonic, Haitink. London 414667-2 [CD].

There is a case to be made that Dmitri Shostakovich never wrote a more audaciously original work than this youthful masterpiece, composed as a graduation exercise from the Leningrad Conservatory when he was only nineteen. In it, many of the Shostakovich hallmarks—the sardonic humor, the grand gestures, the often brilliantly eccentric orchestration—are clearly in evidence, together with a freshness and almost palpable joy in the act of composition that none of his fourteen subsequent symphonies would ever really recapture. (Within several years of its premiere, the Symphony had made Shostakovich a world-famous figure, and hence, from the mid-1920s onward, a man that Soviet officialdom would try to keep on an increasingly tighter leash.)

In spite of its dry and slightly antiquated sound, Leonard Bernstein's recording from the early 1970s remains the most exciting and provocative performance of the Symphony that is currently available. The conductor loses no opportunity to milk the piece for the last drop of its color, wit, and drama; in fact, the interpretation has an abiding mixture of sadness and sarcasm that has never been captured in the recording studio before or since. On a somewhat more understated level, Bernard Haitink's excellent London recording is easily the first choice among all versions on compact disc. While less immediate and personal than the Bernstein recording, it is nevertheless a powerful, deeply committed reading, and one which is exceptionally well played and recorded.

Symphony No. 5, Op. 57

**New York Philharmonic, Bernstein. CBS MY-37218
[LP], *MYK-37218* [CD], MYT-37218 [T].**

Not to be confused with their second recording of perhaps the most famous twentieth century Russian symphony—a performance taped on tour in Tokyo in 1979—this is the celebrated recording that Bernstein and the Philharmonic made two decades earlier, after returning from a highly publicized tour of the Soviet Union. The reasons why this remains the most satisfying of all recordings of the Shostakovich Fifth—a work that Bernstein's mentor, Serge Koussevitzky, found as indestructible and universal as the Fifth Symphony of Beethoven—are as clear today as they were when the recording was first released a quarter of a century ago.

The success of Bernstein's interpretation rests on the fact that he refuses to view the Symphony as an ironic or paradoxical work, but rather as one which marks the culmination of the nineteenth century Russian symphonic tradition. Which is not to say, exactly, that he treats the work as though it might have been written by a harmonically advanced Tchaikovsky, but that *does* seem to be the overall impression he wants the Symphony to make. From the crushing opening statement of the principal theme, through the unusually expansive (and expressive) *Adagio*, through the giddy, helter-skelter *Finale*, this is a Shostakovich Fifth which is as direct, vibrant, and open-hearted as any large scale orchestral work that any Russian ever composed.

And if, in light of some of the more recent performances of the work, Bernstein's view might seem a bit *too* Romantic and literal, it should be remembered that the composer often said that Bernstein was his favorite American interpreter. The New York Philharmonic plays as well as they ever have in their history, and the recorded sound—especially in the compact disc version—barely shows its age.

Symphony No. 8, Op. 65

Amsterdam Concertgebouw Orchestra, Haitink.
London *411616-2* [CD].

Completed only two years after the windy and prolix "Leningrad" Symphony, the Shostakovich Eighth, with the single possible exception of the Tenth, is undoubtedly the masterpiece among the composer's mature orchestral works. Beginning with one of the greatest symphonic *adagios* written after Mahler, the Eighth is a dark, sprawling, grotesque, and enervating work, a combination of a stark outcry against the terrors of the Second World War and the soundtrack for some unimaginable Hollywood horror movie that, fortunately for everyone, was never made. The reactions this great and controversial work continue to provoke are perhaps more extreme than those caused by all of Shostakovich's other works put together: Koussevitzky considered it the greatest orchestral work written in this century; Stalin—as well as other infinitely more civilized listeners—considered it unpleasant, irredeemable trash.

In one of the finest performances from his admirable Shostakovich cycle, Bernard Haitink makes a strikingly strong case for the work. (A brilliant Angel recording, by André Previn, has shamefully been allowed to fall out of print.) As always, Haitink is more than content to let this powerful, often overwhelming music speak for itself. Climaxes and textures, though perfectly judged, are never pushed or overdone, and while the more grisly elements are given their full due, they are never needlessly emphasized. At the conclusion of the performance—the acid test of any interpretation of the Shostakovich Eighth—you do feel very much as though you'd been run over by a freight train, which was *precisely* the effect the composer intended.

Sadly, not *one* performance of this great and courageous work is available as an LP or cassette tape.

Symphony No. 10 in E minor, Op. 93

London Philharmonic, Haitink. London 7061 [LP].

Philharmonia Orchestra, Rattle. Angel *CDC-47350*
[CD].

If we are to believe Shostakovich in his posthumously published *Testimony*, the Tenth Symphony was the composer's rueful, bitter, sardonic refections on the Stalin years. In fact, the composer even went so far as to tell us that the diabolical *Scherzo* of the work was a portrait of that murderous psychopath himself. Whatever the immediate source of the Tenth Symphony's inspiration, it is one of the greatest symphonies of the twentieth century and one of the most compelling works a Russian composer has ever produced.

In the late 1960s, Herbert von Karajan, in one of his last palatable recordings left a staggeringly brilliant account of the Tenth, which has since been superceded by one of his typical smooth-shod monstrosities that is to be avoided at all costs. Until Bernard Haitink's sober, sobering, yet ultimately triumphant London recording makes its debut on compact disc, Simon Rattle's more recent version with the Philharmonia Orchestra is easily the performance to own. As usual, the depth and maturity of the interpretation completely belies this gifted young musician's years. The playing of the Philharmonia Orchestra is exemplary, as is Angel's recorded sound.

Sibelius, Jean (1865–1957)

Concerto in D minor for Violin and Orchestra, Op. 47

Perlman, violin; Pittsburgh Symphony, Previn. Angel AM-34769 [LP], *CDC-47167* [CD], 4AM-34769 [T].

In many respects, Jean Sibelius remains the most mysterious composer of modern times. A national hero in his own country while still quite a young man, and a composer who, during his lifetime enjoyed as much critical and popular adulation as any composer who has ever lived, Sibelius simply closed up his musical shop in the mid-1920s, writing nothing of significance for the next thirty years. (Rumors of a completed Eighth Symphony circulated for more than three decades, although no such work was found in his papers at the time of his death.)

The popular Violin Concerto dates from 1903, the period of some of his finest theatrical music (*Pelleas et Melisande*), the tone poem *Pohjola's Daughter*, and the Second Symphony. Beginning with a famous early electrical recording by Jascha Heifetz and Sir Thomas Beecham, the Concerto has always been brilliantly represented on records: from an unforgettable performance recorded in the late 1940s by the French violinist Ginette Neveu, to the most recent—and finest—of Itzhak Perlman's two recordings. Compared to his earlier recording with Erich Leinsdorf and the Boston Symphony, the new version with André Previn and the Pittsburgh Symphony is at once more dramatic and more relaxed. While tempos, especially in the first two movements, tend to be on the leisurely side, there is nothing in the performance which could be considered even remotely lethargic or slack. The interpretation has a wonderful feeling of expansiveness to it, a performance cast—and executed—on the grandest possible scale. The support that Perlman receives from Previn and his forces is, as usual, exemplary, and the recorded sound in all three formats is absolutely first rate.

Symphonies (7)

Boston Symphony, C. Davis. Philips 6709011 [LP], *416600-2* [CD], 7699143 [T].

There was a time, not so terribly long ago, when some of these seven extraordinary works were heard with the same frequency as the nine symphonies of Beethoven. In fact, for a time during the 1930s and 1940s, they were probably the most frequently performed orchestral works written during the preceding hundred years. Much of the credit for Sibelius' popularity—aside from the power and originality of the music itself—was due to a group of gifted and tireless champions, including Sir Thomas Beecham, Leopold Stokowski, and Serge Koussevitzky, men whose compelling, highly individual interpretations made the Finnish symphonist's name a household word throughout the musical world.

From Koussevitzky's time to the present, the Boston Symphony has remained one of the world's great Sibelius orchestras. And while several individual interpretations might be marginally preferable—Koussevitzky's white-hot reading of the Second is still available from RCA Victor (AGM-1-5232), and Simon Rattle's dazzling Angel recording of the Fifth (*CDC-47006*) deserves all the lavish critical praise it has received—the BSO's complete set of the symphonies under Sir Colin Davis is one of the best imaginable introductions to the music, either for the novice or for the most jaded of collectors. As a Sibelius conductor, Davis represents a golden mean between the audacity of his predecessors and the somewhat cooler approach of the modern school. All the strength and cragginess of the music remains intact, though Sir Colin is also meticulous with textures and details. In short, these are performances that, while they remove some of the bark, leave the trees healthy and intact.

The Boston Symphony plays this music like no other orchestra in the world, and Philips' recorded sound, after more than a decade, remains a model of clarity and warmth. As a bonus, the generously-packed recordings include superlative performances of the ever-popular *Finlandia, Swan of Tuonela,* and *Tapiola.* All in all, one of the few authentic bargains on the market today.

Smetana, Bedřich
(1824–1884)

Prodaná Nevěsta *(The Bartered Bride)*

> Běnáčkova-Capová, Dvořsky, Novák, Czech
> Philharmonic Chorus and Orchestra, Košler.
> Supraphon 3511/13 [LP], *C-37-7309-11* [CD].

Three Dances

> Cleveland Orchestra, Szell. CBS MY-36716 [LP],
> *MYK-36716* [T], MYT-36716 [T].

As immensely and eternally entertaining as *The Bartered Bride* certainly is, its historical importance in the development of Czech music is all but impossible to calculate. Prior to *Prodaná Nevěsta*, Bohemia had been widely known as "The Conservatory of Europe," a tiny province of the sprawling Austro-Hungarian empire that had always supplied the courts of Europe with some of their finest musicians. Yet Czech composers, before Smetana, were indistinguishable from their German and Austrian counterparts; many, in fact, in order to secure important positions, Germanized their names.

The Bartered Bride was Bohemia's musical Declaration

of Independence. A work that not only was based on decidedly Czech themes, but also captured the essential spirit of Czech folk music and dance, *Prodaná Nevěsta* made its difficult, irascible composer a national hero. (While it is the only Czech opera that has entered the standard repertoire of every major opera house, in Czechoslovakia it is revered as a national monument.) Without it, the masterworks of Smetana's maturity are virtually unthinkable, and had it never been written, composers like Dvořák and Janáček might never have evolved as they eventually did.

While a number of fine recorded performances of the opera have been available through the years, none can begin to approach the brilliant Supraphon recording which will undoubtedly set the standard for *Bartered Brides* for decades to come. In the title role, Gabriela Beňáčkova-Capová—the reigning queen of Prague's Theatre and one of the finest dramatic sopranos in the world today—will probably not be bettered for the remainder of this century. She sings with an ease, warmth, femininity, and freshness that only Elizabeth Schwarzkopf, in a few tantalizing German-language excerpts from the late 1950s, could begin to match. Peter Dvořsky is equally outstanding as the wily hero Jenik, and the rest of the cast—especially the marriage broker of Richard Novak—could not have been bettered either on records or off.

Although Zdenik Košler's interpretation is as zestful and refreshing as any the opera has ever received, the principal selling point in a recording loaded with selling points is the playing of the great Czech Philharmonic. They perform this music as no other orchestra possibly could, and the lusty, brilliantly trained chorus is as rowdy, rousing, and tender as anyone could wish.

For those poor misguided souls who think they can do without a complete recording of *The Bartered Bride*—but then, too, there are probably people who can live without sunshine, root beer popsicles, and sex—George Szell's classic recording of the three popular dances (the Polka, Furiant, and Dance of the Comedians) is the greatest single performance ever given of the opera's most frequently heard orchestral excerpts. Actually, this is one of the most valuable recordings of Czech music ever made, including as it does what may easily be the definitive versions of Smetana's popular *The Moldau*, and the "Carnival" Overture of Dvořák.

Ma Vlast *(My Fatherland)*

Vienna Philharmonic, Levine. Deutsche Grammophon *419768-2* [CD].

Boston Symphony, Kubelik. Deutsche Grammophon 2707054 [LP].

Dresden State Orchestra, Berglund. Angel 4AM-34749 [T].

Smetana began work on what would prove to be his only major contribution to symphonic thought in the same week of 1874 that he resigned his post as Director of Prague's Provisional Theatre. At the age of fifty, the composer of *The Bartered Bride* was totally deaf. What had at first been diagnosed as a minor ear infection proved to be the first symptom of the tertiary neurosyphilis that would also claim his sanity, and ultimately, his life.

Ma Vlast, his magnificent, uneven, terribly moving collection of six symphonic poems is perhaps the greatest musical love letter a composer ever wrote to his native country. While *The Moldau* has become justly famous, the entire cycle contains much of the best that the father of Czech music had to give to nineteenth century music. It is a cornerstone of Romantic art and one of the purest expressions of the nationalistic spirit ever heard in Western music.

As a performance of the cycle, no modern recording has ever managed to efface the memory of those two versions that the great Václav Talich made in the mid-1930s and late 1940s. (A third version, from 1941, is one of the rarest recordings that any major conductor has ever made.) Although James

Levine might not have the same instinctive grasp of the man who was probably the greatest Czech conductor of all time, his recent version of the cycle is the most impressive to have appeared in years. The Vienna Philharmonic play with tremendous bite and conviction, and while Levine is at his best in the more dramatic, declamatory passages, he also infuses the performance with considerable sensitivity and finesse. *From Bohemia's Woods and Meadows* has rarely sounded more delicately shaded, and the moonlit passages of *The Moldau* have magic that only a handful of other recordings (Szell's in particular) can equal.

While Levine's compact disc is now an easy first choice among all recorded versions of the cycle, Rafael Kubelik's fine LP version with the Boston Symphony clearly leads the field in that medium, as Paavo Berglund's electrifying East German recording does among the tapes. On the other hand, when some enterprising little label reissues the final Talich recording on compact disc, the situation will change completely.

Quartet No. 1 in E minor, "From My Life"

Juilliard Quartet. CBS MS-7144 [LP].

Smetana Quartet. Denon *C37-7339* [CD].

There is no more poignant chamber work in music than this autobiographical string quartet that Smetana completed shortly after he was engulfed by the deafness that would remain with him throughout the remaining ten years of his life. While the final movement, which contains the famous high-pitched E in the first violin—the initial symptom of what would develop into a fatal, agonizing disease—is one of the most shattering moments in nineteenth century music, the Quartet is in fact a predominantly buoyant and cheerful work. It looks backward to the composer's youth with a charming and gentle nostalgia, and even manages to look forward to the troubled future with great dignity and courage.

Either of the fine recordings by the Juilliard or Smetana Quartets will please the most demanding listener. In terms of technical prowess, the Juilliard's was recorded at something close to the height of that legendary ensemble's powers. The Smetana's performance is also very well played, is slightly more idiomatic in its stylistic flavor, and has the advantage of superb compact disc sound. A choice between the two—apart from the LP or the compact disc format—may rest with your preference for the couplings. The Juilliard offers Dvořák's popular "American" Quartet, while the Smetana gives us the rare opportunity to examine the composer's rarely heard Second String Quartet. Unfortunately, no acceptable cassette version is presently available.

Sousa, John Philip
(1854–1932)

Marches

Philip Jones Brass Ensemble, Howarth. London
410290-1 [LP], *410290-2* [CD], 410290 [T].

What, I hear you ask, is an entry on John Philip Sousa doing in a book dealing with Official Classical Music? Has the man (myself) no standards? Is nothing sacred? The answer to both of the above questions is "No."

If, like me, you find the music of the March King irresistible, then by all means snatch up one of the three greatest Sousa March collections ever released. (The others were a collection led by Henry Mancini, an ace piccolo player and a top-notch bandsmen in his day, and an old Capitol Album called "The Military Band," presided over by the hugely gifted Felix Slatkin.) The playing on this London recording is as sharp as the most demanding drum major could wish. Rhythms are crisp, the ensemble is razor-sharp, and for a British ensemble this group can certainly teach us a thing or two.

In short, fellow Sousa cuckoos, rejoice. The rest, it's the back a' me hand ta yas.

Strauss, Johann II
(1825–1899)

Die Fledermaus

Gueden, Koth, Resnik, Zampieri, Wächter, Kmentt,
Berry, Kunz, Vienna State Opera Chorus, Vienna
Philharmonic, Karajan. London *421046-2* [CD].

Varady, Popp, Kollo, Prey, Rebroff, Bavarian State
Opera Chorus and Orchestra, C. Kleiber. Deutsche
Grammophon 415646-1 [LP], *415646-2* [CD],
415646-4 [T].

More than a century since the first production of *Die
Fledermaus*, it is difficult to imagine how Vienna could have
been so cool to the greatest operetta ever written—that is, of
course, unless you know and love the Viennese. The fact that
they were overwhelmingly indifferent to the original production of *Die Fledermaus* in 1874 places it in some very good
company. The city was also unqualified in its scorn of
Mozart's *Don Giovanni*, Beethoven's *Fidelio*, and countless
other new works, proving that although it was at one time the
musical capital of the world, Vienna was as reactionary as its
brutally despotic emperor, Franz Joseph.

Die Fledermaus has never had a more effervescent recording than London's "Gala" production of the late 1950s.
In addition to memorable "star turns" from many of the finest
singers of the day in the Act II party scene (Leontyne Price's

version of Gershwin's "Summertime" is especially haunting), the rest of the production is an unqualified triumph. As in her earlier London recording from the late 1940s, the scrumptious Hilde Gueden was and remains the ideal Rosalinde—wise, wily, sexy—and captured here in wonderful voice. The supporting cast, led by Regina Resnik as the marvelously dissolute Prince Orlovsky, and the ageless Erich Kunz as the drunken but irrepressible Frosch, is one of the best ever mustered in a recording studio. The Vienna Philharmonic plays *Fledermaus* as only *they* can play *Fledermaus*, and Herbert von Karajan, in one of his last successful recordings, conducts with tremendous joy, delicacy, and verve.

As an LP or tape alternative, the performance led by Carlos Kleiber is only slightly less engaging than London's classic release. The choice of the Russian bass Ivan Rebroff as Prince Orlofsky—generally a mezzo-soprano role—had a particularly daffy inspiration to it, and Kleiber, as always, finds many new and interesting things to say.

Waltzes, Polkas, etc

New York Philharmonic, Bernstein. CBS MY-37771 [LP], *MYK-37771* [CD], MYK-37771 [T].

Vienna Philharmonic, Boskovsky. London *417706-2* [CD], 421223-4 [T].

Vienna Strauss Orchestra, Boskovsky. Angel 37892 [LP], *CDC-47052* [CD].

Chicago Symphony, Reiner. RCA Victor LSC-2500 [LP], *RCD1-5405* [CD], RK-1020 [T].

The next time you hear a serious music snob say something demeaning about the waltzes and polkas of Johann Strauss, tell them they're full of crap. Or even better, haul off and kick them in the shin. Johann Strauss II was admired by Brahms, Wagner, and almost every other important musician of his time. His waltzes are every bit as important as, and even more memorable and entertaining than, those of Chopin; to dismiss them as "light music" or mere pops concert fare is to entirely miss the point. Almost all of them are brilliantly made, ingeniously crafted little tone poems that will undoubtedly survive long after most of the serious music of that era is forgotten.

The recordings listed above have much to offer both the beginning and the experienced collector. At something over fifteen minutes, Leonard Bernstein's version of "Tales from the Vienna Woods" is easily the longest (and sexiest) performance ever recorded. The recordings made by the longtime concertmaster of the Vienna Philharmonic, Willi Boskovsky, are graceful, stunningly played, and close to the last word in idiomatic grace. And finally, the generous RCA Victor compact disc of recordings made by Fritz Reiner and the Chicago Symphony in the late 1950s is a bargain that no Strauss lover can afford to resist. The interpretations are full of Viennese lilt and schmaltz, and the performances are more zestful and precise than any others I know.

Strauss, Richard (1864–1949)

Also sprach Zarathustra, Op. 30

**Chicago Symphony, Reiner. RCA Victor ARP1-4583
[LP], *5721-2* [CD], ARE-4583 [T].**

Since Stanley Kubrick's *2001* made it a popular hit,
Strauss' tone poem after Nietzsche, *Also sprach Zarathustra*,
has had dozens of recordings, most of them with some outer-
space scene cleverly placed on the cover of the record jacket.
(Say what you will about them, but recording companies are
no dolts when it comes to marketing.)

In spite of the flood of new *Zarathustras*, the one that
continues to speak most eloquently is Fritz Reiner's phenomenal 1954 recording with the Chicago Symphony. One of
Victor's very first stereo recordings, and one of the first recordings that Reiner made with his new orchestra, no one
could have expected quite so *great* a recording as this one. The
playing remains a wonder of alertness, fire, and whiplash
attacks, while the recording—as old as it may be—is as warm,
detailed, and sensual as many recordings made in the 1970s.
Incidentally, Fritz Reiner was one of Strauss' favorite conductors. This classic recording will show you why.

Death and Transfiguration; Don Juan; Till Eulenspiegel's Merry Pranks

Cleveland Orchestra, Szell. CBS MY-36721 [LP], *MKY-36721* [CD], MYT-36721 [T].

The young Richard Strauss initially made his reputation with this trio of early tone poems that remain the most popular and frequently performed of his orchestral works. Although there may have been finer individual recordings of each (a live Salzburg Festival recording of *Death and Transfiguration*, led by Victor de Sabata, is so white-hot in its intensity that it might melt the plastic elements in your speaker system), no collection of all three has ever been more successful than this one has.

The Cleveland Orchestra is honed to a fine state of perfection by George Szell, who leads them through a *Till Eulenspiegel* of enormous wit and character, a *Death and Transfiguration* of great power and grandeur, and a *Don Juan* which is a model of swagger and romance. Given the 1960s vintage, the sound is surprisingly good in all three formats, although the compact disc remastering, like most of CBS's efforts with recordings from this period, tends to be on the hissy side. This is a minor drawback, though, to one of the great Strauss recordings of modern times.

Don Quixote, Op. 35

Harrell, cello; Cleveland Orchestra, Ashkenazy. London 417184-1 [LP], *417184-2* [CD], 417184-4 [T].

Not counting the shamelessly self-indulgent *Ein Heldenleben* (*A Hero's Life*), *Don Quixote* is easily the greatest of the mature Strauss tone poems. The structure—a set of variations "on a theme of knightly character"—is beautifully worked out, the orchestration is a wonder of subtle ingenuity, and the dramatic content (who can forget the final, sliding note in the cello as old Don dies?), is among the most powerful and moving of all Strauss' works.

While I continue to have great affection for Fritz Reiner's Chicago Symphony recording, now available on an RCA Victor compact disc (5734-2), this recent version by Vladimir Ashkenazy is not only a breathtaking example of state-of-the-art recording technology, but also a genuinely wonderful performance. The orchestra seems to take tremendous delight in playing for the fine Russian pianist-turned-conductor. At almost every turn they uncover some felicitous detail that we've never heard before, and in general play with the wit, precision, and fire that characterized their work during the height of the golden Szell days. Cellist Lynn Harrell acquits himself magnificently in the "title role," and the recorded sound is among the most natural I have heard from a compact disc.

Elektra

Nilsson, Collier, Resnik, Stolze, Krause, Vienna Philharmonic, Solti. London 417345-2 [CD].

In many ways, *Elektra* is the most successful and satisfying of all Strauss operas. For one thing, it is loaded with all those ingredients that make an opera great (cruelty, horror, bloodshed, and revenge), and for another, it is *not* twenty minutes too long (a charge which has been leveled at every other Strauss opera, with the exception of the equally compressed and gory *Salome*).

There is only one complete recording of the opera currently available, and a very great one it is. In the title role, Birgit Nilsson gives one of her most absorbed and shattering recorded performances: from the savage confrontations with her mother, Klytemnestra, sung to chilling effect by Regina Resnik, to one of the most beautiful and moving versions of the thrilling Recognition Scene. The rest of the cast is splendid. Sir Georg Solti's conducting is vividly dramatic and intense, and the recorded sound in the compact disc format—the only one currently available—will rattle the rafters of the best-built house.

RCA Victor has recently issued on another compact disc some generous selections from the opera, together with excerpts from *Salome*, of the classic recordings made by Inge Borkh (my favorite Elektra of all time) and the Chicago Symphony conducted by Fritz Reiner. As much as I tend to dislike operas chopped up into what George Bernard Shaw used to call "bleeding chunks of meat," this recording is a very special one and shouldn't be passed up. (RCA Victor *5603-2-RC*.)

Ein Heldenleben, Op. 40

> Cleveland Orchestra, Ashkenazy. London 414292-1
> [LP], *414292-2* [CD], 414292-4 [T].

Richard Strauss was not, by any stretch of the imagination, a loveable, or even particularly likable man. He collaborated openly with the Nazis from the late 1930s onward, was shamelessly mercenary throughout his life, and was probably the only composer in history whose ego could be compared with Richard Wagner's. The great German conductor Hans Knappertsbusch may have summed it up best when he said, "I knew him very well. We played cards every week for forty years and he was a pig."

In spite of the fact that it is one of the most self-indulgent pieces in the history of art, *Ein Heldenleben* is a very great work. The "Hero's Life" which the tone poem celebrates is, of course, Strauss' own. And though we blush for the sheer audacity of the man, he does blow his own horn (in fact, all eight of them) magnificently.

Until Bernard Haitink's wonderful recording with the Amsterdam Concertgebouw Orchestra is returned to print (the tone poem was dedicated to them, and to their then music director, Willem Mengelberg), Vladimir Ashkenazy's triumphant Cleveland recording should satisfy nearly everyone. The interpretation is brash, lush, romantic, and impetuous. The orchestra plays stupendously and the recorded sound is state-of-the-art.

Der Rosenkavalier

Schwarzkopf, Ludwig, Stich-Randall, Edelmann,
Philharmonia Chorus and Orchestra, Karajan.
Angel *CDCC-49345* [CD], 4CDX-3970 [T].

Shortly after his new and dreadful Deutsche Grammophon recording of Strauss' loveliest opera was released, Herbert von Karajan, tactful gentleman that he has always been, said something to the effect that he was *so* happy to have finally made a recording of *Der Rosenkavalier* with what he has called "an adequate cast." Taking nothing away from Anna Tomowa-Sintow, just what did that slime bag think he had in Elisabeth Schwarzkopf thirty years ago? Chopped liver?

The first Karajan *Rosenkavalier* has all the tenderness, charm, impetuosity, and dramatic tension that his newer recording lacks. And with Madame Schwarzkopf, he clearly has the finest Marschallin since Lotte Lehmann was singing the role in the 1930s. From either the compact disc or the tapes, the recording emerges as what it has clearly been since it was first released: one of the great operatic recordings of the century. The LPs, alas, have recently been withdrawn, and aside from Karajan's hideous new version, no other version of the opera is available in that format.

Salome

Nilsson, Hoffman, Stolze, Kmentt, Wächter, Vienna Philharmonic, Solti. London *414414-2* [CD].

As with *Elektra*, there is now only *one* recording of this path-breaking masterpiece available to American consumers, and only on compact disc. Fortunately, it also happens to be one of the finest operatic recordings yet made, and I suppose we should be thankful that the compact disc saved it, too, from oblivion.

As Strauss' terrifying, over-sexed adolescent, Birgit Nilsson gives one of the most powerful performances of her long and brilliant career. The closing twenty minutes, when she has that grisly "duet" with the head of John the Baptist, are among the most terrifying ever captured. Sir Georg Solti, here as elsewhere, lends the kind of sympathetic though never sycophantic support about of which most singers only dream. The rest of the cast, especially Gerhard Stolze as King Herod, is overwhelming, and the remastered sound will take your breath away.

Stravinsky, Igor (1882–1971)

The Firebird (Complete Ballet)

Concertgebouw Orchestra of Amsterdam, Davis.
Philips 9500637 [LP], 400074-2 [CD], 7300742 [T].

At a fashionable party, Igor Stravinsky was once thanked by an effusive *grande dame* for writing her favorite work, *Scheherazade*. "But Madame, I did not write *Scheherazade*," he tried to explain. To which the woman allegedly replied, "Oh, all of you composers are so modest."

With Igor Stravinsky's first great popular success, *The Firebird*, it's easy to hear why the poor woman was so confused. In its opulence, drama, and brilliant orchestration, *The Firebird* is a direct descendant of Stravinsky's teacher's masterwork. Only in the closing bars, with its majestic *apotheosis* in 7/4 time, does this early ballet give any clue to the rhythmic experimentation that eventually changed the course of twentieth century music.

Although many great *Firebird* recordings have come and gone over the years (including another Philips recording by the London Philharmonic and Bernard Haitink that desperately needs to be returned to print), this stunning version by Sir Colin Davis and the Amsterdam Concertgebouw Orchestra is as fine as any. Davis' approach is extremely colorful and dramatic. The *scherzo* barely rises above a whisper, and some of the more aggressive moments suggest that this was, indeed, a work by the future composer of *The Rite of Spring*. The orchestra is virtually unbelievable in its ease and power of execution, and the recorded sound, in all three formats, is top drawer.

Petrouchka (Complete Ballet)

London Symphony, Abbado. Deutsche Grammophon 413209-1 [LP], *400042-GH* [CD], 413209-4 [T].

First performed the year after *The Firebird* made Stravinsky an international sensation, *Petrouchka* not only confirmed the young Igor Stravinsky's remarkable gift, but also proved he was neither a flash in the pan, nor a composer who was willing to simply go on repeating himself for the rest of his life. Harmonically, structurally, and most importantly, rhythmically, *Petrouchka* marked a significant leap ahead of *The Firebird*, and was one of his earliest works that the elderly Stravinsky professed to like. (He often said that aside from some of the orchestration, he found *The Firebird* utterly uninteresting.)

While there are at least a dozen superlative recordings of the ballet available today, the most thoroughly satisfying is Claudio Abbado's London Symphony version for Deutsche Grammophon. No nuance of texture, no quirky rhythm, no elegant phrase or ingratiating tune escapes Abbado's attention. And unlike the composer's own celebrated recording (CBS *MK-42433*)—a more or less "revisionist" interpretation that tried to prove the ballet was a little drier, more acerbic, and more "modern" than it actually was—Abbado refuses to deny *Petrouchka*'s Romantic roots, and in so doing performs a great service for both the listener and the work itself.

Le sacre du printemps (The Rite of Spring)

Columbia Symphony, Stravinsky. CBS MG-31020 [LP], *MK-42433* [CD], MGT-39015 [T].

Philadelphia Orchestra, Muti. Angel *CDC-47408* [CD], 4AM-34708 [T].

Le sacre du printemps is one of the two seminal works, with Schoenberg's *Pierrot Lunaire* (first performed only a few weeks apart), that began modern music. While *Pierrot* remains under a cloud of polite neglect, *The Rite of Spring* has nearly become a pops concert staple. (As early as 1940, a mauled and emasculated edition of the ballet was used as part of the soundtrack of that tedious Disney classic *Fantasia*.)

For one of the clearest and most provocatively objective of all the ballet's many recordings, the composer's own is irreplaceable. As in so many recordings of his own music, Stravinsky the conductor—though by this time, much of the nuts and bolts rehearsal work was being done by his protégé and amanuensis, Robert Craft—sought to tone down the overtly barbarous moments in the music in favor of greater clarity and restraint. In short, he seemed intent on proving, late in life, that stylistically there wasn't all that much separating his music from that of Rossini, Mozart, or Bach.

The approach, needless to say, casts some fascinating light on this great twentieth century watershed. But for those who want a vicious, untamed, and yet to be housebroken version of the ballet, Riccardo Muti's Angel recording is a bracing tonic to the composer's own version. The Philadelphia Orchestra plays as though they were possessed, and the recorded sound will rid you of any loose putty on the living room windows and possibly even the family cat.

Symphony in Three Movements; Symphony in C

Israel Philharmonic, Bernstein. Deutsche Grammophon 415128-1 [LP], *415128-2* [CD]; 415128-4 [T].

Stravinsky said a few indiscreet things about Leonard Bernstein, both behind his back and in print. Yet on balance, the mercurial conductor is, and has always been, one of Stravinsky's finest interpreters, as these gleaming performances of the Neo-Classical *Symphony in C* and *Symphony in Three Movements* clearly prove.

While keeping a very firm reign on the proceedings—the slow movement of the *Symphony in C* is especially moving in its compassion and restraint—Bernstein never loses the opportunity to make the dramatic best of this music. The *Finale* of the wartime Symphony in Three Movements is as unbridled in its joyousness as any performance of any Stravinsky work yet recorded. The Israel Philharmonic responds with great precision given the live-performance conditions, and the recorded sound has tremendous clarity, warmth, and depth.

Symphony of Psalms

CBC Symphony, Toronto Festival Singers, Stravinsky. CBS *MK-42434* [CD], MS-6548 [T].

If *Le sacre du printemps* was not Stravinsky's masterpiece, then this proud, aloof, deeply stirring sacred work probably was. Written "To the Glory of God and Dedicated to the Boston Symphony Orchestra" (Serge Koussevitzky never forgave Stravinsky that his orchestra was given second billing), the *Symphony* is one of the half dozen great sacred works of modern music. In fact, with a small handful of companion pieces—Poulenc's *Gloria*, Schoenberg's *Moses und Aron*, Vaughan Williams' *Hodie*—it is among the few works of this century that has kept the divine spirit in music alive and well.

Stravinsky's own performance from the 1960s is still available on a CBS LP, and it has recently been reissued on a compact disc. Here, for once, the composer's predilection for a drier sound in his music than most conductors favored, serves this particular masterpiece extremely well. The *Symphony* emerges with all of its pride in, devotion to, and admiration (as opposed to adoration) of the Supreme Being, blissfully intact.

Among the cassette tapes currently available, Riccardo Chailly's London recording (414078-4) is a perfectly acceptable performance of the music, nicely sung and neatly played, but very little else.

Suppé, Franz von
(1819–1895)

Overtures

Montreal Symphony, Dutoit. London 414408-1 [LP],
414408-2 **[CD], 414408-4 [T].**

In some quarters, an enthusiasm for Suppé Overtures (the operas and operettas they served to introduce have long since disappeared) is looked on very quizzically. It is as if the person who professes the enthusiasm also admits a fondness for cheap detective movies of the 1940s, spy novels, and long summer afternoons in front of the television, watching baseball and nursing a few tall, cold beers.

I admit that, like millions of others, I am thoroughly addicted to these cornball classics. And listening to these crisp, no nonsense, and most importantly, *uncondescending* performances by Charles Dutoit and the Montreal Symphony may even make a believer out of you. Dutoit and his forces play these familiar classics as though they were crammed to the gunnels with zest, unforgettable melody, and brilliant craftsmanship. In short, they only show us why these imperishable warhorses deserve to be just that.

Suppé-lovers, rejoice. Suppé-haters, in your ear.

Tchaikovsky, Piotr Ilyich (1840–1843)

Capriccio Italien; Marche Slave; Nutcracker Suite; 1812 Overture

Montreal Symphony, Dutoit. London 417300-1 [LP],
417300-2 **[CD], 417300-4 [T].**

Although an enormous percentage of music lovers first made their way into Serious Music via the works of Tchaikovsky, many seem strangely loath to admit it. As our tastes mature and we become ever more knowledgeable and sophisticated, we tend to drop—or perhaps even be ashamed of—our youthful enthusiasms. (Who was it who said, "Don't let the young confide to you their dreams, for when they drop them, they'll drop you"?)

Although he can be extremely obvious, bellicose, cheap, and vulgar, Tchaikovsky more than earns his position as one of the three or four most popular composers. He never cheats his listeners, giving them huge doses of overwhelming (and often surprisingly complex) emotions, a keen sense of orchestral color, and one of the greatest melodic gifts that any composer possessed. In short, if you love Tchaikovsky, don't be ashamed. And don't think you're alone. Uncounted millions of us can't *all* be wrong.

This superb and unusually generous London collection brings together four of the composer's most popular works in performances which are as civilized as they are exiting, as brash and brazen as they are thoughtful and refined. Although the *1812 Overture* could be a bit noisier for my taste (remember the great old Mercury recording with Antal Dorati and the Minneapolis Symphony, and Deems Taylor explaining how they got the bells and cannon blasts?), these are the performances I turn to whenever the mood strikes me.

*P*iano Concerto in B-flat minor, Op. 23

Cliburn, piano; RCA Victor Symphony, Kondrashin.
RCA Victor ARP1-4441 [LP], *5912-2-RC* [CD],
RK-1002 [T].

It's no accident that this is one of the best-selling classical recordings of all time. Naturally, much of it had to do with the ballyhoo that attended Van Cliburn's winning of the Tchaikovsky competition in Moscow during one of the chilliest moments of the cold war. (Yes, the Russians had a definite jump in the space race—remember all those films of our rockets blowing up on the pad?—but we had this long, lanky Texan who beat them, and beat them *decisively*, at their own game.)

Three decades later, in the midst of the *glasnost* thaw, it's time we started judging this recording on its own merits and not its historical context. I have. And simply stated, in *any* context, this is one hell of an exciting performance. Cliburn's mixture of elfin delicacy and animal ferocity has remained intact since the recording was first released. It is a poetic, explosive, lyrical, and deeply humane interpretation which no recording of the last thirty years begins to match.

Concerto in D Major for Violin and Orchestra, Op. 35

Heifetz, violin; Chicago Symphony, Reiner. RCA Victor
AGL1-4883 [LP], *5933-2-RC* [CD].

Oistrakh, violin; Philadelphia Orchestra, Ormandy.
CBS Odyssey YT-30312 [T].

From a purely technical point of view, there has never been a recording to match Jascha Heifetz' famous version with Fritz Reiner and the Chicago Symphony. Although the violinist was placed uncomfortably close to the microphone, which accounts for the unaccustomed rasp in his famous tone, the playing is genuinely spellbinding. Listen especially to the first movement *cadenza*, in which the soloist uses one of his own devising that makes Tchaikovsky's original seem like child's play.

On the other hand, if you're after the warmth, color, and abiding romance of the Tchaikovsky concerto, then David Oistrakh's meltingly lovely recording with Eugene Ormandy and the Philadelphia Orchestra is clearly the one to own. Unfortunately, the recording is currently available only on cassette.

The Nutcracker (Complete Ballet)

L'rchestre de la Suisse Romande, Ansermet. London
417055-1 [LP], 417055-4 [T].

Berlin Philharmonic, Bychkov. Philips *420237-2* [CD].

If ever a recording deserved the designation "Imperishable," it is that triumphant early stereo version of *The Nutcracker*, which has more sheer interpretive magic than you can shake a sugar plum at. Although the sound has definitely begun to show its age, the performance never will. Ansermet's conception brings out every ounce of charm and color in this often hackneyed work, and he does it with a touch so light and sure that we're reminded once again of what we all owe this great pioneer of the early stereo age.

While the Philips compact disc recording by Simyon Bychkov and the Berlin Philharmonic can't quite match the charm and delicacy of the Ansermet, it still has much to recommend it. In addition to some razor-sharp playing from one of the world's great orchestras, this compact disc will introduce many to a stupendously gifted young conductor. (It is rumored that Herbert von Karajan has chosen Bychkov as his successor in Berlin. This means, of course, a considerable wait, since Karajan, like all truly evil men, will live to be at least 150.)

*R*omeo and Juliet (Fantasy Overture): *Francesca da Rimini*

Israel Philharmonic, Bernstein. Deustche Grammophon 410990-1 [LP], *410990-2* [CD], 410990-4 [T].

Here is a virtually ideal recording of two of Tchaikovsky's most popular tone poems, each of which is throttled to within an inch of its life by one of the most compelling score-throttlers of this century. For those who like to play it safe, there are three or four dozen other recordings that more than fill the bill. And, for those who are familiar with Bernstein's earlier CBS recording, or for those who prefer a more straightforward approach, Bernstein's readings will seem astonishingly madcap, self-indulgent and willful— as though these might be a pair of forgotten masterworks written not by Tchaikovsky, but by Gustav Mahler in one of his most neurotic moods. But, for a pair of emotional roller-coaster rides you'll never forget, snap this one up as soon as you can.

Symphony No. 4 in F minor, Op. 36; Symphony No. 5 in E minor, Op. 64; Symphony No. 6 in B minor, Op. 74, "Pathetique"

Leningrad Philharmonic, Mravinsky. Deutsche Grammophon *419745-2* [CD].

This series of recordings, made in London when the Leningrad Philharmonic was on tour in the early 1960s, is among the few studio recordings made by one of the most important and enigmatic conductors of the twentieth century, the late Yevgeny Mravinsky. A friend of Shostakovich who led many premieres of the composer's symphonies, Mravinsky, over a period of nearly a half century, galvanized the Leningrad Philharmonic into the Soviet Union's greatest orchestra.

These performances of the last three Tchaikovsky symphonies are among the most exciting, pulverizing, uplifting, and wacky ever made. For instance, Mravinsky sets a pace for the *Finale* of the Fourth that no orchestra could possibly *play*, and yet there they are—playing with such superhuman virtuosity that it takes at least a dozen hearings to believe it. The interpretations are larger than life; the orchestral execution is a wonder of unanimity, courage, and bravado, and the recorded sound is remarkably detailed and clear.

Alas, for those who have yet to acquire compact disc players, only a few reasonable alternatives exist. Leonard Bernstein's early CBS recording of the Fourth (CBS MY-37766, *MYK-37766*, MYT-37766) still packs plenty of wallop and highly individual pizzazz. Claudio Abbado's brooding yet exhilarating performance of the Fifth ranks with the finest of his Chicago Symphony recordings (CBS IM-42094, *MK-42094*, IMT-42094). And, among non CD-versions of the "Pathétique," I've always retained a special fondness for Fritz Reiner's unsentimental, though still enormously intense and personal version with the Chicago Symphony, which, happily, is still in print. (RCA Victor AGL-1-5258, AGK1-5258.)

Telemann, Georg Philipp (1681–1767)

During his lifetime, Georg Philipp Telemann completely overshadowed his near contemporary, an obscure German organist and composer named Johann Sebastian Bach. Later centuries slowly realized that what had made Telemann so fashionable during his lifetime—the clear, uncomplicated structures, the easy to follow contents of a music which had nothing profound to say—ultimately gave him next to no staying power, especially in comparison with the *real* Baroque giants, Handel and Bach.

While I can make no specific recommendations for recordings of the man's music (it all sounds more or less the same to me), I will offer a few general hints for the Telemann shopper. 1. Avoid any recording with a reproduction of an eighteenth century landscape painting on the front cover. 2. Avoid any concerto for more than one instrument (anything more complicated seems only to have confused him). 3. Avoid any recording featuring Nikolaus Harnoncourt, his wife Alice, or their friend Gustav Leonhart. If you see them in the cut-out or used record bins, and I mean *anything* produced by the Telemann society, avoid them as though your life depended on it. (Several people have laughed themselves to death listening to their well-intentioned, but hopelessly feeble efforts.) 4. If the temptation to buy a Telemann recording proves irresistible, make certain your cupboard is well stocked with strong, and I do mean *strong*, coffee.

Tippett, Sir Michael
(1905–)

A Child of Our Time (Oratorio)

Armstrong, Palmer, Langridge, Shirley-Quirk, Brighton Festival Chorus, Royal Philharmonic, Previn. MCA *MCAD-6102* [CD].

Sir Michael Tippett, England's greatest living composer, has spent most of his career in the tremendous shadow cast by his far more famous contemporary, Benjamin Britten. In many ways, Tippett is the more interesting composer (and this from someone who has always adored Britten's music). Unlike Britten, Tippett has ventured down several important modern roads in recent years. His idiom has become increasingly harsh and dissonant, while his expression has become ever more concentrated and precise. Late Tippett (from, say, the early 1970s onward) can be a very thorny, though immensely rewarding row to hoe.

A Child of Our Time, completed in 1941, is not only one of Tippett's most accessible pieces, but also one of the most shattering, yet heartbreakingly lovely choral works of the last hundred years. Patterned consciously after the Passions of Bach, Tippett's Oratorio presents black spirituals in place of the familiar chorales at key moments in the drama. Their effect, especially in a recording like this one, is overwhelmingly moving and beautiful.

While the Oratorio has been recorded twice before—and

handsome performances they were, led by John Pritchard and Sir Colin Davis—this new version by André Previn is not only one of the conductor's finest recordings to date, but also the greatest recorded performance *A Child of Our Time* is ever likely to receive. The complex textures of the work are untangled with a pristine clarity, and the soloists are inspired to give some of the finest performances of their careers. And the way Previn has the often gigantic forces "swing" their way through the spirituals is enough to raise the hair on the back of your neck. (In "Steal Away," there's no hair on *any* part of my anatomy which isn't rustled at least once.) In short, this is an indispensable performance of a great modern classic that belongs in every recording library.

For Tippett admirers—and the man certainly deserves millions more than he has so far attracted—two other important recordings can also be recommended without reservation. The first is Sir Colin Davis' definitive version of that most exuberant and mysterious modern English opera, *A Midsummer Marriage* (Philip 6703027, LP only), and the second is the London recording of the four symphonies the composer has written to date, in stunning performances led by Davis and Sir Georg Solti (414091-1, 414091-4 [T]).

Vaughan Williams, Ralph (1872–1958)

Fantasia on a Theme by Thomas Tallis; Symphony No. 2, "A London Symphony"

London Philharmonic, Boult. Angel AE-34438 [LP], *CDC-47213* [CD], AE-34438 [T].

For those who have yet to acquire the gentle addiction of Ralph Vaughan Williams' music, this superb Angel recording should do the trick. On it are two of Vaughan Williams' finest and most characteristic pieces, the ravishing *Fantasia on a Theme of Thomas Tallis* and that greatest of modern English musical travelogues, "A London Symphony."

Although both works have had marginally finer, but currently unavailable performances (Sir John Barbirolli's version of the Symphony ranks with the great orchestral recordings of modern times), the Boult performances are excellent in every way. A close friend of the composer, Boult has unimpeachable credentials as a Vaughan Williams conductor that shine through every bar of these works. The *Fantasy* has enormous dignity as well as sensual beauty, while the performance of the Symphony, if not quite as colorful a tour as Barbirolli's, is unforgettable. The London Philharmonic is at the top of its form in both performances and the remastered sound of the compact disc is extremely impressive.

Serenade to Music

**London Philharmonic, Boult. Angel 36902 [LP],
4XS-36902 [T].**

Written to a text from Shakespeare's *The Merchant of Venice*, the *Serenade to Music* may be the most bewitchingly beautiful work that Vaughan Williams ever wrote. And to say that of the man who wrote *The Lark Ascending*, the *Fantasia on a Theme of Thomas Tallis*, *Flos Campi*, and the folk-opera *Sir John in Love* is to say a very great deal indeed.

Although usually performed with a full chorus, Sir Adrian Boult gives a gleaming performance of the work as it was originally written. Composed for Sir Henry Wood's Golden Jubilee, the *Serenade* included solo parts for sixteen singers with whom Sir Henry had been especially close. Although the performance is not yet available on compact disc, it should be soon, given the fact that Angel seems bent on reissuing every Boult recording in their vaults. If you can't wait, a very fine performance of the voiceless orchestral edition of the score, conducted by Vernon Handley, is available from Chandos (*CD-8330*).

Symphony No. 5 in D Major

London Symphony, Previn. RCA Victor *6782-2* [CD].

The Fifth is not only the most beautiful of the nine Vaughan Williams symphonies, but also one of the most completely characteristic. In it, we hear an impeccable craftsman with a complex, yet thoroughly humane mind—an utterly modern man who was content with stirring us deeply and left probing the depths or shaking the heavens to others.

There are many who feel that André Previn is the most persuasive of all living Vaughan Williams conductors, and I agree. This Fifth, part of Previn's cycle of all nine symphonies for RCA, remains one of the best recordings the conductor has made so far. In general, Previn brings more life and freshness to this great work than any conductor ever has. The great themes of the first movement unfold with an ease and naturalness that not even Boult can match. For a very different view of the work and one that *is* available on LP and cassette, the Boult performance for Angel, coupled with a wild performance of the aggressively dissonant Fourth Symphony is also highly recommended (Angel AE-34478, 4AE-34478).

While space, alas, does not permit a complete discussion of all nine Vaughan Williams symphonies, the other Angel recordings by Sir Adrian Boult and those by André Previn on RCA Victor can be recommended enthusiastically. The Boult interpretations have the advantage of the conductor's long friendship with the composer and his fifty-year immersion in the music. Previn, on the other hand, brings an engaging spontaneity to the music and a youthful, interpretive insight that make his recordings no less valuable. The wise collector will want them all, especially since all have been reissued on compact disc.

Verdi, Giuseppe (1813–1901)

Aida

**Milanov, Barbieri, Bjorling, Warren, Christoff, Chorus
and Orchestra of the Rome Opera House, Perlea.
RCA Victor *6652-2-RG* [CD], ALK3-5380 [T].**

**Price, Bumbry, Domingo, Milnes, London Symphony,
Leinsdorf. RCA Victor LSC 6196 [LP].**

Verdi is unique among the great composers in that his
posthumous fame is virtually of the same magnitude as the
fame he acquired during his lifetime. In 1842, the year of
Nabucco, Verdi became a national hero in his own country,
and within the next few years he was lionized throughout the
operatic world. Although there were occasional setbacks (the
famous initial failure of *La Traviata*, for instance), he enjoyed
more than a half century of increasing honors, and he died, at
the age of eighty-seven, steeped in wealth and adulation.

    Aida, which was to have been his final opera, is a good
indication of why Verdi, now as then, is the very heart of
Italian opera. Amid all its pomp and spectacle, *Aida* is essentially a work about human conflict—the conflicting emotions
of its central characters, both with each other and within
themselves. Given an even halfway decent production, *Aida*
easily demonstrates why its power is virtually indestructible,

and why it remains one of the three or four most popular works of the operatic stage.

As a performance, no recording has yet to supersede the brilliant version made in Rome in the mid-1950s, which featured what was, and remains, an ideal cast. Beginning with Zinka Milanov, who is as poignant as she is powerful in the title role, all of the parts are covered by superb choices—from the glorious Rhadames of Jussi Bjorling to the menacing, ink-black Ramfis of the young Boris Christoff. The conducting of the vastly underrated Jonel Perlea is full of fire and poetry, and the recorded sound is much better than you expect from that era.

For the best modern LP version of the score, Leontyne Price's RCA recording easily sweeps the field. Although not quite as intense and probing as in her London recording with Sir Georg Solti, the singing clearly shows why Price, after Rosa Ponselle, was the greatest Verdi singer America has produced.

Un ballo in maschera (A Masked Ball)

M. Price, Pavarotti, Ludwig, Battle, Bruson, National Philharmonic Orchestra, Solti. London 410210-1 [LP], *410210-2* [CD], 410210-4 [T].

At first glance, this didn't look at all promising. (Actually, it did, but I hate to tell you exactly *what* it seemed to promise.) At the time, Pavarotti was obviously in serious vocal trouble, Margaret Price was merely getting louder and louder, and Sir Georg Solti hadn't made an operatic recording with any genuine passion in it for nearly a dozen years.

The surprising result is a milestone in recent operatic history. This *Ballo* takes off like a shot and refuses to let up until the very end. The cast could not have been better (Pavarotti sounds like the Pavarotti of old), and there is no praise too high for Solti's alert, incisive conducting. In short, this is a *Ballo* for you.

Falstaff

> Schwarzkopf, Moffo, Merriman, Barbieri, Alva, Gobbi, Philharmonia Chorus and Orchestra, Karajan. Angel *CDCB-49668* [CD].

> Ligabue, Freni, Simionato, Krause, Evans, RCA Italiana Opera Chorus and Orchestra, Solti. London 417168-1 [LP], 417168-4 [T].

More obvious than in his two recordings of Strauss' *Der Rosenkavalier*, the Jekyll-Hyde nature of the old and new Herbert von Karajan is most apparent here. His Angel recording from the early 1960s is one of the most nearly perfect operatic recordings of the stereo era. Each member of the cast is coaxed into an imperishable performance by a conductor who obviously cares as much for his singers as he does for the score. (In his later Deutsche Grammophon catastrophe, it is equally apparent that all Karajan currently cares about is Karajan himself.) In its recent transfer to compact disc, this early performance sounds even more brilliant and endearing than ever. The opera rushes by, as it should, like quicksilver, and the lyrical moments are given more than their due.

Among available tapes and LPs, the performance led by Sir Georg Solti is nearly as exciting. Apart from a tendency to throttle some of the swifter passages, the interpretation is excellent and features Sir Geraint Evans as the only Falstaff who begins to compete with Titto Gobbi in the Karajan recording.

La forza del destino

Price, Cossotto, Domingo, Milnes, Bacquier, John
Alldis Choir, London Symphony, Levine. RCA
Victor CRL3-2951 [LP], *RCD2-2951* [CD],
CRK3-2951 [T].

Of all the great middle-period Verdi operas (from
Rigoletto of 1851 through *Aida*, 1871), *La forza del destino*
is easily the most incredible. And by "incredible," I mean in
the literal sense—as something which can barely be believed.
The plot of the opera is hopelessly twisted and complicated,
and the irony is so extreme that it would have made Charles
Dickens blush. And yet, in spite of the unintentional silliness
of its goofy and frequently embarrassing plot, *Forza* is one of
the greatest of Verdi's operas. And in spite of its great length, it
is one of the most compressed of all Verdi's operas. In its
musical concentration and dramatic power, *Forza* is the one
early Verdi work that clearly points the way to *Aida* and,
ultimately, to *Otello*.

After Rosa Ponselle, Leontyne Price was probably the
finest Leonore of the century. The power of her middle regis-
ter, the incomparable beauty of her high notes, and the enormous strength and dignity of her characterization turn this
performance into the stuff of legend. While it is clearly Price's
show, the rest of the cast is splendid. Domingo and Milnes are
almost as fine as they are in their superb *Otello* (see below),
and Levine, here, offers some of his most assured and sympathetic conducting on records. Without question, this is one of
the best operatic recordings of the last three decades, and
quite clearly it is the *one Forza* to own.

*O*tello

**Domingo, Scotto, Milnes, National Philharmonic,
Levine. RCA Victor CRL3-2951 [LP], *RCD2-2951*
[CD], CRK3-2951 [T].**

The choice of a recorded *Otello* inevitably becomes a
choice between the two great Otellos of modern times, Jon
Vickers and Placido Domingo. On balance, I tend to favor the
Domingo version, but only by a hairbreadth. The Domingo
Otello is a large, powerful, beautifully sung, and ultimately
withering experience. While the Vickers is no less enthralling,
both of his recorded versions have drawbacks: a spotty cast
and strangely inert support from Tulio Serafin in the RCA
Victor recording, and Herbert von Karajan's heavy hand in
the more recent version for Angel.

However, the Domingo *Otello* is not without its flaws. It
features the often shrill Desdemona of Renata Scotto and
conducting from James Levine that is occasionally so enthusiastic some very important singing is lost. (In the opening
"Esultate," for instance, Domingo is practically drowned out.)
Nevertheless, with the splendid Iago of Sherill Milnes, this
Otello is an outstanding performance, and we are not likely
to hear a finer one any time soon.

*R*equiem

**Schwarzkopf, Ludwig, Gedda, Ghiaurov, Philharmonia
Chorus and Orchestra, Giulini. Angel *CDCB-47257*
[CD].**

This is the one recording of the Verdi *Requiem*—that
magnificent opera disguised as a sacred work—guaranteed to
make even the most unregenerate sinner *believe*. (If the Day of
Judgement isn't as overwhelming as Verdi and Giulini make it
sound, I, for one, will be extremely disappointed.) In the
quarter century since its release, this version of the *Requiem*

has totally dominated the catalogues. In its compact disc format, the performance is even more thrilling than ever, and if this recording doesn't spur you on to buy a compact disc player, nothing will.

If any recording on tape or LP came within an inch of this one's instep, I'd be the first to recommend it. To date, no such recording exists.

Rigoletto

Callas, Di Stefano, Gobbi, Zaccaria, La Scala Chorus and Orchestra, Serafin. Angel AVB-34069 [LP], *CDCB-47469* [CD], 4AVB-34069 [T].

The ultimate test of any performance of *Rigoletto* is your reaction to the final scene. Are tears rolling down your cheeks, or are you laughing so hard you're afraid of committing an indiscretion on your seat? *Both* reactions, by the way, are perfectly plausible. Consider the bare bones of the scene itself. A hunchback jester opens a gunny sack, thinking it contains the corpse of the heartless rogue who deflowered his daughter. Much to his surprise, he discovers his daughter herself, who while bleeding to death, sings one of the most demanding duets in all of opera. (If you think *singing* on your side isn't a tough trick, just try drinking a glass of beer that way.)

Whenever I hear the final duet in this historic version of Verdi's early masterpiece, I am *never* tempted to laugh. One of the most enduring of the many great recorded collaborations of Maria Callas and Titto Gobbi, this *Rigoletto* virtually defines the phrase "Grand Opera." To Callas and Gobbi, add the slightly edgy but still magnificent Giuseppe Di Stefano as the Duke, and the firm yet flexible conducting of Tulio Serafin, and you have something close to a *Rigoletto* for the ages. The mid-1950s recorded sound is more than adequate, and in the compact disc transfer its bite and clarity are amazing.

La Traviata

Sutherland, Pavarotti, Managuerra, London Opera Chorus, National Philharmonic, Bonynge. London 410154-1 [LP], *410154-2* [CD], 410154-4 [T].

Unfortunately, this fair but generally uninspired run-through of Verdi's popular opera is now the preferred recording of *La Traviata*, although only by default. Everyone, especially Sutherland, sings well enough yet the performance simply will not grab you by the throat and refuse to let go. Sadly, none of the other versions of this usually foolproof opera comes any closer. Until London gets around to reissuing one of the great treasures in their vault, the Tebaldi *Traviata*, this perfectly serviceable release will have to do.

Il Trovatore

Milanov, Bjorling, Barbieri, Warren, RCA Victor Chorus and Orchestra, Cellini. RCA Victor AVM2-0699 [LP], *6643-2* [CD], CLK2-5377 [T].

This (to use a phrase without which every sportscaster in America would be unable to do his job) really *is* what it's all about. Add a Leonore made of fifty percent volcano and fifty percent pathos, a gleaming, heroic Manrico (his high C in "Di quella pira" will shake you down to your socks), and a sinister, brooding, old-fashioned Azucena "whose very urine" (to use Philip Wylie's immortal phrase), "would probably etch glass," and you have one of the most electric operatic recordings ever made. The combination of Zinka Milanov, Jussi Bjorling, Fedora Barbieri, and Leonard Warren, the same team responsible for that greatest of all recorded *Aida*s, is all but unstoppable here. Even the occasionally phlegmatic Renato Cellini catches fire and turns in what is undoubtedly the performance of his career.

For those who are bothered by the monophonic, mid-1950s recorded sound—and if you're listening to sound instead of music, then you might want to make sure you have the *right* hobby—another fine RCA Victor release (LSC-6194, *6194-2-RC*) with Price, Cossotto, Domingo, Milnes, and Mehta at the top of *their* forms is the best recent alternative.

Villa-Lobos, Heitor
(1887–1959)

Bachianas brasileiras Nos. 1, 5 and 7

**Hendricks, soprano; Royal Philharmonic, Bátiz. Angel
DS-38334 [LP], *CDC-47433* [CD], 4DS-38334 [T].**

Almost everyone who discovers the music of South America's foremost composer, the Brazilian Heitor Villa-Lobos, does so through the wordless aria from the hauntingly beautiful *Bachiana brasileira No. 5*. A startlingly imaginative transposition of the spirit of Bach to the soil of Brazil, this, and indeed *all* of the *Bachiana*s are major contributions to the music of the twentieth century, as is the work of Heitor Villa-Lobos in general.

Not since the Brazilian soprano Bidu Sayao made her famous recording with the composer in the 1940s has there been a more heart-stopping version of the work than this gleaming Angel recording by Barbara Hendricks, who certainly has the talent, the drive, and the looks—she is a dazzlingly pretty woman—to become a dominant voice in the waning years of the twentieth century. This stunning Angel recording is one of her best to date. The singing has a lush yet other-worldly quality which suggests an over-sexed seraphim, and the accompaniment she receives from Enrique Bátiz is a model of sympathetic support. For something slightly off the beaten track, i.e., as a gift for the collector who seems to have *almost* everything, you can't go wrong with this lovely recording, even if you simply give it as a gift to yourself.

Vivaldi, Antonio
(1678–1741)

I'm the first to admit that I have a total blind spot when it comes to this composer. Everyone loves Vivaldi, don't they? At very least, he is the perfect Yuppie composer, a man whose tuneful, relentlessly good-natured, cleverly made music turns up more frequently at cocktail parties than the compositions of anyone else. And the music *is* inventive, distinctive, and exceedingly well made. Yet apart from the surface details (what instrument is playing, what key is the work in, and so forth), most of his music seems exactly the same to me. Stravinsky certainly had a point when he said that Vivaldi wrote the same concerto several hundred times. This explains why there is only a single entry devoted to this composer. Vivaldi lovers, forgive me. Besides, isn't your BMW double-parked?

The Four Seasons

Loveday, violin; Academy of St. Martin-in-the-Fields, Marriner. Argo 414486-1 [LP], *414486-2* [CD], 414486-4 [T].

Standage, violin; English Concert, Pinnock. Deutsche Grammophon 2534003 [LP], *400045-2* [CD], 400045-4 [T].

With the possible exception of Pachelbel's *Kanon*, nothing makes me want to start throwing things more, and I mean *literally* throwing things, than a half dozen bars of *The Seasons*. I hate it with the same irrational intensity that I reserve for peanut butter and for reasons that remain as difficult to explain. Like all of his other concertos, these four are exceedingly inoffensive and exceptionally graceful. In me, alas, they stimulate nothing but violence and, if allowed to go on too long, peristalsis.

The recording I have found least offensive over the years is the Argo version by Alan Loveday and Sir Neville Marriner. The playing is as exciting as it is tidy and communicates a deep and abiding sense of enjoyment. Among period instrument recordings, the interpretation by Simon Standage and Trevor Pinnock's superb English Concert is undoubtedly the best.

Wagner, Richard
(1813–1883)

Der fliegende Holländer (The Flying Dutchman)

**Martin, Kollo, Bailey, Talvela, Chicago Symphony
Chorus and Orchestra, Solti. London *414551-2*
[CD].**

It was in this, the first of his operas destined to occupy a place in the standard repertoire, that the musical world encountered the man who, after Beethoven, would become the most influential composer in history. Although much of *The Flying Dutchman* places it in the company of traditional nineteenth century opera (the discreet arias, choruses, and other set pieces), there is much to indicate that as early as 1843, Wagner the arch-revolutionary was beginning to evolve. For one thing, *The Flying Dutchman*, in its original version, was cast in a single, continuous act. (Two and a half hours without a break was an outrageous demand to make on mid-nineteenth century derrières.) Also we can hear the composer flirting with odd harmonies, dissonances, and an embryonic version of the *Leitmotif* technique, which would eventually lead to those vast music dramas that changed not only opera, but also the course of Western music itself.

Until Angel gives us a compact disc version of that famous, withering performance conducted by Otto Klemperer, Sir Georg Solti's dazzling London recording is clearly the one to own. With a very strong cast led by Norman Bailey, the finest Dutchman of the last twenty years, Solti leads a performance that is as incisive as it is atmospheric, as brilliantly played as it is wonderfully sung. Unfortunately, the performance is now available only on compact disc, and there is no tape or LP version which warrants a serious recommendation.

Lohengrin

Norman, Randová, Domingo, Nimsgern, Fischer-Dieskau, Vienna State Opera Chorus, Vienna Philharmonic Orchestra, Solti. London 421053-2 [CD].

Never expect to hear a *Lohengrin* like this at your neighborhood opera house. For one thing, your local opera company couldn't afford to mount one with this caliber of singers. For another, it's not every day you hear the likes of the great Vienna Philharmonic in the pit. The reasons why this is the finest recording of Wagner's early opera have as much to do with the conducting as with the choice of the tenor for the title role. Given the wonderful idea of casting Placido Domingo as Walter in *Die Meistersinger* a number of years ago, it's a bit surprising that no one ever thought of doing it again until now. No, Domingo is obviously *not* a Wagnerian in the grand tradition: his command of the language is questionable, and his sense of the character is at times rather sketchy. Yet what a pleasure it is to hear a world-class voice *singing* the part, instead of the usual grunting, howling, and groaning that passes for Wagnerian singing today.

For the remainder of the cast, London has put together a formidable ensemble, and Sir Georg Solti's conducting is precisely what it needs to be—neither overly measured, nor uncomfortably rushed. The Vienna Philharmonic has not sounded this impressive since their epoch-making recording (also with Solti) of Wagner's complete *Ring*, and the recorded sound will send shivers down your spine.

Alas, none of the existing tapes or LP versions can be recommended with any enthusiasm. Even the live 1962 Bayreuth production on Philips pales beside this astonishing achievement.

*D*ie Meistersinger von Nurnberg

> Bode, Hamari, Kollo, Bailey, Weikl, Moll, Vienna State Opera Chorus, Vienna Philharmonic, Solti. London *417497-2* [CD].
>
> Ligendza, Ludwig, Domingo, Fischer-Dieskau, Chorus and Orchestra of the German Opera, Berlin, Jochum. DG 2713011 [LP], *415278-2* [CD], 3378068 [T].

While *Tristan und Isolde* is probably his masterpiece, and the *Ring*, taken as a whole, his most significant achievement, *Die Meistersinger* finally showed the world the human side of Richard Wagner. Given the nature of the beast that Wagner was, his human side proved to be shockingly warm, generous, and complete. In the only operatic comedy worthy of comparison with Verdi's *Falstaff* and Mozart's *Figaro*, Wagner succeeds in showing us not only what is finest and best in the German people, but also by inference, what is finest and best in ourselves. For this one Wagner opera, cast on a completely human scale, is about friendship and trust, young love and mature wisdom, tradition and rebellion—in short, the human condition itself.

Among available recordings of the opera, the difficult choice is between the versions conducted by Sir Georg Solti and the late Eugen Jochum. Each has its particular strengths and weaknesses. The Jochum recording suffers from the disappointing Hans Sachs of Dietrich Fisher-Dieskau, which is as badly over-acted as it is over-sung. On the other hand, Placido

Domingo as Walter is a vocal revelation. As in the recent recording of *Lohengrin*, it's a pleasure to hear a voice of this stature in the part.

The Solti recording, which features the marvelous Hans Sachs of Norman Bailey, has to contend with a very wobbly Walter (René Kollo) and conducting from Solti which is only marginally less graceful and stately than what we hear from Jochum. For my money, neither can begin to match that virtually flawless, but now out of print, mid-1950s Angel recording conducted by Rudolf Kempe. But if a choice must be made, then it's Solti by a nose.

Parsifal

Dalis, Thomas, London, Hotter, Neidlinger, Bayreuth
Festival Chorus and Orchestra, Knappertsbusch.
Philips 6747250 [LP], *416390-2* [CD].

There used to be an ancient Metropolitan Opera curse that one still hears from old timers. "May you be trapped in a performance of *Parsifal* without a sandwich." The implication is, of course, that *Parsifal* does tend to go on and on and on. As a matter of fact, nothing can be more thoroughly numbing than an indifferently prepared production of the opera, just as nothing can be more genuinely stirring when all the parties involved are giving the opera all it demands, which is to say, *everything*.

Recorded live at the 1962 Bayreuth Festival and captured on a Philips recording, this performance proves more conclusively than any other that *Parsifal* was in fact a fitting conclusion to Wagner's career, containing as it does many of the most inspired pages the composer ever wrote. With a cast that includes George London, Jess Thomas, and the great Hans Hotter among others, the recording features some of the finest Wagner singing heard on records. *Parsifal* was always a great house specialty of Hans Knappertsbusch, and he leads a performance of unparalleled dignity, depth, and majesty. Although the recording is of an actual performance, the foot-shuffling, coughing, and vocal drop-outs are kept to a bare minimum, and besides, the thrill of hearing those incomparable Bayreuth acoustics more than compensates for the occasional glitch.

At present, there is no tape version available except for Karajan's, which I wouldn't wish on a dog.

Der Ring des Nibelungen (Das Rheingold, Die Walküre, Siegfried, Götterdämmerung)

Nilsson, Flagstad, Crespin, Watson, Ludwig, Madeira, Windgassen, Svanholm, King, Stolze, London, Fischer-Dieskau, Hotter, Frick, Neidlinger, Vienna Philharmonic, Solti. London 414100-2 [CD], 414100-4 [T].

It is only fitting that one of the most titanic outbursts of the human imagination inspired one of the genuine cornerstones of recording history: the now legendary English Decca/London version of Wagner's *Ring*. In spite of its obvious flaws, and there are several, this will undoubtedly be our once and future *Ring*—an achievement so massively ambitious, audacious, and successful that it boggles the mind.

True, this is not the ideal performance of Wagner's sprawling fifteen hour tetralogy. But then again, much evidence suggests that Wagner himself at last concluded that an ideal *Ring* existed only in his mind. The major flaws in the recording include a Siegfried who is barely adequate (although Wolfgang Windgassen was the best the world had to offer at the time) and the rather wobbly Wotan of the once-great Hans Hotter.

In spite of these important drawbacks, the great moments far outnumber the uncomfortable ones. Here is Kirsten

Flagstad, singing the *Rheingold* Fricka, a role she learned especially for this recording. Here, too, are those extravagant bits of casting, including Christa Ludwig as Waltraute, and Joan Sutherland as the Forest Bird. Through it all, one still feels the spirit of the late John Culshaw (the most imaginative recording producer of his generation) who here, with Sir Georg Solti in the pit and the finest cast that could then be assembled, puts together not only his greatest monument, but also those of many who were involved.

On LP, the best alternative is the strange yet frequently compelling cycle mounted by the Italian Radio in 1953, with Wilhelm Furtwängler leading a generally excellent cast in a performance preserved in barely adequate sound (Seraphin IN-6148). The only other LP editions currently available are those of Karajan and Boulez. The former is a smooth-shod travesty; the latter, a well-intentioned and often beautifully conducted bit of evidence that at least vocally, Wagner has now entered a Dark Age.

Tannhäuser (Paris Version)

Dernesch, Ludwig, Kollo, Braun, Sotin, Vienna State Opera Chorus, Vienna Philharmonic, Solti. London 415581-2 [CD].

While Sir Georg Solti has now recorded every Wagner opera from *The Flying Dutchman* to *Parsifal*, none of those recordings is finer than this stupendous version of the Paris edition of *Tannhäuser*. In Helga Dernesch and Christa Ludwig he has a pair of ladies for whom any conductor would give what remains of his hair. And René Kollo, who has had serious vocal problems over the years, here sounds more free and fresh than he ever has on recordings. Nevertheless, Solti's conducting, as languorous and limpid as it is ferocious and exultant, makes this one of the great Wagner recordings of the last twenty years.

As is now so frequently the case, there is no recording of the opera available on LP or cassette.

Tristan und Isolde

Flagstad, Thebom, Suthaus, Fischer-Dieskau, Greindl, Philharmonia Chorus and Orchestra, Furtwängler. Angel ID-6147 [LP], *CDC-47321* [CD].

Behrens, Minton, Hofmann, Weikl, Sotin, Bavarian Radio Chorus and Orchestra, Bernstein. Philips 6769901 [LP], *410447-2* [CD], 410447-4 [T].

The famous 1952 recording of *Tristan und Isolde*, most collectors concede, is the greatest single Wagner recording ever made. In spite of a frequently negligible Tristan and an Isolde who was crowding sixty at the time, no other version of this passionate masterwork has captured as much black magic or animal intensity as this one. The legendary Kirsten Flagstad is quite literally *that* in her finest studio recording. This Isolde beguiles and terrifies with equal ease, and is more convincingly and beautifully sung than any we are ever likely to hear.

Furtwängler's conducting is similarly inspired and more than confirms his reputation as the greatest Wagner conductor of his time. The dynamic contrasts range from the merest whisper to the most shattering climaxes. Phrases are stretched out to unimaginable lengths, and in general the performance creates a feeling that no Wagner opera ever does—that it is far too short.

The most amazing thing about Leonard Bernstein's amazing Philips recording is how favorably it compares to what has been for years an incomparable recording. Although his Isolde is no match for Flagstad, the Tristan of Peter Hoffman is virile, exciting, and exceptionally musical, and the rest of the cast is extremely strong. Nevertheless, the conducting is so obviously the center of attention that the voices seem to disappear. Rarely has anyone taken so many chances with what is already a very chancy work (some of the tempos are so slow that Furtwängler's seem brisk in comparison), and rarely have such chances paid off as handsomely . In another thirty years, posterity will probably view this *Tristan* with the same hushed reverence that we now reserve for the Flagstad-Furtwängler recording. Wise collectors will acquire them both.

Walton, Sir William
(1902–1983)

Belshazzar's Feast

Luxon, baritone; Royal Philharmonic Chorus and
Orchestra, Previn.
MCA MCA-6187 [LP], *MCAD-6187* [CD],
MCAC-6187 [T].

The only disappointing thing about André Previn's new-
est and finest recording of the most lurid, prurient, suggestive,
and rousing of all twentieth century sacred works is the album
cover photo. While perfectly acceptable, it is certainly no
match for the dazzling image that adorned his early Angel
recording, which fortunately remains in print. In every other
respect, however, this exhilarating version of Walton's colorful
Oratorio is easily the most impressive yet made. The chorus
and huge orchestral forces are managed with the ease of a
Haydn symphony, and over the years the interpretation has
become both more thoughtful and more rambunctious. The
unbridled joy that Previn coaxes out of the final cry of "Alleluia" is as exciting as anything you've ever heard.

And if there remains any doubt that Previn is now the
world's foremost exponent of Walton's music, two other recordings will more than convince you. The first, an Angel
version of the Viola and Violin Concertos with the brilliant
Nigel Kennedy (*CDC-49628*, compact disc only) contains the

most admirable and adult interpretation either work has yet received. And in his latest version of the great Symphony No. 1 in B-flat minor (Telarc CD-80125, compact disc only), Previn releases all the beauty, vitality, and majesty of a major twentieth century symphony.

Weber, Carl Maria von
(1786–1926)

Der Freischutz

Janowitz, Mathis, Schreier, Weikl, Adam, Dresden State
Opera Chorus and Orchestra, C. Kleiber. Deutsche
Grammophon 415432-1 [LP], *415432-2* [CD].

The next time you're trapped in a game of musical trivia
and need a question that will stump everyone, ask "What is
the second most frequently performed opera in Germany
today?" The totally unexpected answer is Albert Lorzing's *Zar
und Zimmermann*. In fact, the work that occupies the number
one spot will also come as a surprise to most people simply
because it isn't performed very often outside the German-
speaking world. The reasons for the phenomenal popularity
of *that* opera, Weber's *Der Freischutz*, are as obvious now as
they were when it was first performed. Along with its wonderfully dark atmosphere (Germans love anything set in a forest),
Der Freischutz boasts a succession of unforgettable arias,
choruses, and other set pieces. Also, with *Der Freischutz*,
Carl Maria von Weber brought Romanticism into the opera
house, and thus composers as diverse as Meyerbeer, Berlioz,
Wagner, and Strauss owe Weber an incalculable debt.

This splendid Deutsche Grammophon release marked
Carlos Kleiber's recording debut as an operatic conductor,
and what an auspicious debut it proved to be. Kleiber leads

the superb cast and the always impeccable Dresden State Opera forces with tremendous energy, enthusiasm, and imagination. Only in the most darkly brooding moments of the second act do hints of Weber's poetry escape him. Still, this is a bracing introduction to a wonderful opera. Unfortunately, a tape is not available.

Webern, Anton (1883–1945)

Complete Works

Various Ensembles, Boulez. CBS M4-35193 [LP].

Anton Webern was the most tragic member of the so-called Second Viennese School, whose other members were his teacher, Arnold Schoenberg, and his fellow pupil, Alban Berg. Accidentally shot by an American soldier during the post-war occupation of Austria, Webern's tragedy had in fact begun years earlier. Both of his daughters were married to high-ranking Nazi officials, and he himself seems to have been extremely sympathetic to the cause, not because he was evil, but because he was incredibly naive. On the day the Nazis marched into Vienna, Webern allegedly said, "Well now at least we will be able to hear Mahler!"

Until quite recently, this pathetic, lonely figure was one of the most influential composers of the twentieth century. In fact, "Post-Webern" became a designation that was once used as frequently as "Neo-classicism" or "New Romanticism." This four- record set from CBS collects Webern's entire output as a composer and is something no person interested in contemporary music should be without. The performances of these rarified, delicate, often startlingly original works, run from adequate to extraordinary, and the recorded sound is excellent.

Wolf, Hugo (1860–1903)

Songs

After Franz Schubert, there were only three incontestably great composers of German *lieder*: Schumann, Brahms, and Hugo Wolf. And if Schubert practically invented the form, then it was Wolf who presided over its final, bittersweet flowering. In the work of no other composer are words and music so intimately connected, and in no other German songs do we encounter so much effortless perfection.

Among the available recordings of Wolf songs, and there are shamefully few, the Nonesuch recording (78014, T-78014 [T]) of the *Italian Song Book* is exceptionally appealing. Elly Ameling sings flawlessly, and Tom Krause gives one of his best performances in years. Similarly, the classic Deutsche Grammophon recording (412226) of the *Spanish Song Book* with Elizabeth Schwarzkopf and Dietrich Fischer-Dieskau is among the most nearly perfect *lieder* recordings ever made. And finally, although certainly not perfect from a technical point of view, that famous recording of a Wolf recital given at the 1952 Salzburg festival is currently available on a Fonit-Cetra compact disc (*CDC-21*). The young Schwarzkopf was never more enchanting than in these twenty-two songs, and the accompaniments are highly unusual and individual, given the fact that the pianist was Wilhelm Furtwängler.

Zemlinsky, Alexander von (1871–1942)

Die Seejungfrau (The Mermaid); Psalm XIII

**Berlin Radio Chorus and Orchestra, Chailly. London
417450-2 [CD].**

Until quite recently, the name of Alexander von
Zemlinsky only came up in relation to his one-time pupil and
brother-in-law, Arnold Schoenberg. Actually, he was one of
the most respected teachers and conductors of his era and, as
we're beginning to discover only now, one of its most interesting and original composers. For the collector who has everything, or for anyone who is simply interested in making the
acquaintance of a fabulously beautiful work, this recent
London recording of Die Seejungfrau cannot be recommended too highly. The piece itself is a startling amalgam of
Mahler, Strauss, and the composer's own elusive originality.
The performance, led by Riccardo Chailly, could not have
been more poised or luxuriant, and the version of Zemlinsky's
Psalm XIII is similarly enthralling. For those who find either
or both works to their taste, they might want to explore the
LaSalle String Quartet's brilliant recording of the four
Zemlinsky quartets (Deutsche Grammophon 423316-1, LP
only) or the wonderful recording of the large and fascinating
Lyric Symphony, also from Deutsche Grammophon
(419261-2, compact disc only).

Index